7-9·73

ATLA Monograph Series
edited by Dr. Kenneth E. Rowe

1. Ronald L. Grimes. *The Divine Imagination: William Blake's Major Prophetic Visions.* 1972.

2. George D. Kelsey. *Social Ethics Among Southern Baptists, 1917-1969.* 1973.

3. Hilda Adam Kring. *The Harmonists: A Folk-Cultural Approach.* 1973

4. J. Steven O'Malley. *Pilgrimage of Faith: The Legacy of the Otterbeins.* 1973.

PILGRIMAGE OF FAITH:
The Legacy of the Otterbeins

by
J. Steven O'Malley

ATLA Monograph Series, No. 4

The Scarecrow Press, Inc.
Metuchen, N.J.   1973

Library of Congress Cataloging in Publication Data

O'Malley, John Steven.
    Pilgrimage of faith.

    (ATLA monograph series, no. 4)
    Thesis--Drew University, 1970.
    Bibliography: p.
    1. Reformed Church--Doctrinal and controversial
works. 2. Pietism--History. 3. Otterbein, Georg
Gottfried, 1731-1800. 4. Otterbein, Johann Daniel,
1736-1804. 5. Otterbein, Philip William, Bp., 1726-
1813. I. Title. II. Series: American Theological
Library Association. ATLA monograph series, no. 4.
BX9422.2.O4 1973   284'.2   73-5684
    ISBN 0-8108-0626-6

To my wife and daughter,
Angie and Sarah

TABLE OF CONTENTS

Editor's Foreword   vii

Introduction   ix
    Acknowledgments   xi

Abbreviations   xii

PART I.   THE ROOTS IN EUROPE

1. The Herborn Tradition of Reformed Theology   2

   a. The Reformed Church in Nassau and the
      Herborn High School   2

   b. Anti-Scholasticism at Herborn and
      Catechetical Exposition "Without Bond-
      age to Word and Form"   16

   Notes   30

2. Streams of Reformed Pietism   44

   a. The Interpretation of the Cathechism by
      the Dutch Master Theologians of the
      Seventeenth Century   44

   b. Reformed Pietism Comes to Herborn   57

   Notes   78

PART II: THE OTTERBEINS

3. A Theology of the Catechism for a Day of Crisis   94

   Notes   104

4. The Pilgrimage of Faith   109

    Notes   120

5. Kingdom and Church: The Identity of the Pilgrim   126

    Notes   143

6. Gratitude: The Apotheosis of the Pilgrim   151

    Notes   160

    PART III: PHILIP WILHELM OTTERBEIN AND
               THE AMERICAN EXPERIENCE

7. Otterbein and the Rise of German-American
    Evangelicalism   166

    Notes   185

8. The Legacy of the Otterbeins   189

    Notes   195

Bibliography   197

Index   209

EDITOR'S FOREWORD

The indebtedness of Protestantism to Pietism has long been acknowledged. However, the nature and extent of this indebtedness has never been fully assessed. Part of the reason for this is undoubtedly due to the complexity of the movement itself. For the 17th century extension of the reform principle to the Christian life (a principle which the earlier Reformers applied chiefly to doctrine and polity) took many shapes in England, Germany and the low countries.

Studies in Pietism have tended to concentrate on the Lutheran variety in Germany, with its roots in Arndt, Spener and Francke, or on the Puritan variety in England, with its roots in Baxter, Bunyan and Taylor. Little attention has been paid to the Reformed variety in western Germany and the Netherlands. Professor O'Malley's study, however, focuses squarely on Reformed Pietism with its roots in the mellowed Calvinism of the Heidelberg Catechism and especially on the Herborn tradition and its interpreters, the brothers Otterbein--Georg Gottfried, Johann Daniel and Philip Wilhelm. This tradition has run parallel with Lutheran and Puritan Pietism, but with significant differences that deserve more attention than they have thus far received. Its significance for the American religious scene has also been largely unexplored. Yet out of this tradition, transplanted in the "Dutch" communities of the Middle Colonies in America in the 18th century and nurtured by spiritual leaders like Philip Wilhelm Otterbein, came two American religious communities--the German Reformed and the United Brethren in Christ.

Happily, Professor O'Malley stands with one foot firmly planted in Western Europe and the other in the Middle Colonies, for Philip Wilhelm Otterbein, Domine of the Pennsylvania and Maryland "Dutch," cannot be understood--in terms of either his life or his thought--apart from his roots in the warm piety of the Herborn tradition of Reformed Pietism.

Although most American and Canadian doctoral dissertations in religion are available to scholars on microfilm or expensive xerographic copies, distribution and scholarly use is limited. A number of studies are submitted each year which deserve a better fate than to remain in the drawers of library microfilm cabinets.

The American Theological Library Association has undertaken responsibility for a modest dissertation publishing program in the field of religious studies. Our aim in this monograph series is to publish, in serviceable format and at reasonable cost, at least two dissertations of quality in the field of religious studies each year. Titles are selected by the Committee on Publication from titles nominated by Graduate School Deans or Directors of Graduate Studies in Religion.

John Steven O'Malley studied theology at Yale Divinity School and Drew University, having received the doctorate from Drew in 1970. He has taught in the Department of Philosophy and Religion at Indiana Central College in Indianapolis and is currently Assistant Professor of Historical Theology and Methodist Studies at the Graduate Seminary of Phillips University in Enid, Oklahoma.

We are pleased to publish his study as number four in our series.

Kenneth E. Rowe, Editor

Drew University Library
Madison, New Jersey

INTRODUCTION

Modern historical scholarship has witnessed a remarkable surge of interest both in Reformation studies and in the recasting of this tradition since the time of Schleiermacher. However, scholars have tended to ignore theological development on the continent in the two intervening centuries --the period of Protestant orthodoxy. Without a recognition of the continual shaping of the Reformation faith which took place in this period, particularly in adjusting the faith to the developing scientific world view, our knowledge of the tradition is impoverished. Barth and Pelikan recognized that Pietism played a significant role in shaping the Protestant self-understanding in this transition, though the precise nature of this influence--particularly in the Reformed tradition--has yet to be delineated. The delineation of this influence is the intended purpose of this case study of the Otterbeins.

The particular concern of this study is to determine whether the content of Reformed theology, as expressed by Calvin and the Heidelberg Catechism, was significantly altered in the 18th century exposition of the Catechism by Georg Gottfried Otterbein and Johann Daniel Otterbein, who used it as a means of edification and the polemical defense of the faith against their rational opponents. As prolegomena to this task, the study describes the Herborn tradition of Reformed theology, with its roots in the Reformation, and the revisionist tradition of Reformed Pietistic Orthodoxy which prevailed there during the Otterbeins' day. The evaluation of their exposition of the Catechism will focus on their view of Scripture and tradition, the role of reason and experience in theology, and their exposition of the great Christian doctrines.

In this focus upon the Otterbein brothers, my attempt is to deal in a controlled way with an incredibly scarce and generally inaccessible body of literature. Because of the Pietists' propensity to use publication as a means of edification and polemical defense of the faith against orthodox and rationalistic opponents, there are many hundreds of devotional and theological works by dozens of pastor-theologians in the Dutch and German Reformed traditions, few of which have ever been read by English-speaking scholars. In view of this vast corpus, a study of the Otterbeins is particularly appropriate. They were the principal exponents of the Herborn tradition of pietistic orthodoxy in the latter half of the eighteenth century. The father, Johann Daniel Otterbein (born 1696), was pastor of the Reformed Church in Dillenburg, capital of the principality of Nassau, which had established and maintained the high school and later the university at Herborn. Six of his sons graduated from the university and became pastors in the vicinity, while one, Johann Heinrich, became a professor at Herborn. According to contemporary reports, the published works on the Cathechism by Georg Gottfried Otterbein and Johann Daniel Otterbein became the most influential of their kind in the Reformed territories of northwestern Germany and in the German Reformed areas of the American colonies. Because the Otterbeins stood as leaders within the church tradition, their exposition reflects the thinking of the evengelical wing in the churches of the day, and they avoid the excessive mysticism and radical separatism which characterized many eighteenth century pietistic authors. Above all, they regarded themselves as staunch defenders of the old faith against the massive inroads of rationalism in the life of the church.

The relevance of the continental theology of the Otterbeins for American scholarship lies in its role in nurturing the German Reformed piety of the Middle Colonies. The concluding section of this study shows how this tradition of Reformed Pietism became a mediating factor in the development of the broader tradition of American evangelical Protestantism through the influence of a third member of the family, Philip Wilhelm Otterbein.

The theological traditions which shaped the early development of American religion were often obscured amid the pervasive and leveling impact of the revivals, and with the rise of denominationalism. Among these early theological traditions were the writings of the German Reformed and the varied pastoral activities of their clergy. As Tanis has observed, the many-sidedness of Pietism renders obscure the common epithet that Frelinghuysen was the "Father of American Pietism." While Frelinghuysen was the leading spirit of the Dutch Reformed in colonial New

Jersey and New York, it was Philip Wilhelm Otterbein, pastor of the leading colonial German Reformed congregations, who occupied a similar position among his churchmen. The volumes of sermons on the <u>Catechism</u> by his brothers in Germany were circulated in Pennsylvania by Philip Wilhelm Otterbein, and the volume by Johann Daniel Otterbein was reprinted at Lancaster in 1790. It is my intention to assess Philip Wilhelm Otterbein in the context of the Reformed tradition in which he labored, rather than primarily in terms of his associations with Asbury and the German preachers who, partially under Methodist influence, organized the Church of the United Brethren in Christ. These associations came only in the latter decades of his eighty-nine year life. Thus, he will be placed in the continental historical and theological context with which earlier denominational historiography has been little concerned.

Acknowledgments

I wish to express appreciation to the members of my dissertation committee in the Graduate School, Drew University, and especially to Dean Bard Thompson, for his perceptive guidance and encouragement in this project. To Arthur Core, the preeminent authority on Philip Wilhelm Otterbein, whose suggestions and encouragement in my work were invaluable, I am especially indebted. Kenneth Rowe, the editor of the American Theological Library Association series, has been most generous in providing assistance in the final editing. Donna Walter of Phillips Seminary has given helpful assistance in typing and proofreading. And last, but certainly not least, I am grateful to my wife Angie, who has been an encouraging companion and aid from the beginning of my studies.

ABBREVIATIONS
(Used in Notes throughout)

CNTC   Calvin's New Testament Commentaries, 12 vols. ed. by D. W. and T. F. Torrance, Grand Rapids, Michigan, Eerdmans, 1959-

COT   Calvin's Commentaries on the Old Testament, 30 vols. Edinburgh, Calvin Translation Society, 1845-1855.

Inst.   Institutes of the Christian Religion by John Calvin. 2 vols. (Library of Christian Classics) Philadelphia, Westminster Press, 1960.

Gnad.   Friedrich Adolph Lampe, Geheimnis des Gnadenbundes. 6 vols. Bremen, Verlegts Nayhansel Saurmann, 1748.

GWC   Georg Gottfried Otterbein, Der Geist des wahren Christenthums nach Paulus: eine Reihe praktischer Erklärungen des zwölften Kapitels des Briefes an die Römer; ein Erbauungsbuch. Erste Halfte. Frankfurt and Leipzig, F. A. Julicher, 1792.

HM   Philip Wilhelm Otterbein, Die Heilbrigende Menschwerdung und der Herliche Sieg Jesu Christi Deu Teufel und Tod. Edited by Arthur C. Core and translated by Ehrhart Lang. Philip William Otterbein: Pastor, Ecumenist, Dayton, Otterbein Press, 1968.

JKB   Johann Daniel Otterbein, Jesus und die Kraft seines Bluts Ganz besonders Verherrlichet an Johann Jost Weygand einem armen Sünder, der einen Mord begangen; und den 21ten October, 1785, auf der Richtstätte vor Berlenburg, mit dem Schwerd vom Leben zum Tod gebracht worden. Lancaster, Neuen Buchdruckerey, 1790.

LDS   Georg Gottfried Otterbein, Lesebuch für deutsche Schulkinder; herausgegeben von Georg Gottfried

Otterbein; mit Veränderungen und Zusätzen, zum Gebrauch Nor-Amerikanischer Schulen, Philadelphia, Carl Cist, 1795.

PHK   Georg Gottfried Otterbein, Predigten über den Heidelbergischen Katechismus, 2 vols. Duisburg, Helwing, 1800, (and) Lemgo, Meyer, 1803.

UHC   Georg Gottfried Otterbein, Underweisung in der Christlichen Religion nach dem Heidelbergischen Catechismus... Zweyte Auflage. Frankfurt, Julicher, n. d. (1788?).

PART I

THE ROOTS IN EUROPE

Chapter 1

THE HERBORN TRADITION OF REFORMED THEOLOGY

a. The Reformed Church in Nassau
and the Herborn High School

The establishment of the Reformed Church in Nassau
was due to the labors of that princely Reformer, Count
Johann VI of Nassau-Dillenburg (1535-1606). Born in Dillenburg, the capital of the principality, he was the second
son of Wilhelm the Elder and Juliane of Stollberg.[1] His
father had been a participant in the Diet of Worms (1521).
Lutheranism had been introduced into his principality in
1529, when the Lutheran Heilmann Bruchhausen of Crombach
came as head chaplain to Dillenburg.[2] As a youth, Johann
studied law and theology at Strassburg, which was then characterized by a non-polemical, evangelical Lutheranism, and
later he studied at Wittenberg under Melanchthon himself.
In 1559, he married the Countess Elizabeth of Leuchtenburg
and, with the death of his father the same year, he began
his reign.[3]

As Cuno has shown, Count Johann desired to be "a
man after the heart of God," rather than a military leader
in the tradition of his elder brother, Willem of Orange.
The Nassau Chronicle dubbed Johann a

> scrupulous, righteous father of the fatherland, an
> administrator of justice and equity, protector and
> defender of his subjects, and patron and admirer
> of a learned and skillful people.[4]

The emergence of what Steitz calls a "later Reformation" (Nachreformation) in Nassau was a complex development in which political and religious motives were inter-
twined.[5] In 1566, Johann established a church council
(Kirchenrath) for his territory which, together with an administrative chamber (Kammer) and a court of justice
(Hofgericht), became the ruling body for his realm (Landescollegium).[6] He also projected a codification of law

(Gesetzbuch).[7] His residence city (Residenzstadt) was the ancient castle at Dillenburg, where he and his brother Willem the Silent were born.   Through his Landescollegium, Johann attempted to order Nassau in terms of an irenic, Melanchthonian Lutheranism, and he sought to extend the Reformation to the surrounding territories.   This work was to be supervised by his superintendent, Bernhardi, who was also responsible for the composition of the evangelical church order of Dusseldorf in 1567.[8]

The Count was not inferior in piety to his colleague, the Elector Frederick the Pious of the Palatinate, under whose auspices the Heidelberg Catechism was prepared.[9] Johann also did not remain free from the controversy between Gnesio-Lutherans and Crypto-Calvinists, which was then raging in Heidelberg to the south.   According to the terms of the Peace of Augsburg (1555), each prince was entitled to decide which religion would be established in his realm, though there were to be no religious rights extended to any except Roman Catholics and adherents of the Augsburg Confession.[10]   The so-called "Crypto-Calvinistic controversy" threatened to remove Melanchthonian Lutherans from the protection of the Empire.   A review of the events surrounding this controversy will shed light on the precarious position of Count Johann in Nassau.

It should be recalled that the mild, conciliatory spirit which was ascribed to Melanchthon was accompanied by his doctrinal deviation from Lutheran orthodoxy with regard to free will and the Lord's Supper.   Concerning the former, Melanchthon shifted from agreeing with Luther's denial of the freedom of the will in the Loci Communes of 1521 to insisting that the work of conversion should be attributed to three "connected causes" (copulationem causarum), in which the human will is a causa concurrens.[11]   With regard to the doctrine of the Lord's Supper, Melanchthon shifted from his position in the Augsburg Confession of 1530, where he agreed that the body and blood of Christ are "truly present (vere adsint) under the form of bread and wine," and that they are "distributed" (distribuantur) to those who eat.[12]   Soon afterward, Melanchthon became convinced that the Fathers did not support Luther's sacramental realism,[13] but he did not subscribe to the Zwinglian position.   Rather, he asserted a real life-union of the person of Christ with the soul of man--a substantial life-union which Calvin could appreciate. In 1540, Melanchthon revised the tenth article of the Augsburg Confession by removing the words vere adsint ("truly

present"), by replacing the word distribuantur ("distributed")
with exhibeantur ("tendered"), and by adding cum pane ("with
the bread"). [14] In short, the amended text of the Confession
taught that, with the bread and wine, the body and blood of
Christ are tendered to the communicants.

Melanchthon's position on the Lord's Supper became
surrounded with controversy when it was attacked by the
Gnesio-Lutheran, Joachim Westphal, who assailed Calvin and
implicated the Melanchthonians as perverters of Luther's
doctrine. [15] The Gnesio-Lutherans began calling the Melanchthonians "Crypto-Calvinists" after Calvin agreed with Melanchthon's reinterpretation of the tenth article of the Confession
in the replies to Westphal. At Heidelberg, severe conflicts
raged from 1557 to 1559 among Lutherans, Melanchthonians,
Zwinglians, and Calvinists in the divinity faculty, and in
1559, the new Elector Frederick III appealed to Melanchthon
himself for a resolution of the issue. [16] Melanchthon's Re-
sponsio, which was congenial to the Reformed doctrine, appealed solely to the Pauline theme that the bread which is
broken is "the communion of the body of Christ." [17] During
this defection of the Palatinate, the Lutheran princes met at
Naumburg in 1561 to solidify their position vis-a-vis a re-
vived Roman Catholicism, and in this colloquy the unaltered
Confession was reaffirmed. [18] In view of this mounting opposition, Frederick III resolved to establish a church in the
Palatinate which would be founded upon the Scriptures and
would be catholic and evangelical--a plan which led him to
summon new Reformed leadership in the persons of Zacharias Ursinus and Casper Olevianus.

It was Frederick's intention to create an instrument
which would edify the infantile Palatinate Church "according
to the pure and consistent doctrine of the holy gospel." [19]
By appealing to the Word of God as its sole authority, it was
hoped that this Catechism would dispel the controversy between Gnesio-Lutherans and Crypto-Calvinists. The document
followed the threefold division which had shaped the Catechesis
Minor of Ursinus: man's misery, his deliverance, and his
gratitude for deliverance. There remains considerable confusion with regard to the composition of the text. It is assumed that Boquin, Tremellius, Ursinus, Olevianus, Erastus,
Diller, and Zierler took part in the preparation of the
draft, [20] though the tradition that Olevianus was responsible
for its final redaction, which gave it a warm, experiential
character, has recently been challenged by Walter Hollweg. [21]
At the Diet of Augsburg in 1566, Frederick was confronted by

his adversaries, who charged that the Catechism represented
a defection from the Evangelical Church of Germany and thus
excluded the Palatinate from the privileges of the Peace of
Augsburg. His successful reply, in which he upheld both the
Catechism and the Confession, was a pious defense of the
Catechism on the ground that the Palatinate Church had appealed to the authority of sola Scriptura above all temporal
authorities. [22]

While these events were transpiring in the Palatinate,
Count Johann, who had declared himself and his realm in
favor of Melanchthonian Lutheranism, [23] was still hesitant in
his attitude toward Calvin. As late as 1565, he remained
hostile toward the Reformed position, which was known to
him as "sacramentarian." From Dillenburg he wrote to his
brother, Ludwig, at Wittenberg, complaining that "the people
called Calvinists are gaining power in many places, especially in Hesse and Wittenberg," and that "the Almighty should
check this and all other wicked rabble and sects." [24] However, in a letter to this brother which was dated September,
1566, he showed signs of discouragement with the polemical
attacks upon the Calvinists, and recognized that no position
held by any Protestant prince was free from prejudice. He
noted that the princes had better seek the glory of God,
rather than their own, and the salvation of their peoples, for
it would be better if doctrinal instruction would "be pursued
in order to edify and instruct the whole man in the Word of
God." [25]

The influence of the Netherlands was initially more
instrumental than the Palatinate in wooing Count Johann from
Lutheranism. His brother Willem had already supported the
Reformed Church in Holland, where the Catechism had been
introduced in 1566 by Petrus Gabriel, and in 1567, Willem
influenced Johann to permit a noted Huguenot pastor, Pierre
Loyseleur de Villiers, to preach in Dillenburg. [26] In 1568,
the Reformed theologian Gerhard Geldenhauer, Noviomagnus,
came to Herborn from Hesse and proceeded to direct Nassau
toward a Reformed confession. Since Noviomagnus had the
reputation of a Reformed "heretic," he was received in Herborn with suspicion, and the most determined opposition
came from the Superintendent, M. Bernhard Bernhardi of
Dillenburg, "keeper of the Lutheran Zion," who demanded
that Noviomagnus undergo a doctrinal test (examen orthodoxie). [27] In a short time, the erudite newcomer turned the
mistrust of the people into genuine esteem, and Count Johann
himself became convinced of the lucidity and the solid biblical

basis of the Reformed dogma. Images and tapestries, which
had persisted from pre-Reformation times, were now removed from the churches, and exorcism in baptism and the
practice of private, auricular confession were also aban-
doned--all measures which were initially unpopular with the
populace, particularly in rural areas.

However, care must be taken not to reduce our conclusion to Good's statement that the Count was "converted to
Calvinism."[28] As in the case of Frederick III of the Palatinate, both the political realities of Nassau and the piety of
Johann prevented him from conceding that the Church of Nassau had forfeited its participation in the evangelical community of the Augsburg Confession.[29] Wishing to hold to the
Reformed dogma in such a way as to live in as much harmony as possible with the Lutherans, the Count wrote to Willem
of Orange in April, 1576, with a new outlook, saying

> [concerning] the disdain of the German Lutherans
> for the Reformed, the church cannot be without its
> cross and yet flourish; however, everything stands
> in God's hands.[30]

A predominant theme in his correspondence was his affliction
with theological dissension, which was the subject of a letter
to the prince in 1576:

> It is truly to be pitied that we evangelicals are so
> often cold, blind, and faint-hearted; ... we will
> now take efforts to be awakened from our prejudice
> and the corruption of such indolence.[31]

Being particularly distressed by the Formula of Concord and
its condemnation of the Reformed, Count Johann followed the
neighboring Hessian Church in repudiating the document.
There is evidence that he became implicated in the charge
of Crypto-Calvinism, which was then being directed against
the Melanchthonians in Saxony.[32] In 1577, he opened his
realm as a refuge for persecuted Calvinists from Saxony,
notably Pezel and Widebram, and from the Palatinate, where
Lutheranism had been reintroduced after the death of the
Elector Frederick III by his son, Elector Ludwig.   Ludwig
turned against Olevianus and Tossanus, the court-preachers
of his father.   He even prevented them from speaking at his
father's funeral, preferring instead Paul Schecksius, the
Lutheran court-preacher whom he had brought from Amberg.[33]
When Tossanus caused a breach in the electoral family by con-

ducting a private funeral service at the request of the Elec-
tress, he was forced to seek refuge in Nassau. [34] Ludwig
censored Reformed pastors, forbade the sale of Reformed
books, and discouraged the use of the Heidelberg Catechism.
Olevianus, who had had considerable influence with the father,
was expelled from the consistory, forbidden to preach, placed
under house arrest, and even forbidden from holding private
religious conversations in his home. [35]

Having emerged as a leading Reformed prince in Germany, Johann now became committed to the preservation and
extension of the Reformed faith. In 1577, he assembled his
pastors for the celebration of the Lord's Supper with broken
bread rather than wafers, and without the use of the communion cloth under the elements--an act which symbolized
their commitment to the Reformed faith. These pastors then
prepared the people for the transition by instructing them in
the Reformed doctrine of the Lord's Supper, in the division
of the two tables of the Decalogue followed by Calvin, [36] and
in the inappropriateness of certain forms and ceremonies
which had been preserved in the Lutheran service. A general synod of twenty-two ministers was held at Dillenburg in
1578, [37] where a confession of faith was prepared primarily
through the efforts of Pezel, after the main points of disa-
greement between the Reformed and the Gnesio-Lutherans
were discussed. Above all, it was the Count himself who
brought about confessional agreement through his own moder-
ate, clear-headed appeal to Scripture. This confession was
the first to use the name "Reformed" as the official title of
the Calvinistic branch of the Reformation. [38]

The Nassau General Synod of 1582 established uniformity in worship and church life by setting forth Reformed
dogma, with its distinctive treatment of Word, sacrament,
and church discipline, along the lines set forth in the Palatinate Church Order of 1563. This Church Order has been
called a "life ordinance" (Lebens-ordnung) because it embraced the life of faith and emphasized discipleship to the
Word in parochial life. [39] The Heidelberg Catechism was intended to be an integral part of this Order, with its great
attention to correct belief and polity. As embedded in the
Church Order, the Catechism stood between the sacrament
of baptism and the Lord's Supper, with the first signifying
entry and the second the abiding of the believer in the
church. [40] What is more, in Reformed theology, baptism is
made one's own, and entrance to the Lord's Table is allowed
only when the child of twelve or so is able to say the Cate-

chism in the midst of the congregation. This Order, together with the Catechism, was published in Nassau to promote "correctness and uniformity" in ceremonies, the true
observance of the sacraments, and a "correct knowledge of
God's Word and Will" among the congregations.[41]

The Catechism took its place alongside the Kinder-
fragen of the fifteenth-century Bohemian brethren and the
catechisms of Luther, which were neither guidebooks for
priests nor texts solely for the religious instruction of children. Rather, they were lay folks' manuals to promote lifelong discipleship to the Word. As such, the Heidelberg Catechism was designed to embrace the entire spectrum of life in
the church. Above all, it was to be received by adults
through the vehicle of catechetical preaching, which was a
requirement both of the Palatinate Church Order and the Nassau Church Order.[42]

Walter Hollweg, in a recent study,[43] has asked whether the Catechism was originally intended to be a confessional
document, or whether this was a later development. He believes the latter to be the case, and thereby seeks to clarify
Goebel's supposition[44] that the document was intended to be
used simultaneously as a confessional symbol, as doctrinal
theology, and as a catechism. Similarly, Heppe, the great
Marburg church historian, wrote that "the Catechism was
supposed to assume the role of a confession and a public
norm for teaching for the entire church."[45] "The Catechism
is at the same time a confession and a book of instruction."[46]
Hollweg concludes that the Catechism had been first designed
to prepare the faithful for understanding the office of preaching, and to this end its authors intended it to live in the
church orders, and vice versa.[47] Thus, the tendency to
treat the Catechism as a separate confession was a later development. He marshals the following evidence as support
for his position:

> 1. Frederick III did not regard the Catechism as
> a separate confession when the Emperor Maximil-
> ian II charged Frederick with opposing the Augs-
> burg Confession.

> 2. It had not yet attained this status by 1570, for
> in that year, Olevianus in Heidelberg opposed the
> proposal that it be treated as a confession.

> 3. As the Lutherans established the radical dis-

tinction between themselves and the Reformed with the 1580 edition of the Formula of Concord, attempts emerged to publish a unifying confessional document for all Reformed churches. In 1581, Frances Salluardo proposed to unify all Reformed confessions in a 'Harmonia Confessionum,' which would include the Heidelberg Catechism. The plan was rejected, chiefly through the opposition of Ursinus. [48]

The evidence indicates that the intended integral relation between Catechism and Church Order was carefully maintained by Count Johann in Nassau. The Reformed Nassau Confession of 1578[49] does not mention the Catechism. Its "General Articles" express agreement with the fundamental evangelical doctrines, notably justification by faith. Its "Particular Articles" set forth the distinctive Reformed teachings with regard to the Person of Christ and the Lord's Supper.[50] With Calvin, the Confession rejects the Gnesio-Lutheran view that the divine qualities of Christ are communicated to His human nature, which had made possible the Lutheran explanation of the real presence in the Lord's Supper as a "local inclusion" of Christ's divine nature within the elements. [51]   On the contrary,

Christ in this [human] nature is raised from death, and in the same body is seated at the right hand of His heavenly Father, and thus He is exalted to His kingly and priestly office, and is established as the Head of His Church. ... [52]

The similarity of this statement with Question 50 of the Catechism is unmistakable:

Q. Why is it added, And sitteth at the right hand of God?

A. Because Christ ascended into heaven for this end, that He might there appear as Head of His Church, by whom the Father governs all things. [53]

The Confession also fails to affirm "double" predestination, which is in accord with the Catechism and in direct contrast with the high, "supralapsarian" Calvinism of Beza, Pezel, and others. [54]   These areas of similarity indicate that the spirit and teaching of the Catechism is maintained in the Nassau Confession although it makes no explicit references

to it. The possibility that the Confession is implicitly con-
fessionalizing the Catechism by drawing upon its content
should be acknowledged.

As the Catechism began to assume a confessional
character, the phrase "holy Catechism" begins to emerge
alongside "holy Scripture."[55] Beginning in the 1560's, there
were isolated instances of eccentric pastors in the Rheinland
who had become convinced that the Catechism was free from
error, that whoever believes its truth would never perish,
and that whatever is opposed to it is false and sacrilegious.[56]
It was believed that the Catechism was given by the dictation
of the Holy Spirit, and it was regarded as the only means to
a correct knowledge of Scripture.[57] This line of thought
found a milder expression in 1619 at the Synod of Dort when
the Emden pastor Ritzius Lucas affirmed that it was more
important to teach the Catechism than to preach from the
Scriptures.[58] Representatives from Nassau participated at
the Synod.[59]

The Nassau Church Order which was adopted at the
Dillenburg General Synod of 1581 made provisions for the
parochial life in Nassau which remained as ideals for the
Otterbeins. Its purpose was to direct the life of believers
from baptism to the grave. Prominence was given to the
office of preaching, since the sermon was given by our Lord
to lead the elect to eternal life. The content of preaching
was comprehended in the threefold structure of the Cate-
chism--to bring men to the knowledge of their sin and misery,
then to their redemption from this condition, and finally, to
an attitude of thankfulness for deliverance.[60] The pastors
were to instruct the people "according to their lowly, limited
understanding,"[61] and were to relate as many of their sermons as possible to the Catechism. As in the Palatinate,
several questions were to be read from it on a systematic
basis in Sunday morning worship, and catechetical services
were held on Sunday afternoons for the purpose of examining
the children and for expounding the questions and answers to
the people on a yearly cycle.[62]

In the service of worship, congregational singing was
advocated for the "edification of the church," although it was
typically restricted to the singing of the German Psalms.[63]
The Church Order provided that the Lord's Supper should be
celebrated at least monthly in the cities and every two
months in the villages of Nassau, and in all congregations on
Easter, Pentecost, and Christmas. Where desired, it was

"Christian and correct" that it be held more often. [64] The
sacrament was always to be announced on the preceding Sunday, and a personal examination of the communicants was to
be made on the preceding Saturday. In conducting the examination, the pastor included the chief heads of doctrine,
the Decalogue, and the "Unser Vater," as set forth in the
Catechism. [65] However, the pastor should be prepared to extend a charitable judgment to those whose testimony was un-
clear for reasons of timidity. By guarding against unworthy
participation at the Table, the Church Order sought to main-
tain the integrity of sacrament and church, however much it
may have neglected the Eucharistic character of the sacrament. This emphasis on the integrity of the church was also
enhanced by the minister's authority to levy ecclesiastical
penalties, in accordance with the distinction between private
and public offenses as stated in Matthew 18. [66]

These provisions for discipline in the life of the
church reflect the emphasis of Calvin[67] and Ursinus[68] upon
the "third" use (tertius usus) of the law as its "true and
proper use." The law is primarily intended as a stimulus
and guide for the believer, in order that he might progress
in a life of sanctification. [69] The convicting use of the law,
which was primary for Luther, was "accidental" to this true
and proper use, said Calvin. [70] He does not mean to imply
that the existence of the true church is dependent upon the
holiness of its members, as in Donatism, for its marks are
limited to the true preaching of the Word and the proper administration of the sacraments. However, since the church
remains the church only when it exercises itself in the world,
discipline provides the sinews which enable it to be itself.
Discipline induces men to repent and serves as a restraining
influence which provides a moral example for society. [71]
The third section of the Catechism and the provisions for
discipline in the Church Order bear witness to this Reformed
emphasis upon the demands of grace. There is no contra-
diction between divine election and the alleged importance of
the means of grace in the visible church. In the Catechism,
the doctrine of election is presented not as ethereal speculation but as our "only comfort in life and death" (Question 1),
as "the stimulus of our moral life" (Question 32), and as
"the basis of our undoubted membership in the church" (Question 54).

After the adoption of the Church Order and the Catechism in the Nassau General Synod of 1582, subsequent General Synods had the purpose of promoting them and instruct-

ing pastors in their use--a program which was extended
throughout the local parishes by means of house visitations.
In addition, these sessions sought to examine and ordain
pastors, fill vacancies in churches and schools, and admonish negligent magistrates. [72] The fourfold order of pastor,
teacher, deacon, and elder was to be established, according
to the provisions of the Order. To effect the exercise of
church discipline and the reproof of "public" violations, the
elders were to meet in conventus with their pastor every
fourteen days or four weeks. [73] Each congregation was directed by a presbyterium, which was composed of the pastor
and selected elders. A group of congregations was organized
as a Konvent, over which an inspector presided. All pastors, together with an elder from each parish, held membership in this Konvent, and from their number general synods
(Landes-Konvente) were organized. [74] The consistory was
the body which stood between the nobility and the synod.

Discovery of the Visitations Record for 1608-1609,
which was published in 1611, permits us a glimpse at the
actual situation which prevailed in the churches during the
period. [75] For one thing, there was confusion among the pastors as to whether the Luther Bible or the new version produced by the Herborn professor, Johannes Piscator, should
be used. The inspectors decided in favor of the Luther version. [76] In some churches and chapels, the inspectors found
baptismal fonts in the Roman Catholic style (ausem Papstum)
and these were to be replaced by a mere basin. [77] All manner of variations were found with regard to the preparation
for and the administering of the Lord's Supper. Hence, the
provisions of the Church Order were strictly enforced and
the sacrament was to be celebrated at least six times a year,
depending upon whether the congregation was large or small.[78]

Of greater importance was the discovery of considerable confusion with regard to the meaning of the term "catechization." Some pastors were using questions which they
had composed independently, and these varied greatly in content. Others used the catechisms of Luther or Calvin, and
still others had devised such difficult questions that the youth
were left in an unedifying quandary. As a consequence, the
uniform use of the Heidelberg Catechism was strictly imposed. [79]

As in Calvin's Geneva, the coercive arm of the state
could be summoned to augment the persuasive doctrine of the
church. The local magistrates were asked to assist the pas-

tors in restraining the violation of the Sabbath, the neglect
of alms and charities, disobedience of elders and neglect of
children by parents, and the dissipating frivolities of excessive drinking, gluttony, dancing, trifling, profanity, and
slander. [80]

Steubing indicated that, at the time he was writing (c.
1800), Nassau-Dillenburg was the only Reformed territory
which was still maintaining the Reformed tradition of house
visitations. [81] Elsewhere, parish life had been shattered by
the debilitating effects of rationalism and secularism. At
this time, the following rubrics were being observed for the
visitations being conducted in the region where the Otterbeins
were pastoring. The inspection was to take place annually
on a Sunday afternoon, with the pastors and elders in charge.
They were to examine the parents, children, and house serv-
ants in the questions of the Catechism, to test their understanding by asking related questions, to inquire whether family prayers were being regularly offered, and to determine
whether the Psalms were sung and the Scripture read in the
homes. [82] In addition to inquiring into the regularity of
church attendance, the inspectors asked whether the sermon
was discussed at home after the service. [83] In this fashion,
the standards of Catechism and Church Order were not intended to effect a reformation in doctrine alone; they were
to permeate the full scope of parochial life.

Although the Catechism did become a confessional
document after the Synod of Dort in 1619, in Nassau it remained primarily a book of instruction in church, school,
and home. [84] There was no detached veneration, as in the
case of the symbols of the Formula of Concord, for it was
preeminently the layman's guide to God's Word. In Nassau,
the place of the local congregation assumed prominence, especially with the division of the kingdom after the death of
Count Johann (1606). As the Catechism gained confessional
status, it was in relation to the local congregation, not the
synod. Hence, the diminution of the idea of a "church confession" in Nassau in favor of the designation "congregational confession. "[85]

This development significantly affected the role of
dogma in the life of the church. Because of the centrality
of the local congregation, the chief mode of dogmatic expression became the congregational hymnal. The first hymnal
had been published in Herborn in 1586 under the direction of
Count Johann, and it included not only the Psalms (as well

as other hymns, notably Luther's Ein Feste Burg), but was
also equipped with annotations so that it could be used as a
book of instruction. [86] The Heidelberg Catechism was included, together with several prayers, which means that this
book assumed the character of a "house-book" (Hausbuch),
which could be used in times of crisis without regular pastoral assistance. [87] This Herborn hymnal had undergone
thirty-nine editions by 1694, [88] and it was used in many Reformed churches throughout Germany--thus making the comforting doctrine of the Catechism accessible to the faithful in
times of political oppression and rationalistic skepticism.
At the same time, the Catechism began to assume an autonomous character in the diminution of its role as a "church"
confession.

This latter development was, of course, not antici-
pated by Count Johann, for whom the Catechism was only to
be used in relation to the Church Order, and vice versa.
His task of establishing a durable parochial life in Nassau
along the lines set forth in the Nassau Confession, the Church
Order and the Catechism, required that provision be made
for a teaching church by the establishment of an educational
center for his realm.   Earlier in the century, Latin schools
had arisen in several towns, including Herborn. [89] The Count
planned a German school for every parish, where candidates
for the ministry would be sought.   Until 1594, parish schools
were established in this fashion, and, here and there, town
schools were also established in the larger communities. [90]
He even planned a school for women, which heretofore had
been unknown.   In all schools, the Catechism was to be the
principal educational tool; it was even used as a reading
primer.   Yet, familiarity with the Catechism was never intended as an end in itself; above all, it was intended to promote discipleship to God's Word, to which it bore witness.

Johann's greatest project was the creation of the "high
school" (hohe Schule) at Herborn, which consisted of two
parts.   There was the pedagogium, or gymnasium, consist-
ing of five classes which would continue the classical education which a student had begun in the Latin school; and the
"academy," for clerical education. [91] Instead of "academy,"
the term "university" is used in Schem's German Cyclopedia.
In the Cyclopedia of Education by Kiddle and Schem, it is
said, "The academy connected with the gymnasium, after
Sturm's plan [which the school at Herborn resembled], approached but did not entirely reach the standard of a university." [92] Each class in the pedagogium had its own precep-

tor, and here students completed a two-year course in logic,
math, philosophy, and Greek and Roman classics and history.
After completing their examinations, students could choose
among medicine, jurisprudence, or theology in the academy.[93]
The majority of students selected theology, which required a
three-year period of study. [94] In addition to the theological
curriculum, which was divided into dogmatic, exegetical, and
practical theology, the students were required to preach twice
a week before one of the theological professors, and each
Sunday afternoon a different student was appointed to conduct
a Bible study with the students. [95] Although committed to
Reformed dogma, the Count's "high school" was to reflect
the irenic spirit of Melanchthon.

Count Johann's plan was heartily received by the re-
nowned Olevianus, who had by now fled the persecution of
Ludwig in the Palatinate and was serving as court-preacher
at Berleburg. [96] Johann wished to locate the school either at
Siegen, Dillenburg, or Herborn, where he owned a castle
which could serve to house the school. Herborn was selected
after Olevianus had accepted a call to become pastor there in
1583. [97] The Count's objectives for the institution can be
learned from the record of his consultations with the pastors
on the projected school, which were part and parcel of his
efforts to increase the understanding of the Reformed faith in
his kingdom. [98]

In 1584, the institution was opened with a theological
faculty of ten members, led by Olevianus himself. [99] It was
called the "Johanneum," after its founder. In the first quarter, Johannes Piscator and Jakob Alstedt were added to the
faculty, the former arriving from Heidelberg and the latter
being influential in Dutch circles. Alstedt was to serve as
the representative from Herborn at the Synod of Dort. [100]
Piscator, who had also been sought by the University of Leiden in the Netherlands, joined with Olevianus in becoming
the "soul" of the institution. [101] Its "golden age" came in
the first twenty years, when its enrollment rose to four hun-
dred and included students from all parts of Germany and
even from Poland and Hungary. [102] This flowering took place
in the midst of a dearth of Reformed schools in Germany.
In 1602, Matthias Martinius wrote that this school was celebrated throughout the entire Christian world. [103] With Heidelberg having "lapsed" into Lutheranism, Herborn briefly
became the principal Reformed school in Germany. [104]

In this celebrated era of the school's history, Olevianus read dogmatics from his abridgement of Calvin's Institutes and Piscator lectured from his Aphorismen, which were based upon the Institutes and were dedicated to Beza. [105] Both men also specialized in exegetical discourses, and Olevianus became known for his persuasive, rhetorical manner of preaching. The death of Olevianus in 1587 was a great loss for the fledgling institution, and Count Johann was racked by anxiety with regard to the future prospects for the school. However, its first professor had laid a careful foundation, and the school was able to withstand the circumstances which threatened its existence after its initial period of growth. On two different occasions, the school was moved from Herborn to Siegen in an attempt to flee from the plague (from 1594-1599, and again from 1605-1609). [106] During the destruction of the Thirty Years' War, it was besieged by plague, famine, and by the burning of Herborn in 1627. [107] In the period of reconstruction which followed, the school found itself in combat with a new foe, rationalism, which was formally banished from the institution in 1681. [108] In the eighteenth century, the school continued to decline, while nearby Marburg flourished. It continued to function until 1817. [109] While other Reformed schools became enmeshed in rationalism, Herborn continued throughout the eighteenth century as a "nursery of the true Reformed faith."[110]

This resilient tradition of pietistic orthodoxy as Herborn is incomprehensible apart from the continuing influence of the Heidelberg Catechism. Antonius von der Linde has estimated that some forty editions of the Catechism were published in Nassau, mostly at the Herborn press, in addition to the editions of the Herborn hymnal, which included the Catechism in an appendix. [111] The manner in which this catechizing was conducted was an expression of the formal opposition to scholastic methodology which prevailed at Herborn. This Herborn tradition will emerge in its uniqueness when it is seen in contrast to the pervasive Protestant scholasticism which prevailed in the late sixteenth and the seventeenth centuries.

b.   Anti-Scholasticism at Herborn and Catechetical
      Exposition "Without Bondage to Word and Form"

The Heidelberg Catechism is defined in the Church Order as

... a short and simple verbal statement of the

principal items of Christian teaching, in which the
young and the innocent are ever nurtured anew by
what they have learned. [112]

The word "catechism" was associated with "echo," notes
Achelis,[113] for after the catechist had recited a portion of
the Catechism, the question brought about the echo of the
student, even "as the valley or the forest gives an echo of
our call." Graffmann notes that the following four terms
were used in the age of orthodoxy for catechetical instruction: einprägen (to impress upon one's memory), erklären
(to explain), beweisen (to demonstrate), and anwenden (to apply). [114] Of these, the first was the favorite.

Evangelical catechizing distinguished itself from the
medieval in that the Decalogue, confession of faith, Lord's
Prayer, and the other catechetical items were no longer regarded as "holy formulas," a formal knowledge of which had
an intrinsic power of protection. Rather, it explained (erklärte), as in the case of Luther's Small Catechism with its
typical, interpretative questions, "Was ist das?" and "Wie
geschiehet das?" Thus, the catechism was not only to present the principal teachings of Scripture by asking the question of its meaning. [115] It also followed that an explanation
(erklärung) of the catechism was superfluous, because it
would merely be an exposition of the exposition of doctrine
(Erklärung der Erklärung der Hauptstücke). [116] Graffmann
asserts that the catechetical instruction of the Reformation is
to be distinguished from that of the Middle Ages in that, in
the former, the fixed expressions of the dialogue, as well as
the texts themselves, now had to be memorized. [117] The result, he argues, was a catastrophic memory device (Memor-
ier-mechanismus), of which we at this juncture can hardly
conceive.

It was against this background of catechizing in the
age of Protestant orthodoxy that the uniqueness of the Herborn method of interpretation emerged. In order to appreciate better its uniqueness for its day, let us present a pre-
liminary evaluation of the philosophical and theological features of Protestant scholasticism and of the corresponding
antischolastic tradition which emerged at Herborn in the late
sixteenth century.

The ponderous manner of catechizing which emerged
in orthodoxy was already apparent in Ursinus' commentary
on the Heidelberg Catechism, in which he couches his evan-

gelical insights in the formal, deductive methodology of Aristotelianism. Thus, the questions and answers of the Catechism which, in themselves, provide a highly lucid presentation of Reformed doctrine, form the basis for a scholastic
reformulation of the faith. Note, for example, his exposition
of Question 54:

> Question 54. What believest thou concerning the
> 'Holy Catholic Church' of Christ?
>
> Answer. That the Son of God, from the beginning
> to the end of the world, gathers, defends, and pre-
> serves to himself, by his Spirit and word, out of
> the whole human race, a church, chosen to ever-
> lasting life, agreeing in true faith; and that I am,
> and forever shall remain, a living member there-
> of. [118]

The same scholastic tendency is present in Ursinus'
definition of the causes of predestination. This becomes the
basis for his exposition entitled "Of the Eternal Predestination of God," which is divided, in scholastic fashion, into
the questions: "Is there any predestination?", "What is it?",
"What is the cause of it?", "What are the effects of it?",
"Is it unchangeable?", "To what extent may it be known by
us?", "Are the elect always members of the church, and the
reprobate never?", "Can the elect fall from the church, and
may the reprobate always remain in it?", and "What is the
use of this doctrine?"[119] In each case, the question is an-
swered, and all objections are met. Also, in defining the
causes of predestination, distinctions are made between the
"efficient" cause of predestination, which is the "good pleasure of God," and its "final" cause, which is the "manifestation of the glory of God."[120] With regard to reprobation,
with which the Catechism does not deal, he also defines its
efficient cause as the good pleasure of God, and its final
cause as the manifestation of the glory of God. However,
"the cause of damnation, which is sin, is wholly in men."[121]
Thus, what Ursinus intended was an exposition and clarifica-
tion of the principal themes of the Catechism through a many-
sided interrogation. [122]

Melanchthon, his teacher, had already prepared the
way for this scholasticism with his famous "loci" methodology. With Melanchthon, there emerged the outline of a new
theme which would gain dominance both in Lutheran and Reformed orthodoxy: the concept of the dual nature of theology.

It has been said that a consequence of this concept was the
elevation of the text of the Bible as a whole, rather than the
evangelical doctrine of the Word of God, into the infallible
repository of doctrine.[123] Let us consider the development
of this scholasticism, which came to play such a prominent
role in determining the direction of catechizing.

On the one hand, the Loci Communes, which first appeared in 1521, was "something radically new in the theological science--a system of doctrine drawn from Scripture," and
on the other hand, for Melanchthon, Scripture is also to be
read in proclamation and meditation for the purpose of "learning Christ."[124] It was Troeltsch, in his Vernunft und Offenbarung bei Gerhard und Melanchthon,[125] who first recognized
this double nature of doctrine in Melanchthon. Theology as
"knowledge" is the exposition of the contents of Scripture in
an objective manner: theology as "true knowledge" (vera
cognitia) of Scripture is the knowledge which results when
Scripture is concretely proclaimed and heard as the vox Dei.
In the former, theology is publicly studied as a university
discipline, whereby the characteristic humanistic tools of
classical learning and philology are employed. It is assumed
that classical learning providentially concurs with the vera
cognitia, resulting from the hearing of the Word whereby
"The Holy Spirit strikes terror in consciences through the
preaching of repentance and lifts them up again through ...
the proclamation of the forgiveness of sins."[126] A disci-
plined study of Scripture, Melanchthon hoped, could resolve
the majority of controversies, but a true knowledge could
come only from the hearing of the word.[127]

In his Commentary on the Heidelberg Catechism, Ursinus made use of his teacher's concept of theology: in
preaching and meditation, the Catechism imparted the true
knowledge of salvation to believing hearts (vera cognitia); in
formal instruction, it was the basis for that knowledge of
faith (cognitia) which could be defined in terms of scholastic
concepts and therefore be rationally self-evident. In the
Commentary, the latter (cognitia) provides the formal structure in which the former (vera cognitia) is conveyed. Note,
for example, his use of substantial terminology to convey
the meaning of "comfort," as used in the Catechism:

> Comfort is that which results from a certain pro-
> cess of reasoning, in which we oppose something
> good to something evil ... The substance of our
> comfort therefore is briefly this: that we are

Christ's, and through Him reconciled to the Father,
that we may be beloved of Him and saved, the Holy
Ghost and eternal life being given unto us. [128]

Thus, explanation (Erklärung) was regarded as a matter of logic, as understood in the Aristotelian fashion whereby the particular is derived from the general as a matter of
logical necessity. The task of explanation tended to be reduced to the task of logical demonstration. The highest principles of explanation were none other than the four principles
of metaphysics: matter, form, purpose, and cause. [129] The
metaphysical assumption of this thought was that the actual
comprehension of truth is attained by a knowledge of the general premise and its recognition of the idea. [130] The chief
theological ideas in the catechetical answers were made the
theme of his study. Though Ursinus, who had also prepared
a commentary on the logic of Aristotle, [131] had achieved a
precise explanation of the concepts of the Catechism, this
strength was also his weakness. His detailed, massive Commentary gives the appearance of a rather vacuous classifica-
tion of properly defined concepts.

Graffmann calls this scholastic procedure, as used in
preaching and instruction, "explanation as dismemberment"
(the Zergliederungsmethode). [132] By this, he means that explanation is the investigation of the hidden logic behind the
expression of the text, or, an attempt to discern the steps
of thought implied in the text. Thus, while Ursinus' chief
concern was the explanation of the chief theological concepts
in the Catechism, the analysis of the logical structure of the
answers and even the questions became an end unto itself.
Ursinus realized that when he presented a text to his students, their first impression was characterized by unanalyzed
uniformity. Therefore, scholastic dialectic was the device
for penetrating the content of a particular text and its place
in relation to the whole. This concern with the grammatical
and logical, as well as the theological aspects, had first appeared in the writings of Lutheran and Roman Catholic po-
lemicists in the sixteenth century, but it came into general
use with the first school edition (Schulausgabe) of the Heidelberg Catechism in 1609. [133]

As well as being concerned with an analysis of the
various parts of the Catechism, Ursinus was also interested
in the exposition of the Catechism as a whole. By this, it
is meant that the principal teachings of the Heidelberg Catechism were not simply placed beside one another in an un-

connected fashion, as in Luther's Small Catechism, but were
unified in the teaching of the Catechism as a whole. [134]   In
the Small Catechism, the Decalogue, the Creed, the Lord's
Prayer, and the section dealing with baptism, confession,
and the Lord's Supper are set forth without any overarching,
connecting scheme. [135]   In the Heidelberg Catechism, all
heads of doctrine are ordered by the three aspects introduced
in Question 2: man's misery, redemption, and gratitude;
though this order has been decried by modern Lutherans as
an impossible pedagogical scheme, [136] it was important for
Ursinus.   He attributed its origin to the existence of his
Catechesis, which "includes the sum of Christian teaching." [137]
He explained that his "succinct and plain explanation of Christian teaching and its chief points" is needed by everyone because "... the foundation of religion must be known in such
a manner by all, learned and unlearned. "[138]   Here he refers
to the faithful knowledge necessary for salvation (Melanchthon's
vera cognitia).   The other knowledge of faith, the treatment
of the loci communes in the theological schools, have provided students with a 'full-blown system of Christian teaching,
as it were, a 'corpus'. "[139]

     Both the sum of Christian teaching presented in the
Catechism and the scholastic exposition of its content in
terms of the loci communes are intended ultimately to lead
to the true knowledge of faith (vera cognitia) which results
from the earnest reading and meditation upon Scripture itself.
This is the reason why the catechizing and dogmatics are
studied.   Yet, there is particularly close relationship between the simple order of the Catechesis and true, faithful
knowledge, for the saving truth of any given point of doctrine
is only apprehended in its relation to the whole. [140]   Ursinus
writes that a problem in the exposition of the Catechism is
thus "the correct demonstration of the parts and the order
and the interpretation of the words and sentences. "[141]   This
organic nature of the Catechism would become an important
factor in its exposition by the Reformed Pietists, as we shall
see later.

     As a student of Melanchthon, Ursinus structured the
Heidelberg Catechism within the scheme of law and gospel.

> The Decalogue contains the sum of the law, the
> symbol of the Gospel ... The Decalogue belongs to
> the first part--for it is a mirror of our sin and
> misery, and the third part--for it is the rule of
> true thankfulness.   Because the confession of faith

explains the method and mode of redemption, it belongs to the second part. Herein the sacraments
belong as appendages and seals of the doctrinal
teaching. [142]

Ursinus' commitment to the scholastic exposition of
the Catechism, which became the predominant mode of interpretation in seventeenth century Reformed orthodoxy, found a
distinct counterpart in the anti-scholastic tradition which
emerged at Herborn with Olevianus and his associates. The
ponderous, scholastic mode of exposition produced alarm
here, and the demand began to be raised in the General Synod
of Nassau-Dillenburg that the Catechism should be explained
(erklärte). [143] One of the clearest statements of the problem
was made by Wilhelm Zepper, a professor in the Academy
who was heavily influenced by the anti-scholastic logic of
Ramus. In 1595, he wrote that it is not sufficient for a
teacher to "think that he has fulfilled his duty if the catechumen can recite the dictated words of the Catechism like a
parrot, so that the tongue utters without understanding."[144]
In this case,

> ... the mark of truth does not penetrate at all,
> but remains on the periphery and cleaves to the
> surface, so that it soon vanishes, because nothing
> is as unreliable as the memory if its own judgment
> or insight into the matter is not exercised. [145]

Although Hollweg has recently questioned the assumption that Olevianus, in a final redaction, rendered the Catechism its non-scholastic, experiential character, it remains
valid that Ursinus was inclined toward Aristotle while Olevianus favored Ramus. It is difficult to establish with certainty that such questions from the Catechism as "what profit
does this doctrine have for you"?[146] should be attributed to
the Ramist outlook of Olevianus, as Good suggests. [147] It
resembles Luther's use of "What is that?" (Was ist das?)
in his catechisms, but as Tanis notes, it derives from the
Emden Catechism and can be traced through Ursinus' Larger
Catechism. However, Olevianus did publish a commentary
on the logic of Ramus at Herborn, [148] and his lectures on the
Catechism reflected the directive of the Nassau General Synod
of 1582, which held that the Heidelberg Catechism should be
set forth in preaching and teaching in such a way that its content would not be bound to the exact words and form in which
they were presented in the questions and answers (ohne
Bindung an die Wörte und die Form). [149] In evaluating this

Herborn tradition, let us first delineate the significant features of the Ramist logic (vis-a-vis Protestant scholasticism), with reference to its implications for Reformed orthodoxy and the interpretation of the Catechism at Herborn.

Peter Ramus (1515-1572) belongs in the rank of Renaissance philosophers who stood in formal opposition to the scholastic methodology. As Windelband notes,

> Instead of the idea, they [the Ramists] require the reality; instead of the artificial word pictures, they require the language of the created world; and instead of the subtle arguments and distinctions, they require a taste for an expressive description of the imagination and disposition of living men. [150]

Moltmann has recently evaluated the significance for Reformed orthodoxy of Ramus' attempt to dislodge the Aristotelian syllogism from its place of prominence. [151] Ramus, the Huguenot philosopher and martyr of St. Bartholomew's Night (in 1572), had been prevented from accepting the Elector Frederick's offer to teach at Heidelberg because of pressure from Aristotelians at the University. [152] However, he was later permitted to deliver a series of lectures there on Cicero, which inspired Ursinus to write of "the shameful, arrogant sophistry and babbling of Ramus."[153]

At a time when Protestantism--both Lutheran and Reformed--was making use of Aristotle, as a traditional method for a traditional range of theological problems, [154] the new intellectual concerns of Ramism were viewed as detrimental to the Protestant cause in its imminent struggle with Catholicism. The chief opponent of Ramus was the Reformed dogmatician Beza, with whom Ursinus sided, [155] and who was stoutly opposed by Olevianus and Piscator at Herborn. Moltmann has shown that the "hohe Schule" was established at Herborn rather than at Siegen because Crellius at Siegen had opposed the Ramists. [156] In a sense, Herborn was the continental counterpart to Cambridge, where, as Perry Miller has shown, [157] Ramism became influential among the Puritans. In brief, Ramism was capable of assimilation with every form of opposition to Aristotelian scholasticism within Protestantism, which included, in addition to Herborn, the late Zwinglianism of Bullinger and Molanus and the heretical humanism of Curione, Castellio, and Dudith. [158] Ramism also became implicated in the charge of "Crypto-Calvinism," for, at Wittenberg and Leipzig, it was held to be "a step toward Calvinism. "159

The question emerges, in what sense was Ramism
capable of being used as an apologetic, "Christian philosophy"
which could support the tenets of the Reformed faith, and the
Heidelberg Catechism in particular? Like Calvin, Ramus
was a Picard who studied at the University of Paris, and in
opposition to the scholasticism at the Sorbonne, Ramus first
enumerated the "heresies" of Aristotle: Aristotle disdains
the creation of the world, the predestination by God, and the
immortality of the soul. 160 Further, Aristotelians "despise
the study of the Word of God and emaciate theology through
the countless sophisms of Aristotle. "161

In particular, Ramus wished to free the arts faculties
of the universities from the dominance of Aristotle as a
counterpart to his opposition to the dominance of Aquinas in
theology. The "knowledge of the knowable" (Wissen des
Wissbaren), rather than the knowledge of abstract concepts,
became the watchword. 162 In freeing dogma from its subor-
dination to Aristotle, he undermined the latter by correlating
the principles of ratio and experientia. His point of departure both in philosophy and theology was emancipation from
the authority of tradition to an "unprejudiced" empiricism. 163
He replaced the syllogism with the grammatical dialectic of
rhetoric, modeled after Cicero's orations. Here was an in-
cipient movement from metaphysics to linguistic philosophy. 164 The motive of this transfer from the formal re-
tionale of the Aristotelian syllogism was practical. Ong
claims that Ramus' training in dialectic is

.... a curious attempt and can be described as an
attempt to set a vaguely Socratic dialectic in a
Ciceronian psychology, to give it a Platonic surface
purportedly in the interests of religion, and to 'sim-
plify' the results for reasons of 'practical' or pedagogical expediency. 165

By following Socrates rather than Aristotle, he did not place
himself under the yoke of any particular school, nor was he
required to regard philosophy as a purely formal system of
ideas. The system of Socrates was that of practical, human
wisdom, open to the common man.

Thus, it was his fiercely anti-Aristotelian record, and
not his mild Zwinglian theology, which led Beza to warn him
away from Geneva and which prompted Ursinus, Erastus, and

others at Heidelberg to refer to him as the "pest of all knowledge. "166

Yet, Ramism had distinct implications for theology. He defined theology as "Christian art of living, " and he also speaks of it as the "doctrine of living well, that is, to God. "167 As the purpose of the Ramist dialectic is "to speak well, to reason well, and to calculate well, " similarly, in theology, it is "the art of living to God. "168 In contrast to all orthodox definitions, which understood theology as the "discourse of God" or as the description of God's self-knowledge,169 Ramus appealed to Calvin himself.170 Against the Renaissance ideal of "living happily, " he adopted the phrase "to live well" as the motto for his Christian humanism, which emphasizes the ethical claim of responsibility resting upon divine grace rather than upon man's fortune.171 More precisely, the Ramist Schultetus even spoke of the imperative "to live rightly. "172

In contrast to the a priori method of scholastic methodology, Ramus' historical empiricism became fundamental for the federal theology which developed at Herborn. After defining God as "eternal Spirit, infinite and best above all, " he proceeds to state that He is only known by His activity among men.173 Thus, the orthodox emphasis upon the divine decrees, as in Beza, is undermined to make room for a theology of man and for a new historical orientation for dogma. Not from objective revelation but from the reach of human experience can the will of God be discerned.174 Ramus also introduces an "economical" view of the Trinity, for he finds the most important distinction between the Old and New Testaments to be in the separate and successive revelation of the Father in the one and of the Son in the other.175 This shift in trinitarian teaching to an historical description of its manner of revelation would be implemented in the Kingdom of God theology at Herborn. Calvin had used many different images to show the similarities and dissimilarities of the two Testaments;176 Ramus disregarded all customary dogmatic constructions of the Heilsgeschichte in the Old and New Testaments in favor of a simple ascending line.177 The distinction between the Testaments is only quantitative. With regard to predestination, Ramus sought to dispel the supralapsarianism which was espoused by Beza. Like Calvin himself, Ramus emphasized the soteriological implications of the doctrine, and he recognized that the varied statements in Scripture could not easily be reduced to a rigid system of decretal theology.178

Ramus' most controversial departure from scholastic
orthodoxy was with regard to the idea of substance in the
Reformed doctrine of the Lord's Supper. To the consterna-
tion of the French National Synod, he eliminated the scholastic notion from Article 36 of the Gallican Confession--a ges-
ture which brought down the ire of Beza upon his head. [179]
In his teaching, the question "What is it?" (Quid est?) is
almost rendered inconsequential, but the question "To what
end?" (Quis finis?) is treated in detail. Similarly, Piscator
at Herborn asserted that the primary question was the purpose for which the sacrament is intended. [180] Remus' emphasis is upon the "commemoration of Christ's benefits (not
His Person) and of the communication of the benefits of His
death. "[181] There is no substantial fellowship of the Body of
Christ, neither "realiter" nor "spiritualiter, " but only a fellowship of the "benefits" and "a consociation between the will
and work of Christ and the will and work of the believer."[182]
Piscator calls the communion of Christians and their faithful,
"obligation to mutual charity"; it follows that "the union
should not be considered substantial, whereby many are united
into one substance, but a personal fellowship of friends. "[183]
In this Ramus-Piscator doctrine, Christ is present not in a
mystical sense, as in Calvin's doctrine of the spiritual real
presence, and not in a physical nor metaphysical sense, but
as an ethical "consociation. "[184]

In opposition to Ramus' view of the Lord's Supper,
Beza advocated the substantia Christi, by which he meant
that Christ's benefits were not to be separated from His Person and that both comprised the gift of the sacrament, to be
grasped by faith. In a letter to Piscator at Herborn, Beza
stated that the real presence is the association of "the life
taken root in the exalted Christ, " in which the vivifying power of Christ's life is communicated to the believer as the
substance of His life. [185] Hence, he denies the assertion of
Ramus and Piscator that believers are only partakers in the
benefits of the suffering and death of Christ. [186] Beza doubt-
less thought he was defending Calvin, who said that it was
not only the beneficia, but also "Christ in Person" of whom
the faithful partake. [187] However, unlike Calvin, he did not
believe that Lutherans could join in the sacramental union. [188]
Ramus and Piscator sought to overcome this dogmatic exclu-
siveness with their doctrine of "ethical consociation. "

At Herborn, Ramus' doctrine of the Lord's Supper, together with the other aspects of his theology which we have

noted, was affirmed on the basis of federal theology, against
the scholastic orthodoxy of Beza and his several scholastic
colleagues.   Here the subjective side of the sacrament was
emphasized, as the "public faithful activity" of the congregation, and only secondarily was it held to be a sign of divine
grace for sinful man.[189] Also, Ramus had joined the "dis-
ciplinarian party" of Olevianus at Heidelberg,[190] and at Herborn, Olevianus advocated that the power of discipline in the
congregation be entrusted to a group of the heads of families
--a tradition which sided the emergence of congregational
autonomy at Herborn and which rigorously opposed the ex-
clusiveness of Beza's pastoral aristocracy.[191]

Under the influence of Ramus' empiricistic opposition
to scholasticism, Olevianus fell back upon the covenant idea
from Ursinus[192] as the basis for developing theology as "the
art of living for God." This rhetoric and empiricism also
became the basis for an accentuated biblical theology.[193]
Increasingly, the heads of doctrine came to be treated under
Ramus' category of de fidei actionibus--a trend which became
more clearly evident in catechizing. From his early days at
Trier, Olevianus had been interested in vernacular catechetical instruction, and though his chief theological work (De
substantia foederis gratuiti ...), which appeared at Herborn
in 1585, made use of the covenant theme as his dogmatic
locus, his primary interest in this theme was centered in its
religious efficacy for the believer.

It was the believer's past experience of salvation
(Heilserfahrung) which became the focal point of the federal
theme.[194] Olevianus was convinced that he was adhering to
the real intent of the Catechism. Did not the answer to the
first question, which speaks of the firma consolatio in life
and death, answer that "God has received me in His grace
(Gnadenbund)?"[195] This union is the reconciliation with God
accomplished through the mediation of Christ and made necessary because the covenant (Foedus) between God and man
had been broken by the fall. His discussion of this covenant
of grace is always in connection with the kingly-priestly role
of Christ (which, as we have seen, played so prominent a
role in the Nassau Confession).

As Schrenk has shown, Olevianus joined the covenant
theme with the threefold office of Christ by accentuating the
relation between "covenant" and "Kingdom."[196] The covenant
of grace (foedus gratuitum) is the Kingdom of Christ (regnum
Christi). More precisely, by means of the former, the latter

is brought into being. The Kingdom becomes established in
us wherever the covenant proceeds from His rule: the con-
foederati are the true citizens of the Kingdom of Christ (veri
regni Christi cives). [197] The sovereignty of God (dominum)
is brought into harmony with the active, faithful participation
of man in unison with God. This covenant is only made with
the elect. [198] In the Substantia, the attempt is made to join
regnum, foedus, and immutabile Dei decretum. [199]

        The theme of the indwelling Christ assumes major
importance in view of Olevianus' warm, practical religious
interest, and his Pauline Christ-mysticism occasionally becomes pervasive, as in his description of the Lord's Supper
as a certain oath (sacramentum) of the union which Christ
wants to make with us:

> A believing soul does not hasten to a visible drink
> in the Lord's Supper, but steps as into a garden,
> and, freeing himself from his drops of bloody
> perspiration, he attains a holy wonder, and re-
> stores and quickens himself over against the fires
> of hell. Indeed, he has feasted with hearty trust
> on the whole Easter Lamb at the cross with His
> crown of thorns, which is quite consoling to the
> disturbed soul ... [200]

        With Olevianus' interest in federal theology for its
religious efficacy, the Ramist method of catechetical explanation assumes a form which cogently distinguishes it from the
scholastic method. Being freed from the scholastic terminology, catechetical explanation acquires a certain lucidity,
which pertains to theology as practical knowledge. The principal example of this method is Olevianus' Vester Grund. [201]
It is clearly pastoral, and wants "Christians who will seek a
consolation from God's Word in this dangerous and afflicted
time," and who, "not knowing wherein they are, exhibit a
firm trust in which they can abide." [202] Thus, the doctrine
of Providence looms prominently in this treatise.

        With the influence of Ramus, it became characteristic
at Herborn to regard the content to which the Heidelberg
Catechism bore witness as being in no way identical with the
text and its particular form. Not only was it thought that its
testimony could be given in other words; even more, it was
felt that a continual repetition of the same words obscures
the ideas. Thus, Zepper advocates

If children can repeat the text and formula of the Catechism, the catechumens should accustom themselves in the questions of the Catechism in an independent manner; that is, to answer in their own words in another order than that of the memorized text and to present a testimony of the one questioned. [203]

This procedure was not intended to supplant the Catechism, for he added that

Through this [procedure] it will become evident in which place and even with which words this is transmitted in the Catechism, and thus the insight and judgment of the catechumen will be better molded. [204]

In this statement, Zepper summarized the practice of catechetical exposition "not bound to the words and the form" (ohne Bindung an die Wörte und die Form) which had already been the practice at Herborn for a decade, [205] and which had been masterfully expressed in Olevianus' Vester Grund, which was formally quite unrelated to the Heidelberg Catechism.

Olevianus' free divergence from the form of the Catechism is further exemplified in his suggestion that the sacramental teaching found in Luther's Small Catechism be "united from God's Word with the teaching of the Reformed churches." [206] He also composed a catechism for the Landvolk of Wittgenstein. [207] Similarly, Piscator, his colleague at Herborn, did not feel hindered by his confession of the Heidelberg Catechism from composing three catechisms of his own; [208] and when Georg Pasor, another colleague at Herborn, wrote his Christlichen Lehrmeister, he expressed in the foreword that "those things which were set forth were the same as in the Heidelberg Catechism" (the principal characteristic of his work was the shortening of the longer answers). [209] Other Herborners who followed the example of Olevianus and Zepper included Matthias Martinius (1572-1630), who composed numerous catechisms which were not bound to the form of the Heidelberg Catechism; and Heinrich Alting, whose catechetical instruction only loosely adhered to the Catechism. [210] In short, the contributions of Olevianus and Zepper represent developments complementary to the anti-scholasticism of Ramus: the one understood catechization as depending not only upon catechetical instruction, but also upon the trust which the catechumen learns to receive into his life; and the other supported this position with his struggle against the mechanism of memory. 211

The Herborn theology found its culmination in the monumental theological system of Johann Heinrich Alsted (1588-1638), who was professor in the theological faculty from 1619 to 1629. 212 He addressed himself to the full range of theological issues from the Ramistic point of view in his Praecognitia (Frankfurt, 1614): the Theologia naturalis, the Catechesis (for beginners), the Theologia scholastica (which was reserved exclusively for the polemical defense of the faith), and the Theologia practica or ecclesiastica (which was his primary section and was devoted to soteriology and ethics).213 This last section was also discussed under the rubric of the Theologia prophetica, thus showing the influence of the federal theology of Olevianus.

With this introduction to the Herborn tradition of Reformed theology, our concern now is with its continual reshaping in the period which I call "Reformed Pietistic Orthodoxy," in the seventeenth and early eighteenth centuries. In this period emerged the diverse interpretations of the Catechism by Voetius, Cocceius, and the Reformed Cartesians. Though their procedures appeared totally dissimilar, distinctive emphases from all three would be combined in the ethos of eighteenth-century theology and, in particular, in the theology of the Otterbeins.

Notes

1. Heinrich Steitz, Geschichte der Evangelischen Kirche in Hessen und Nassau (Marburg, 1965), I, 95.

2. Ibid.

3. Ibid.

4. Friedrich Wilhelm Cuno, Johann der Alter von Nassau-Dillenburg, ein furstlicher Reformator (Halle, 1869), 1.

5. Steitz, I, 96.

6. The Landescollegium was the Nassau provincial council--the highest administrative body, which included representatives from the church council, the Count's ad-

ministrative chamber, and the provincial court of justice.

7. Cuno, 5.

8. Ibid.

9. Bard Thompson, et. al., Essays on the Heidelberg Catechism (Philadelphia, 1963), 25 ff.

10. B. J. Kidd, ed., Documents Illustrative of the Continental Reformation (Oxford, 1911), 363 f.

11. These "interconnected causes" were the Holy Spirit as
the primary agent, the Word of God as the instrumental agent, and the will of man which consents to this
action and freely yields to it. --See Thompson, 25 ff.,
Corpus Reformatorum, 21:659. However, as Sup-
perich notes, it is not clear what Melanchthon meant
by their "interconnection." See Melanchthon: On
Christian Doctrine, Clyde L. Manschreck, ed. and
tr., Library of Protestant Thought (New York, 1961).

12. Philip Schaff, The Creeds of Christendom (Grand Rapids,
1966), III, 13.

13. The principal influence was a treatise on the Lord's Supper by Joannis Oecolampadius. --See Corpus Reformatorum 2, 217; discussed in Thompson, 12.

14. Schaff, III, 13, and Thompson, 13.

15. It should be recalled that Luther himself had substantial-
ly agreed with Calvin on the Lord's Supper.

16. See Thompson, 16-20.

17. "Koininia" is defined as the communion by which union
takes place in the use. Thompson notes that, by in
usu, Melanchthon means that the grace of the sacrament is personal--a personal communion with Christ
--and cannot be realized merely by the consecration
of the elements. --Ibid., 19.

18. See H. Heppe, Die Bekenntnisschriften der altprotestanti-
schen Kirche Deutschlands. (Cassel, 1855), 583-597;
and Thompson, 22.

19. Preface to <u>Heidelberg Catechism</u>, quoted in Thompson,
    25.

20. This is deduced from the statement in Frederick's <u>Pref-</u>
    <u>ace</u> that the Committee included "our entire theologi-
    cal faculty in this place, and all the superintendents
    and distinguished servants of the Church."--Wilhelm
    Niesel, ed., <u>Bekenntnisschriften und Kirchenordnungen</u>
    <u>der nach Gottes Wort reformierten Kirche.</u> (Zurich,
    1938), 138-9; quoted in Thompson, 25 ff.

21. Walter Hollweg, <u>Neue Untersuchungen zur Geschichte und</u>
    <u>Lehre des Heidelberger Katechismus.</u> (Neukirchener
    Verlag, 1961), 1. Folge, 124-152.

22. August Kuckhohn, <u>Die Briefe Kurfürst des Frommen von</u>
    <u>der Pfalz</u>, I, 661-664, quoted in Thompson, 28.

23. Steitz, I, 96.

24. Cuno, 10.

25. <u>Ibid.</u>

26. <u>Ibid.</u>, 11.

27. <u>Ibid.</u>, 12.

28. James Good, <u>Origin of the Reformed Church in Germany.</u>
    (Reading, Pa., 1887), 256 ff.

29. See discussion in Thompson, 29 ff.

30. Cuno, 14.

31. <u>Ibid.</u>

32. <u>Ibid.</u>

33. Johann Steubing, <u>Kirchen und Reformations-Geschichte</u>
    <u>der Oranien-Nassauischen Lande.</u> (Hadamar, 1804),
    85.

34. Cuno, 16.

35. <u>Ibid.</u>

36. Inst. 2, 8, 12.

37. It consisted of twenty-two pastors, the Court-master Nymptsch and Otto von Grunade. --Good, 258.

38. This claim is made by Good, 13.   See also H. Heppe, Bekenntnisschriften der Reformierten Kirche Deutschlands; (Elberfeld, 1860), quoted in Cuno, 17. With this synod, the pastors were free to retain the Augsburg Confession of 1530 in the understanding of the Wittenberg Concord of 1536. --Steitz, II, 164.

39. Ibid.

40. Thompson, 40.

41. Preface to the Nassau edition of the Order, quoted in Steitz, 162.

42. Thompson, loc. cit.

43. Walter Hollweg, Neue Untersuchung zur Geschichte und Lehre des Heidelberger Katechismus. 2. Folge. (Lemgo, 1968), 12.

44. Max Goebel, Geschichte des christliche Lebens in der rheinisch-westphalischen evangelischen Kirche. (Coblenz, 1852), I, 365.

45. Heppe quoted by Hollweg, 2. Folge, op. cit., 9.

46. E. F. K. Müller, Die Bekkenntnisschriften der Reformierten Kirche. (Leipzig, 1903), LI.

47. Herausgegeben von W. Niesel, 1934, V, quoted in Hollweg, 2. Folge, 23.

48. These two points are discussed in Hollweg, 23 ff. He notes that the first collections of Reformed confessions were made in the nineteenth and twentieth centuries, such as that of Müller (op. cit.).

49. This was the Nassauische Bekenntnish (Dillenburger Synode) von 1578, Müller, 720.

50. Ibid.

51. Joseph McLelland, "Lutheran-Reformed Debate on the
    Eucharist and Christology," in Paul C. Empie and
    James McCord, eds., Marburg Revisited. (Minneapo-
    lis, 1966), 42.

52. Müller, 721. This passage is similar in content to
    Question 31 of the Heidelberg Catechism. (Schaff, III,
    317).

53. See Question 50, Schaff, III, 323.

54. The Nassau Confession reads as follows: "Through this
    teaching, God forever and ever gathers unto Himself
    from the human race an eternal church."--Cuno, 21.
    This compares favorably with question 54 of the Cate-
    chism. --Schaff, III, 324ff. As Cuno noted (loc. cit.),
    the definition of the Person of Christ in the Lord's
    Supper is treated in greater detail in the Confession
    because, at the time of its composition in the 1570's,
    the problem of its definition was a more burning issue
    than the question of predestination.

55. Hollweg, 2. Folge, 28.

56. These sentiments were expressed by one Magister Al-
    brecht, a preacher at Rheinstrom; discussed in Holl-
    weg, 2. Folge, 29.

57. Ibid.

58. Steitz, II, 163.

59. Hollweg, 34. --Representatives were present from the
    Rheinland Reformed territories, including the Palati-
    nate court-preachers Schultetus and Fontanus. The
    following statements summarize the action of the Gen-
    eral Synod of Duisburg (1610): "1. The sum of God's
    Word is comprehended in the Heidelberg Catechism,
    and for this reason, the same should also be confessed
    in schools and churches ...
    "2. ... these brethren wish to influence the other
    brethren of churches inside and outside the German na-
    tion with God's Word and therefore with this confes-
    sion." Quoted from the German in Goebel, II, 1852,
    108ff.

60. Steitz, II, 168.

1766334

61. Ibid.

62. August Kluckhohn, Die Briefe Kurfürst des Frommen von
    der Pfalz, I, 661-5; quoted in Thompson, 28.

63. Steitz, II, 169.

64. Ibid., 170.

65. Questions 1-5 deal with one's fitness to approach the
    Table. Only those were invited to the Table who
    sought to enhance their union with Christ, for "None
    should be admitted to the Holy Communion who has
    not confessed a knowledge of his faith according to the
    pure teaching of the evangelical Reformed, according
    to the mode of the church, and whoever does not have
    the sign of a godly life. Without these changes no
    alien person may be admitted."--Cuno, 113.

66. Inst., 4, 11, 1-5.

67. Ibid., 2, 7, 12.

68. Corpus doctrinae Orthodoxae, 491-528, cited in Thomp-
    son, 43.

69. Inst., 2, 7, 12.

70. See Calvin's Commentary on II Corinthians 3:7, CNTC.

71. Thompson, 43.

72. Steitz, II, 173ff.

73. Ibid.

74. Ibid., 166.

75. Ibid., "Visitations-Abschied de Anno 1611, November 25."

76. Steitz, loc. cit.

77. Ibid.

78. Ibid.

79. Ibid.

80. Ibid.

81. Steubing, op. cit., 207.

82. Ibid.

83. Ibid., 208.

84. Steitz, II, 180.

85. Ibid.

86. The Psalms were cast in the style of the Lutheran Ambrosius Lobwasser (1515-85) with the melody of the French Huguenot Psalms of Marot and Goudimel. -- Ibid.

87. Ibid.

88. Ibid.

89. Johann Steubing, Geschichte der Hohen Schule Herborn. (Hadamar, 1823), 166.

90. Steubing, Kirchen und Reformationsgeschichte..., 378.

91. A. W. Drury, The Life of Otterbein. (Dayton, 1898), 35ff.

92. Kiddle and Schem, Cyclopedia of Education, quoted in Drury, loc. cit.

93. Ibid.

94. Steubing mentions that more than 5000 students attended the school up to 1800. --Steubing, 50ff.

95. Drury, 36.

96. Good, op. cit., 263.

97. He succeeded Pezel, who had become pastor in Bremen. --Ibid.

98. His four principal objectives were as follows:
    "1. Because it is recognized that the work of religion would nowhere be as diligently promoted as in school.

"2. Betit is recognized that the Reformed faith is little understood in the Kingdom and that both church and schools are in ill-repute and are persecuted. "3. Because it is recognized that a pure church and school are difficult to attain. "4. Because the present tendency for students to study in other lands prevents youth in this realm from being challenged to attain the ideals of a higher education."--Quoted in Cuno, 33ff.

99. These men were Olevianus, Publianus, Joh. Pincier, Hermann Germberger, Mag. Conrad Ursinus, M. Naum, M. Jakob Dickhaut, M. Heinrich Heidefeld, M. Nobis, and Ehren Pilger. --M. Maurer, Zum 300 jahrigen Gedächtnis der Stiftung der Hohen Schule Johannes zu Herborn. (Herborn, 1884), 9.

100. Ibid.

101. Cuno, 35.

102. Ibid.

103. Joh. Steubing, Geschichte der Hohen Schule Herborn, 128.

104. Cuno, 35. In addition, Johann's brother, Willem of Orange, founded the University of Leiden, and Count Lewis of Nassau founded the University of Franeker in the Netherlands.

105. They appeared in 1627. Olevianus' compendium was entitled Epitome institutionis Calvin.

106. Ibid.

107. Ibid.

108. J. Bohatec, Die Cartesianische Scholastik in der Philosophie u. reformierten Dogmatik des 17. Jhdts. 1 Theil, Leipzig. 1912. 58.

109. Cuno, 37.

110. Ibid.

111. H. Graffmann, Monatschefte für evangelische Kirchen-

geschichte des Rheinlandes. Vol. 9, (1960), 36.

112. Pal. Church Order, quoted by Graffmann, "Erklarung
     in Predigt u. Unterricht...," 63.

113. E. Chr. Achelis, Lehrbuch d. prakt. Theol., Leipzig,
     1898, II, 3; quoted in Graffmann, Ibid.

114. Ibid.

115. Thompson, 34.

116. Graffmann, 63.

117. The Commentary of Dr. Zacharias Ursinus on the Hei-
     delberg Catechism. (Columbus, Ohio, 1852), 285.
     (G. W. Williard, tr. and ed.). (Originally published
     as Explicationes catecheticae in 1591).

118. Ibid.

119. Ibid., 293.

120. Ibid., 297ff.

121. Ibid.

122. Wilh. H. Neuser, Der Ansatz d. Theol. Bh. Melanch-
     thons. (Neukirchen, 1957), 46ff.; quoted in Graffmann,
     64.

123. Rupert Davies, The Problem of Authority in the Conti-
     nental Reformers. (London, 1947), ch. 1.

124. Clyde L. Manschrek, Melanchthon: The Quiet Reformer.
     (New York, 1958), 82, 92.

125. Ernst Troeltsch, Vernunft und Offenbarung bei Gerhard
     und Melanchthon. (Gottingen, 1891), 25-41. (On the
     dual conception of theology.)

126. From Schwarzenau, Die Wandel im theologischen Ansatz,
     17, quoted in Robert Scharlemann, Aquinas and Ger-
     hard (New Haven, 1964), 26.

127. An acoustic, not a theoretical knowledge, to use the dis-
     tinction formulated by Scharlemann in his study,

Aquinas and Gerhard. He uses this distinction, based on Melanchthon, to expose the view that, in Melanchthon, Luther's "existential viewpoint has been replaced by the point of view of the spectator." Given this dual character of theology in Melanchthon and his successors, Scharlemann establishes a continuity between the Reformation and post-Reformation periods, which also indicates the difference between the scholasticism of the thirteenth century and that of the seventeenth. -- Ibid., 27.

128. Ursinus, Commentary... 17, 19. Althaus states that Ursinus accepted the general dogmatic concept of Melanchthon in his definition of fides theologica. -- Opus 1. 105ff., quoted in Althaus, 221.

129. Graffmann, "Erklärung des Heidelberger Katechismus in Predigt und Unterricht des 16. bis 18. Jahrhunderts," Handbuch zum Heidelberger Katechismus, Lothar Coenen, ed. (Neukirchener Verlag, 1963), 66.

130. Windelband-Heimsoeth, Lehrbuch d. Gesch. d. Philosophie. (Tubingen, 1957), 113-131, discussed in Graffmann, loc. cit.

131. Ibid.

132. Graffmann, "Erklarung...," 66.

133. Ferd. Cohrs, "Katechismum u. Katechismusunterricht," R.E., X, 142, discussed in Graffmann, op. cit.

134. Graffmann, 69.

135. Schaff, III, 74-92.

136. Graffmann, 69.

137. Miscellana catechetica (Neustadt, 1600), 51f; quoted in Graffmann, loc. cit.

138. Ibid.

139. Ibid.

140. Ibid.

141. Ibid.

142. Ursinus, Expl. Cat., 16, quoted in Graffmann, 70.

143. Steubing, Kirchen u. Reformations Geschichte, 116.

144. Politia Ecclesiastica, (Herborn, 1714), 352, quoted in Graffmann, 64.

145. Ibid.

146. This phrase is found, for example, in Question 45. -- Schaff, III, 321.

147. James Good, The Heidelberg Catechism in its Newest Light, (Philadelphia, 1914), 119.

148. Ibid.

149. This was the actual wording of the General Synod. -- Steubing, Kirchen u. Reformations Geschichte, 120. Olevianus' lectures were entitled Explicatio Catecheseos Heidelbergensis. (Herborn, 1614).

150. Windelband-Heimsoeth, loc. cit., 308.

151. Jurgen Moltmann, "Zur Bedeutung d. Petrus Ramus fur Philosophie U. Theologie in Calvinismus," Zeitschrift fur Kirchengeschichte. Vol. 68 (1957), 296ff.

152. Good, The Heidelberg Catechism..., 110.

153. Ursinus' letter to Camerarius, July 17, 1570, quoted in Good, 112.

154. This phrase, "traditional method," is used by Beardslee, 8.

155. Beza taught at Geneva; his followers included Ursinus, Pareus, and Keckermann in Heidelberg, and Lubertus, Gomarus, and Voet in the Netherlands. --Moltmann, 296.

156. Ibid.

157. Perry Miller, The New England Mind: The Seventeenth Century. (New York, 1934), 141.

158. Moltmann, loc. cit. ; he also argues that, in the seven-
     teenth century, it entered into the complex streams
     of Arminianism and Amyraldism.

159. Ibid.

160. Ibid. , 298.

161. Ramus, Commentariorum de Religione Christiana libri
     quator, 1576, quoted by Moltmann, 299.

162. Ibid.

163. Ibid.

164. Althaus, op. cit. , 9ff.

165. Walter J. Ong, Ramus: Method and the Decay of Dia-
     logue. (Cambridge, 1958), 172.

166. Moltmann, op. cit. , 303.

167. Com. de Rel. , 6; quoted by Moltmann, loc. cit.

168. Ibid.

169. H. Heppe, Reformed Dogmatics set out and Illustrated
     from the Sources. (London, 1950), 6.

170. Müller, op. cit. , 117ff.

171. Moltmann, 303.

172. K. Reuter, Amesius, (1940), 32; quoted by Moltmann,
     304.

173. Moltmann, loc. cit. , 34ff.

174. Ibid. , 305.

175. Ibid.

176. See Inst. , 2, 10, and 2, 11.

177. Moltmann, 305.

178. Ramus says "1. Scripture states both: by Christ's com-

mand the Gospel is to be preached to all creatures;
yet the Pauline sentence also is correct concerning
the vessel which God has decided for construction.
2. We believe that both statements, which appear in
the weakness of the human capacity for knowledge,
were in the divine purpose... "--Ibid. , 306.

179. This occurred at the French National Synod meeting at
La Rochelle in 1571. --Ibid.

180. Piscator defended the Ramist teaching against the Melanchthonian Pezel at Herborn. --Ibid.

181. Ramus, Comm. de Rel. , 290ff. , Ibid.

182. Ibid.

183. Thes. Theol. I, loc. cit. , 13; Moltmann, op. cit. , 309.

184. Ibid.

185. Ibid. , 310.

186. Ibid.

187. In the Institutes of 1559, 4, 7, 11, Calvin wrote "Ma-
teriam aut substantiam voco Christum cum sua morte
et resurectione. "

188. Calvin had recognized Lutherans as brethren at the
Table, and Melanchthon, in the Variata doctrine of
the Augsburg Confession, was in particularly close
harmony with Calvin, as noted above. --See Wendel,
340ff.

189. Moltmann, 308.

190. Ibid. , 307.

191. Ibid.

192. It is for this reason, notes Tanis, that Olevianus could
say that he was adhering to the real intent of the
Catechism.

193. Moltmann, 317.

194. Gottlob Schrenk, Gottesreich u. Bund im älteren Protest-antismus, vornehmlich bei Johannes Cocceius. (Gütersloh, 1923), 57.

195. Ibid.

196. Expositio, 76, quoted by Schrenk, 60.

197. Exp. 3ff, 5, 9ff, 20, 47, 75ff, 89; Subst. 132, dis-cussed in Schrenk, loc. cit.

198. Exp. 9, Ibid.

199. Subst. 132ff., 140, discussed in Schrenk, Ibid.

200. Olevianus quoted by Goebel, I, 384ff.

201. Graffmann, "Erklärung...," 67.

202. Vester Grund, quoted by Graffmann, op. cit.

203. Zepper, Politia ecclesiastica, (Herborn, 1714), 352; quoted in Graffmann, loc. cit.

204. Ibid.

205. Ibid.

206. From the conclusion of Olevianus' Gnadenbund (Herborn, 1590), quoted in Graffmann, 68.

207. Ibid.

208. Ibid.

209. Ibid.

210. Ibid.

211. Ibid., 69.

212. E. Bizer, Introduction to Heppe's Dogmatik ... (Neukirchener Verlag, 1958), LI.

213. Ibid.

Chapter 2

STREAMS OF REFORMED PIETISM

a. The Interpretation of the Catechism by the Dutch
    Master Theologians of the Seventeenth Century

The conflicts among Voetians, Cocceians, and Cartesians, which characterized Reformed theology in the Dutch
and German Reformed territories during the seventeenth and
early eighteenth centuries, led to new developments in the
history of catechetical instruction, which will be the subject
of this section.

We have seen how Melanchthon's conception of the
dual nature of theology permitted the reception of Aristotle
in seventeenth-century orthodoxy, as a means of clarifying
conceptually the insights of the Reformation vis-a-vis the
Counter-Reformation. This tendency is already evident in
Ursinus' Commentary on the Heidelberg Catechism, in which
he couches his evangelical insights in the formal, deductive
method of Aristotelianism.

However, the limitation of reason in the dual conception of theology was obscured as reason became a methodological principle for understanding the truth of Scripture.
Once the clarity of logic and metaphysics had entered the domain of theology, philosophy increasingly came to have an
independent status and its concepts began to influence the content of theology. Concurrent with the development of Protestant Aristotelianism, the assumption emerged with Galileo
that the book of nature is as significant as the book of
Scripture. Not only is nature on the same plane with Scripture, it is more precise and clear. Implicit in the new science was an independent, natural basis for religion which
would soon be determining the biblical understanding of revelation. [1] This was a clear departure from the Reformers,
who had often found that obscurity in Scripture was a guard
against undue pride of intellect. [2] In the face of the emerging rationalism, orthodoxy could either abandon the dual nature of theology and admit that rational, scientific truth was

not in full harmony with revealed truth, or biblical statements could be affirmed over against the new science. The
latter course was chosen in most instances, thus moving
orthodoxy beyond the authority of the biblical word to the
inerrancy of the text. Calovius, for example, could now
write "No error, even in unimportant matters, no defect of
memory, not to say untruth, can have any truth in all the
Sacred Scriptures. "[3]

At the same time as the use of reason as a proof for
revelation was passing from the hands of the orthodox to the
emerging rationalists, Aristotelianism was being undermined
within the church tradition by the Pietists. In the decade
that Galileo was asserting the clarity of nature over the unclarity of Scripture, Johann Arndt, the Lutheran precursor
of Spener, was asserting the clarity of the Spirit in the reborn, rather than the metaphysical unity of Aristotle and
Scripture, as the methodological principle for understanding
the unclarity of Scripture. [4] It is generally understood that,
for the Pietists, the new birth tended to offset a one-sided
emphasis upon forensic justification; but it is also significant
that their neglect of the philosophical problem is concurrent
with the emergence of the new science. It is to be noted
that Pietism flourished most at Herborn and Franeker, which
had been influenced by Ramus. In Arndt and Spener, among
the Lutherans, and in Lodensteyn, Untereyck, and others
among the Reformed, the clarity of the Spirit in the reborn
replaces metaphysics as the guide for understanding revelation. [5]

The Aristotelian dominance was thereby challenged by
the model provided by natural science, by churchly piety,
and also, from the side of philosophy, by Renaissance humanism. Whereas Melanchthon had introduced classical learning
only as a logistic discipline in the service of revelation, it
became the motive for an attack upon Bezan orthodoxy by the
Dutch humanist Coornhert. The tenets of the "Remonstrants,"
as well as those of the "Anti-Remonstrants," were defeated
at the Synod of Dort (1618-19). [6]

An issue which received no decisive resolution at the
Synod was the question of whether Scripture or creed was
primary--an issue which brought to focus the debate between
scholastics and anti-scholastics. The question erupted anew
in the Voetian-Cocceian controversy of the mid-seventeenth
century, when this issue was to be more clearly drawn. For
Voetius, the prominent Aristotelian at the University of

Utrecht (d. 1676), the Bible was to be interpreted in the light
of the Reformed tradition; for Cocceius, who held forth at the
University of Leiden (d. 1669), creeds were to be interpreted
in terms of Scripture. [7]

The Voetians continued the scholastic tradition of catechetical instruction which began with Ursinus, but they accentuated the emphasis upon correct living as well as correct
teaching. Voetius asserted that it was not enough to take
notice of the chief items of the Catechism; rather, God, in
speaking through his Word, willed that our entire lives be
consecrated in service to Him. [8] This dogmatician wrote
that

> All theology that follows Scripture or is based upon
> it, whether expressed in commentaries, 'loci com-
> munes,' or catechisms ... is practical theology. [9]

Or again, he writes "no theology can be completely and correctly discussed unless developed practically." [10] Casuistry,
or moral theology, is to be distinguished from church dogma,
which he also calls "speculative theology." [11] The necessity
of "precision," or practical theology, is proved

> ...from the necessity of the perfect divine law,
> whose direction in bringing conviction for sin, de-
> sire for grace, humiliation, and saving despair
> concerning ourselves is found in Questions 3 and
> 115 of the Heidelberg Catechism. [12]

In explaining "precision," Voetius wrote that

> The law, with all its requirements about individual
> virtues and vices, even in the smallest cases of
> conscience, remains in force, and therefore the
> law must be explained according to the teaching of
> God's Word by professors and by ministers of the
> Word in sermon and in catechetical instruction. [13]

Here, more explicitly than before, the purpose of catechetical instruction is defined as the proper ordering of life, in
all its detail. In introducing practical theology at Utrecht,
alongside the customary lectures on the loci communes and
the weekly disputations, [14] Voetius wished to treat the subject
in three sections.

The first consists of moral or casuistical theology

based on the third part of the Catechism up to the section on prayer (Questions 86-115). The second is ascetic theology; that is, the practice of devotion, based on the section on prayer and the remainder (Questions 116-29).[15]

The third section indicates the extent to which polity, for Voetius, was an order of salvation.

> The third is ecclesiastical polity, based on our Dutch liturgy, the ecclesiastical constitutions, and the article on the keys of the Kingdom, or ecclesiastical discipline, in the second part of the Catechism (Questions 83-85). In the third section we include what some others call prophetic theology, or homiletical practical theology.[16]

If it be objected that there are more important concerns than the "minutiae" of his casuistry, Voetius answers that this "only confuses practical theology with the actual practice which is the result of this theology,"[17] for

> There is in one system of practical theology, or one commentary on the Decalogue, everything pertaining to all the vices and the corresponding virture, although in the church as a whole, people who are to be converted or who already have been converted cannot always and equally be led to complete implementation.[18]

In settling cases of conscience, which is "the exposition of any moral question,"[19] the subject may be "inherent" (that is, the individual who presents his problem to the casuist), or "adjunct" (which refers to the status of a person or of an act he has committed as he is before God). The predicate refers to the particular moral problem in relation to that person and his status.[20] Further, while the settling of cases of conscience has reference to what is permitted or forbidden, theological guidance (consilia) has reference to effecting what has already been decided is lawful or unlawful.[21]

Unlike the earlier Reformed scholastics (see Ursinus), Voetius stresses the moral over the metaphysical qualities of God, as is indicated in his discussion of obedience to the Decalogue (in the context of the third section of the Catechism).[22] Accordingly, precision, which has the practice of piety as its object, has as its efficient cause the purity,

holiness, and perfection of God, who loves purity and wants
His children to be like Him; and the secondary efficient cause
is the Word of God, which is the sole norm of precision. [23]

Because Voetius utilized conventicles in the Dutch
churches for the practice of piety by "earnest" Christians, [24]
he was admired by the "earnest" followers of Cocceius in
the Netherlands and at Herborn. However, under the influence of the Ramistic, federal thought from Herborn, Cocceius
came to interpret the confessional symbols in the light of
Scripture and without the aid of Aristotelian scholasticism,
which was the reverse of Voetius. Cocceius received his
theological training at Bremen under Martinius and Crocius--
"federal theologians" who had been associated with Olevianus
at Herborn. [25]

For Cocceius, the personal, juristic language of Scripture was seen as the locus of God's self-revelation, and
therefore as the locus for life and doctrine. Dogmatic symbols were not to replace Scripture as the center of life and
thought, which also meant that formulation in theology on the
basis of the proclaimed Word was to be a continuous process
in the church, necessary in every era. He asserted that
both the Old and New Testaments were included under the
covenant of grace and that it was preceded by a covenant of
works between the creation and the fall. [26] The covenant of
grace was understood to have three economies: before the
law, under the law, and after the law in Christ, who is implicitly the center of the covenant of grace in the first two
as well. [27] By making use of the covenant theme as a systematic principle, Cocceius had a basis for counter-acting the
decretal theology of orthodoxy (especially Beza), whereby
predestination was discussed in terms of the doctrine of God
and not in terms of soteriology.

The federalism of Olevianus and Cocceius (as also the
logic of Ramus, which preceded it) tended to mitigate the
rationalism inherent in orthodoxy, whereby Scripture was becoming the handmaiden of creed and Catechism under the
aegis of deductive logic. Though Cocceius was frequently accused by his opponents of Cartesianism, rational philosophy,
with its non-historical mentality, was actually more akin to
scholasticism in its methodology. [28]

Cocceius wrote that

Theology is not a logical construct of man's mind

nor an explication of a system residing in the mind
of God centered about the decree of predestination.[29]

Rather, it can be no more nor less systematic than Scripture,
its subject, will allow. The systematic principle of Scripture is based upon the various stages in the development of
the history of salvation; hence, he distinguishes between
truth as it is in God and partial truth as man perceives it,[30]
for God "distributes His gifts in diverse ways and is always
wishing to see some new light in His Church."[31] Cocceius
concludes that, while we do not have the whole truth, we do
have enough for a life of devotion,[32] and because of this
sense of sufficiency, he can say "theology is practical."[33]
The final test of theology is not in setting forth propositional
truths but "in setting forth the form and delineation of godliness."[34] The meaning of Scripture is not to be tied to an
a priori dogmatic, for there is to be "exegesis from Scripture, not eisogesis into Scripture," and "the words of Scripture mean what they can signify within the whole context."[35]
The immutability of God is understood now not in terms of
the immutability of logic but, as McCoy notes, through the
image of the covenant: God has the consistency of one who
is faithful (foedus is derived from fiducia).[36] Fiducia is defined primarily not in the sense of individual trust, but in
the context of the covenant, the federal community of faith.

In the fiducial knowledge of God there are also ideas
or propositional knowledge, but their truth ultimately rests
upon our faith in God's self-revelation in His covenant. In
contrast, Voetius held that other kinds of knowledge, as well
as knowledge of God, can be derived from Scripture; such as
the knowledge of jurisprudence, politics, philosophy, and scientific knowledge.[37] For Cocceius, the substance of all
knowledge, as of all history, is salvation; he thus speaks of
Heilswissenschaft as well as Heilsgeschichte.[38] Revelation
controls reason, for God's covenant defines the meaning of
covenants between men, and yet the meaning of man's covenant also illumines God's covenant.[39] While Cocceius held
to the doctrine of predestination by saying that the foundation
of the covenant was God's will, he made the doctrine less
specific by holding that God's decree is not determined by
anything external to His will as revealed in the covenant, and
that Scripture reveals to man at the proper time what is need-
ful for him to know of God's purposes. Like Voetius, Cocceius stresses not the metaphysical but rather the moral attributes of God, as life, goodness, and power--God's "com-

municable" attributes, revealed in the covenant and the image
of God in man consists in rectitude, or moral conformity. [40]
Unlike Voetius, he holds that the standard of morality does
not have to do with propositions, as with "cases of conscience," but with God's faithfulness in the covenant.

It was chiefly through his interpretation of the Heidelberg Catechism that Cocceius was led to the conclusion that
instruction in the teachings of Scripture was not to be based
upon citations demonstrating the dicta probantia of Scripture.
In catechetical instruction, Scripture was not to be relegated
to a secondary role by the demands of church dogma, nor
was it to be superimposed upon dogma. [41] For Voetius, the
heart of catechetical instruction is the scholastic procedure
which leads the Christian, in his inner life, through a systematic advancement in Christian living, characterized by
clearness and precision. [42] For Cocceius, the authority of
the Catechism is highly rated because therein is contained
the essential content of God's Word revealed in Scripture.
As Graffmann has shown, [43] this conviction led followers of
Cocceius to over-estimate the pedagogical authority of the
Catechism, with the result that Scripture becomes over-sys-
tematized. Cocceius himself strongly warned against this
consequence in the introduction to his Catechesis: the goal
of catechizing is not the Catechism itself, but Scripture alone.
To him, the explanation of the Catechism and the explanation
of Scripture are the same. [44] In this, he took seriously the
Elector Frederick's intention that the Catechism should promote lifelong discipleship to the Word of God. [45] He writes

> ...that the words of this small book [the Cate-
> chism] must be taken from the model of the saving
> words of our Lord Jesus Christ...for the Christian
> religion can be learned in no way except through
> the words which he taught by the Holy Spirit. [46]

The consequences of this point of view became apparent in the catechetical preaching of Salomon van Til (1613-
1713), whose Homiliae catecheticae maintains the Cocceian
outlook with the strong biblical and philological character of
his sermons. [47] He regularly proceeds from the Old Testament evidence and leads his hearers from here to the New
Testament, thereby preserving the unity of the Testaments. [48]

Let us conclude our discussion of Cocceius and his
significance for the history of interpreting the Catechism by
noting an additional element in his thought beside his use of

the covenant theme. [49] An exclusive emphasis upon Cocceius'
use of federalism overlooks his deeply-rooted symbolic-
apocalyptic interest.   This is an aspect of his thought which
becomes dominant in the catechetical interpretation given by
the Reformed Pietists, notably by Lampe. [50]

With his use of typological, allegorical and prophetic
exegesis, which Schrenck and Moltmann have ascribed to the
influence of Joachim of Floris, [51] Cocceius and certain of his
pietistic followers broke the Reformers' ban on a chiliastic
interpretation of the apocalypse. [52]   In the preface to the
1699 edition of Cocceius' In apocalypsim commentarius,
Joachim is discussed as the precedent for Cocceius' periodization of history, though it is recognized that Cocceius' system differed in that

> The highest are the first and second periods, the
> time of the resurrection and ascension of Christ
> until Constantine, also in part the three period,
> in which the battle against the Arians took place,
> and then again the seventh period, in which the
> conversion both of the Jews and the heathen is
> brought about. [53]

For Joachim, according to Bossuet, [54] "the first six parts of
the apocalypse bring six periods of suffering to the church";
however, "the seventh treats the Sabbath, and the eighth the
eternal rest. " Nevertheless, with Cocceius, the revival of
chiliasm has an important effect in contributing to the development of Reformed Pietism.

> ... in the displacement of certain churchly points
> of view, in the concentration on the prophetic move-
> ment of the Kingdom of God as the spirit of the
> church united with a certain indifference toward the
> state-church form, Cocceius prepares a basis for
> Pietism. [55]

Cocceius' understanding of the progressive stages in
the revelation of Scripture, regarded as an organic whole, is
consonant with the intention of the authors of the Catechism
to interpret that document as an organic whole. [56] Whether
or not there is also a nascent, progressive Heilsordnung with
Ursinus, [57] Cocceius does prepare the way for such an interpretation. As we have seen, Cocceius regarded the exposition of the Catechism and of Scripture as synonymous tasks.
Let us now consider more closely this developmental view of

history in Cocceius' exegetical method, with reference to the
conflicting exegetical views of the seventeenth century rational theologians in Reformed theology. A comparison of the
two schools will also enable us to bring into focus the rationalists' proposals for catechetical exposition--proposals which
were subsequently to be opposed bitterly by the exposition of
the Reformed Pietists, notably the Otterbeins.

In viewing Scripture as an organic entity, Cocceius
differed not only from the Voetian scholastics, for whom
Scripture was interpreted in terms of creed, but also from
the rational theologians, who tried to minimize doctrinal articles in the interest of tolerance. Unlike either, Cocceius'
exegesis makes way for the new and prophetic: "the new
grows as an organic development (Weiterbildung) from the
foundation."[58] Scripture makes clear that God has appointed
times for the church to apprehend new truth.[59] However, it
does not provide a neat, rational pattern, but rather induces
one's trustful adherence to the prophetic message of the
apostles and the prophets. This leads not only to the positive appraisal of the new knowledge but also to a certain valuation of tradition: the symbolic-prophetic teaching of Scripture is the work of many generations and is built upon the
heritage of the past. Heretofore, church history had been
predominantly a polemical discipline for the defense of dogma.

Cocceius' valuation of tradition in his exegesis also
affects his idea of the church, for the historical progression
of the kingdom of God is an influential concept in the doctrine
of the "inner church" in Reformed Pietism. The outer
church and its institutions are secondary and their form is
dictated by the course of this positive, developmental thought
and its valuation of tradition.[60] The Cocceian idea of progress, with its revaluation of tradition, tended to establish
historical tradition as an authority, undergirded by exegesis
and apologetic, which is autonomous from the authority of the
church. This optimism represented a reinterpretation of the
doctrine of hope in Calvin and the authors of the Catechism:
for them, hope was established in the faith in the ascended
and glorified Christ who is the glorified Head of the Church.[61]
However, Cocceius, as a Reformed dogmatician, does not go
to the extreme of a fully autonomous view of history, as did
such spiritualists and mystics as David Joris or Sebastian
Frank.

Cocceius' overarching exegetical conviction, which was

correlative with the view of Scripture as an organic whole, was that Christ is the foundation of Scripture. Christ is at the center of the covenant of grace as the true image of God, who effects the restoration of the lost image of God in man. Humanity grows into this fully-developed image by degrees. The image of God in man before the fall is not a lost ideal of the past to be recovered; it is the first phase of a higher development to the ideal "imago Dei,"[62] which will be attained in the course of time. This does not abrogate the necessity of Christ's work of salvation. Rather, Christ is Lord of both kingdoms. It is only when this Christocentrism is lost in the rational theologians that the idea of progress is secularized as a human attainment--as the work of man's "ratio."

As a result of the influence of Cocceius, the Aristotelian dominance in Reformed theology was effectively checked from within--so much so that his Voetian critics attacked him in the same spirit in which they opposed their antagonists from without, the rational theologians. Voetius used much ink in his attack upon Descartes, whom he correctly regarded as being instrumental in undermining the Aristotelian structure of theology. He was particularly critical of the suggestion that we begin with doubt, then proceed to existence (cogito ergo sum) rather than the traditional formal structure of knowledge. Bohatec, in the first volume of his uncompleted work,[63] has shown the impact of Cartesianism on Reformed theology in the Netherlands and Germany. Though Descartes was inspired by the new science in looking to mathematics for the model of certain and clear reasoning in metaphysics, the rationalist effect of Cartesianism for theology was not basically different from Aristotelianism,[64] and in Dutch theology it was variously amalgamated with Aristotelianism.[65] Cocceius had regarded himself as neither anti-Cartesian nor anti-Aristotelian, assuming that his exegetical theology had freed him from philosophical commitment. Some disciples of Cocceius did associate themselves with Cartesian philosophy, but to the extent that they were not more but less Cocceian. There evolved a relationship between them produced by the attack of scholasticism on both of them, but the alliance between the philosophy of Descartes and the Reformed churches did not last. As Cartesianism, and earlier, Ramism, had helped free Reformed thought from scholasticism, so whatever elements of Cartesianism had entered Calvinism were displaced in turn by Leibniz, Wolff, and then Newton.[66]

Though Cocceius did not succeed in ridding theology
of philosophy, he so undermined scholastic methodology, especially in catechetical exposition, that subsequent theologians
would now make use of whatever philosophical patterns were
in vogue. Thus, for a time there developed a school of
"Reformed" Cartesians, such as Wittich and Bekker in the
1650's, who found it acceptable to hold that theology could
not dictate the truth of philosophy.[67] Bekker also asserted
that Scripture and reason were fully coordinate, with Scripture dealing with salvation and reason with nature. Here,
then, a dichotomy was being made between the heilsgeschicht-
lichen Reich and the Naturreich which Cocceius had joined
under the rubric of his Christology. Here too, was a clear
departure from the Reformers' limitation of reason to the
finite, which had been retained by orthodoxy in its concept
of the dual nature of theology. As we saw, this concept permitted the reception of Aristotle in seventeenth century orthodoxy as a means of clarifying conceptually the insights of the
Reformation vis-a-vis the Counter-Reformation. However,
the entry of reason within the domain of revelation obscured
the Reformers' limitation of reason as reason became a
methodological principle for understanding Scripture.[68]

While "Cartesian scholasticism" found its home in the
Dutch Reformed universities, it also made its way to the
Reformed territories of northwestern Germany. There had
been considerable interchange between these lands since the
time of Willem the Silent and Count Johann. Cocceius had
received his theological training at Bremen under two federal
theologians from Herborn--Martinius and Crocius--and the
pietistic conventicles of the type used by such Dutch Pietists
as Teellinck, Lodensteyn, and Voetius were officially sanc-
tioned at Herborn in the last third of the seventeenth century.[69] Thus, when the Cartesians appeared in Holland at
mid-century, they soon found representatives in the German
Reformed centers of Duisburg and Herborn.[70] The reception
which greeted the Cartesians at these two centers was quite
dissimilar. The University of Duisburg embraced Cartesianism when it was presented by Johann Clauberg, the rector
and professor of theology, who was the first "systematician
of Cartesianism."[71] Clauberg had come to Diusburg from
Herborn, where he, together with Christoph Wittich, had
taught theology and philosophy in the Academy.

At Herborn, these men had espoused a hermeneutical
point of view which was quite foreign to the tradition of Ramist, anti-scholastic, biblical theology and catechetical exposi-

tion "without bondage to word and form. " Cyriscus Lentulus, professor of history at Herborn, attacked them as atheists and innovators, and the rumor circulated that they had denied the resurrection. [72] Their greatest offense was their teaching of the rotation of the earth and its movement around the sun, which appeared blatantly to contradict the teaching of Scripture. [73] Wittich distinguished between philosophical and revealed knowledge, arguing that the former was not given by the testimony of the Holy Spirit but was in accordance with the lumen naturale and assisted the search for truth by the natural man. [74] Descartes had shown that one could arrive at clear and certain conclusions, and such philosophical knowledge could not, said Wittich, detract from the testimony of Scripture, for God would not reveal that which is contrary to reason. When reason appears to contradict the literal meaning of Scripture, as with the miracles, Wittich resorted to a distinction between the outward, literal expression and the inward, rational truth.

This point of view did not prevent Wittich and Clauberg from confessing the testimony of Scripture and the Reformed confessions at Herborn. They held that the controversy should have no particular interest for the faithful; it only concerned them because of their scientific commitment to veracity. [75] At the very least, there must be the freedom to discuss such matters. To be sure, Scripture itself does not distinguish between the expression and its truth, but the question is whether man may do so. Wittich wrote,

If the exegetes have found the general truth which satisfies the text, they should determine whether perhaps a bias was implied in this phrase which was not from the Holy Spirit but from common linguistic usage, and therefore whether the language is 'vulgar' or accurate and whether it brings the pure truth to the phrase. [76]

He sought to justify his deviation from the literal meaning of the biblical text by citing the treatment in Reformed theology of the words of institution of the Lord's Supper: it was the Lutherans, not the Reformed, who vindicated the literal meaning of the text. [77] Further, it is understandable that Cartesians such as Wittich or Clauberg could be attracted to the Coccejan biblical theology, since their separation of the domains of revelation and reason had the consequence that revelation became more strongly bound to Scripture. [78]

In view of the fact that Cocceius placed Scripture in
the foreground of catechetical interpretation in a wholly new
way, [79] it is hardly unusual that these Cartesian followers
of Cocceius also altered the interpretation of the Heidelberg
Catechism.   With the traditional exegesis of Scripture being
severely shaken by the revolutionary advances of modern science, Descartes had proposed that exegetical work be guided
by the assumption that clear and certain principles are the
highest criterion of all truth and that the nature of theology
is determined by reason alone. [80]   Similarly, a Cartesian
such as Van Til, [81] in his commentary on the Catechism, affirmed Cocceius' biblical treatment of the catechetical themes,
yet, on the other hand, affirmed that the developed New Testament understanding is not simply attained through the Old
Testament, but it is also frequently introduced as being pala-
table to the rational faculty. [82]   This tendency becomes most
apparent in Van Til's treatment of Questions 12 to 15 of the
Catechism, which consider whether there is any basis within
man whereby he may escape "temporal and eternal punishment" and be restored into God's favor. [83]   Whereas the
Catechism answers this question in the negative, Van Til
finds here a basis for exalting "godly wisdom" which, he repeatedly emphasizes, man is capable of developing to a certain extent.   In view of this consideration, one must

> ... proceed intelligently and humbly and must not
> succeed by reason alone, but rather must be led
> by the counsel of God Himself, for lowly man may
> not venture to pose as the counselor of God. [84]

To pose as the "counselor of God" is the height of godless-
ness, says Van Til.   Thus, to a greater extent than Clauberg
and Wittich at Herborn, Van Til holds to the formulation
"credo ut intelligam, " though his study of the Catechism does
bear unmistakable traces of the forthcoming Aufklärung, which
completely replaced the Heidelberg Catechism with an anthro-
pomorphic, religious instruction. [85]   It was this less mitigated
rationalism which such eighteenth-century defenders of the
Catechism as the Otterbeins would confront.

At Herborn, the Ramist, anti-scholastic catechetical
exposition of Olevianus, Piscator, Zepper, and others had
advocated catechetical exposition "without bondage to the word
and the form" (ohne Bindung an die Wörte und die Form).
In effect, these men declared that scholastic terms derived
from Aristotle were not necessary to convey the meaning of
God's Word.   Not the clarity of scholastic terminology, but

the clarity of the testimony of the Spirit in the pious believer
was the proper criterion for coping with the unclarity of
Scripture and Catechism. For the Reformed Cartesians, the
proper model for understanding the unclarity of Scripture and
Catechism was the clarity of the book of nature, whose truth
can be demonstrated mathematically. Now the formula has
become "clear and distinct" catechetical exposition. [86]

As a result of the activities of Clauberg and Wittich
at Herborn, Count Ludwig Heinrich of Nassau-Dillenburg
thereupon requested the judgment of the Universities of Leiden, Utrecht, Harderwijk, and Groningen concerning the new
method of teaching. [87] Should it be accepted at the cost of
rejecting the older Ramist philosophy or would this not en-
danger the authority of the theological faculty? The answers
he received, which all spoke negatively of the effects of
Cartesianism, induced Count Heinrich to ban the Cartesian
philosophy from Herborn.

This indicates that Herborn had developed at mid-century a complementary relationship between Ramean philosophy
and Aristotelian metaphysics, notably in the Encyclopedia of
Heinrich Alsted. [88] Wilhelm Heinrich wrote to his cousin
that it was "through the teaching of Clauberg and Wittich at
Herborn that factions originated," which coincided with the
universities' judgment that "philosophy was hazardous. "[89]
Having banished Cartesianism, the way is clear for the tri-
umph of the "Reformed Pietistic Orthodoxy" at Herborn in
the late seventeenth and early eighteenth centuries.

b.   Reformed Pietism Comes to Herborn

The existence of the Heidelberg Catechism indicates
that neither Geneva nor Wittenberg was exclusively responsible for molding the spirit and thought of the German Reformed people. [90] The Heidelberg Catechism, together with
the Palatinate Liturgy, which contained the main outlines in
this development, is often regarded as the "fruit and flower
of the whole German and French Reformation. "[91] The responsibility for fulfilling the threefold office of the Catechism,
as a book of instruction for the young, as a confession of
faith, and as an introduction to theology, was entrusted to
the rulers of the several German Reformed principalities,
though church affairs were administered by a consistory appointed by the ruler and composed of laymen and clergy.

The Reformers' appeal to provisional assistance from the German princes, as "the chief members of the Church,"[92] had led to a condition of permanent control under the absolute pretensions of the rulers. Although there were those benevolent princes who were genuinely concerned with the spiritual welfare of their subjects, such as Count Johann of Nassau-Dillenburg, in the seventeenth century class distinctions often took such extreme forms as insistence on private baptisms, weddings, funerals, and communions in private by the princes and nobility, so that it was only for the common people that these acts continued to be observed in the church.[93] These class distinctions were accompanied by ecclesiastical distinctions between clergy and laity, especially in view of the fact that interconfessional polemics occupied a prominent place in the education of ministers at such Lutheran centers as Wittenberg and Leipzig and such Reformed centers as Geneva and Utrecht. The preoccupation with theological polemics tended to supplant pastoral work, and the arid doctrinal preaching and ex opere operato administration of the sacraments proved to have little efficacy for the layman.

The plight of the peasants and townsmen of Germany was multiplied by the catastrophic effects of the Thirty Years War, which brought mass destruction of life and property, impoverishment, anarchy and licentiousness in its wake. As a result of the Peace of Westphalia (1648), the Reformed faith was recognized, as well as the Lutherans and Catholics, but

> The church had become the heritage of a generation of warriors, who while they preserved and protected her, had developed those passions which destroyed her inner life.[94]

In Lutheranism, Philip Jacob Spener's[95] attempt to take the Christian life seriously led him to encourage lay religion by the holding of private meetings for the cultivation of holiness. In a sermon which he preached at Frankfurt in 1669, he declared

> ... we preachers cannot instruct the people from our pulpits as much as is needful unless other persons in the congregation, who by God's grace have a superior knowledge of Christianity, take the pains, by virtue of their universal Christian priesthood, to work with and under us to correct and reform ...[96]

Luther had never found these "earnest Christians" with whom
the "third order" of service could be inaugurated. [97] With
Spener, Pietism developed within Lutheranism as a party,
and the new birth became acceptable to orthodoxy only as an
addendum to the doctrine of justification. The Melanchthonian dual conception of theology permitted this development.

In the Reformed tradition, there were elements of
classical Calvinism which could more readily be developed
in a pietistic direction, such as lay participation in congregational life, church discipline, and ascetic rigor based on the
important doctrine of "tertius usus," which was emphasized
in the third section of the Catechism. Also, Reformed Pietism did not develop as a party because the most prominent
theologians of mid-century, the scholastic Voetius and the
anti-scholastic Cocceius, were influential in its development.
Pietism was assisted from the side of ethics by the casuistry
and conventicularism of Voetius, and from the side of theological reconstruction by the biblical theology of Cocceius.
With the arrival of Pietism, both in the Lutheran and the
Reformed traditions, something new was added: the priesthood of believers was no longer defined primarily in terms
of baptism and personal faith but in terms of the new
birth. [98]

Given the irenic, Melanchthonian orientation of the
German Reformed and their Catechism, which, according to
Schaff, [99] is "unsurpassed for depth, comfort, and beauty,"
it is not unusual that Pietism should find a warm reception
among them. At Herborn, theology had been developed in a
practical, non-polemical direction, Count Johann had been instrumental in promoting the protestantische Unionspolitik of
the late sixteenth century (vis-a-vis the Counter-Reformation), [100] and the onslaughts of Aristotelian and later Cartesian scholasticism had been effectively checked. Here, too,
the excesses of ecclesiastical and class distinctions were not
experienced, for the place of the local congregation assumed
prominence in Nassau and the confessional status of the Catechism became bound to the local congregation so as to di-
minish the idea of "church confession" in favor of "congregational confession." [101] This developing congregational autonomy had been aided by Olevianus' proposal that the power of
discipline in the congregation be entrusted to a group of the
heads of families--a measure which opposed the exclusive-
ness of Beza's pastoral aristocracy.

However, the vigor of parochial life in Nassau had

been severely shaken by the destruction of Herborn during
the Thirty Years' War[102] and again by the Roman Catholic
invasions under Louis XIV (1685), which took a heavy toll of
churches, schools, personal property, and lives.[103] An
Electoral Edict of 1719 forbade the use of the Catechism in
the Palatinate and in Nassau and the churches were at the
mercy of the Jesuits who controlled the Roman Catholic Electors.[104] During the reign of Elector Charles Philip (1716-
42), such oppressions obliged one quarter of the population
of these regions to emigrate, mostly to America.[105] This
was the most effective means of opposing the Electors' efforts to use the state church principle as an instrument of
social control. Within this context, Pietism represented the
effort to meet this crisis in parochial life; its message was
addressed to the dislocated masses whose destiny was increasingly being determined not by the continuing academic
quarrels concerning justification by faith, election, grace,
and works, but by the forces of secular politics and econom-
ics.

     Again, it was the course of developments in Holland
and in the adjacent German Reformed regions which became
influential in determining the theological outlook of "Reformed
Pietistic Orthodoxy" at Herborn. Before Voetius and Cocceius carried on their academic debates at Franeker and
Utrecht, such preachers as Jean de Taffin (1529?-1602),
Gottfried Udemans (1580-1649?), and Teelink (1579-1629) advocated the practice of piety, rather than the polemical defense of the faith, with an earnestness which distinguished
them from other Reformed pastors of the day.[106] However,
our concern is not with the origins of Dutch Pietism, but
with its theological nature as represented by its principal
spokesman in the late seventeenth and early eighteenth centuries.

     Various factors contributed to the assimilation of
Voetians and Cocceians in a pietistic direction during this
period. While some followers of Cocceius fragmented into
an anti-scholastic, humanistic wing, such as those who came
to accept Cartesian rationalism, there were other Cocceians,
known as de fijnen, who increasingly shared the casuistic
emphases of the Voetians. They reacted against what they
regarded as Cocceius' defective views concerning the Sabbath.
Lodensteyn (1620-1677) and Koelman (1632-1695), prominent
pastors, became alarmed that the effect of Cocceius' conviction that Scriptural laws pertaining to the Sabbath belonged to
the realm of ceremonial law was being reflected in a growing

secularity and impiety. As a result, Lodensteyn refused to
baptize the children of unregenerate church members and,
as Ritschl notes, [107] he regarded "dull church attendance" as
a greater offense than intemperance.

Jean de Labadie (1610-1674), the French Jesuit who
had been drawn to Calvin after reading the Institutes, was so
affected by the lax moral condition of the church that, after
a great struggle with the Reformed church, he lapsed into
schism, announcing as his watchword, "separate ye my people. "[108] Untereyck (1635-1693), who introduced a pietistic
variety of Cocceian federal theology into Germany in his
Hallelujah, agreed with Labadie's views concerning the antagonism of God and the world, which was marked by a pronounced chiliastic strain, [109] though he disavowed separatism.
For the most part, Reformed Pietists were not under any
great necessity of separation, for they were able to appeal
to the instructions of the Synod of Dort, which upheld the use
of the Catechism in Sunday afternoon catechetical sermons
and in weekday meetings for adult catechetical instruction.
As a result of the efforts of these churchly Pietists, many
were dissuaded from abandoning the church in an increasingly secular age.

In many Reformed universities, the theological candi-
date had previously been asked these two questions: "Do
you fear God?" and "To what party do you belong?"[110] The
latter question was now abolished and the long-prevalent par-
tisanship subsided. In most schools, a compromise was
reached whereby a Voetian was placed in the chair of dogmatic theology, and a Cocceian was appointed in biblical theology. In addition, a disciple of the Pietist Lampe was
frequently placed in the chair of practical theology. [111]

Another factor which contributed to the assimilation of
Voetians and Cocceians in a pietistic direction, in addition to
their preoccupation with the Christian life, was the Voetians'
acceptance of the Cocceians' symbolic-prophetic exegetical
method. The demise of Aristotelian scholasticism was no-
where so poignantly illustrated as in the shift from scholastic literalism to the Cocceian-inspired, symbolic-prophetic
mode of Scriptural exposition in numerous Dutch and German
Reformed pulpits. This development has lad Alfred Adam to
assert that "the beginning of the Enlightenment belongs to the
history of the church, not to the history of unbelief. "[112]

A principal spokesman for this "pietistic, prophetic

theology" was the great orientalist at Franeker, Campegius
Vitringa (1659-1722), with whom Lampe was to study. His
chief exegetical work was his Commentary on Isaiah (two
volumes, Leeuwarden, 1714-1720), which was characterized
by the care and accuracy with which he applied the entire
exegetical apparatus to determine the meaning of the text in
its historical context. [113] In his Anakrisis Apocalypsios
Joannis apostoli (Franeker, 1705), prophecy is applied to
anti-Catholic polemicism, and his Latin lectures on the interpretation of the parables were edited in Dutch by the Pietist d'Outrein under the title Verklaringe van de evangelische
parabolen (Amsterdam, 1715). In this work, the persons of
the parables are symbolically made to apply to historical figures. [114] In his Typus theologiae practicae sive de vita
spirituali ejusque affectionibus (Franeker, 1716), the fulfillment of the types and prophecies contained in the miracles
of Christ are sought in the history of the church. [115]

Underlying these exegetical meditations was the assumption that prophecy and history correspond with one another, and that a particular event has implications for the
entire course of events. A prophecy which cannot be signi-
fied in a real, concrete fulfillment really has no significance
at all. [116] The prophetic exegesis sought to unite the spiritual and the corporal in a visible structure. [117] It is only
possible for man to know the will of God when a certain
agreement between prediction and fulfillment, prophecy and
history, can be demonstrated--a task for the godly mind
which is the counterpart for the rationalists' search for truth
in the clarity of mathematics and in an orderly nature.

If it is objected that this method gives free reign to
the most irresponsible kinds of historical interpretation,
Vitringa would reply that: (1) a meaning must be ascertained
in every given historical event or personality, but that the
exegetical procedure must be delimited by carefully defined
rules; and (2) that when a meaning so attained is asserted,
one may not pretend to have fathomed the whole counsel of
the Holy Spirit, for it must always be recognized that later
generations will be granted a deeper understanding of prophecy through God's grace so long as history continues. [118]
Prophecy and history are related to one another as "idea and
reality," as "plan and accomplishment," and even as "cause
and effects," so that in the description of prophetic-pietistic
theology, there is a progression both ab affectis ad causas
(a posteriori) and a causis ad effecta (a priori). [119]

Accordingly, Vitringa wrote in his Hypotyposis historiae et chronologiae that prophecy was more significant
than bare historical knowledge, for the former brings the
reader into proximum Dei commercium and is the real kernel of history, though both are related and illuminated only
in the context of one another.[120] The theme of prophecy is
none other than the history of Christ and His kingdom. Vitringa frequently uses the phrase "the kingdom of the
Church."[121] In a sense, prophecy only finds its meaning in
church history, for he wrote that "truly no prophetic statements concern events of the world except with respect to the
church."[122] Yet, church history is also the kernel of world
history, and since church or kingdom begins with creation,
not with the fall,[123] there is no antithesis between nature
and grace. As Möller shows,[124] this prophetic theology will
become the basis for the idea of progress in secular history
and philosophy. Vitringa's demand that biblical prophecy
should make use of world history had been voiced long before
Cocceius--namely, in the medieval literature of the four kingdoms of Daniel's prophecy. However, this was concerned
with a prophecy whose fulfillment lay in the past.[125] The
chief interest of the Cocceian-Vitringan historical reflection
lay in its orientation toward the future and in unfulfilled
prophecy. This future hope was sustained not only by their
study of the Revelation of John, but even more by their use
of the Old Testament prophecies, which had yet found no concrete fulfillment, and thus were efficacious for explaining
the future history of the church.

Not only did Vitringa assume that prophecy and history
corresponded with one another; he also inherited the Cocceian
idea of time, though there are differences between Cocceius
and the later prophetic-pietistic theology with regard to the
progressive steps of the ordo temporum. The central theological concept of this idea of time, that God reveals Himself in a temporal "economy" of salvation in the Heilsgeschichte, contravened the premise of scholastic orthodoxy that
the movement of God's Spirit in temporal events corresponded to their respective decreta Dei. Vitringa gave as his
motto in the foreword of his Hypotyposis a citation from
Origen, in which the work of God in His church is likened
to the farmer in his field: both order themselves according
to the times and will observe the decorum divinum according
to this temporal economy.[126] The "ratio oeconomiae" is
known in nature as the gradual development of the creatures
according to the plan of the Creator; in history, it is known
as the temporal progression of the plan of salvation.[127]

        Duration is not merely a principle of organization; it
is the concept which replaces the former scholastic concept
of substance.* Schrenk has shown that, after Cocceius, a
distinction between the Testaments could no longer be maintained among his followers: the former distinction between
paresis ("passing over") and aphesis ("deliverance") was no
longer regarded as sufficient to detract from the view that
the kingdom of Christ is already present in the Old Testament. [128] Time is the category of existence in which the
Lordship of Christ is expressed, whether it be in the Old or
the New Testaments.   The status ecclesiae is only distinguished in terms of the time period in which the church finds
itself within the entire economy.   The valuation of time as a
divinely-established framework, which history must fulfill before the kingdom of God can be realized on earth, distinguishes this "biblical" chiliasm from the chiliasm of certain
radical reformers which the Protestant confessions had pro-
scribed. [129] The "revolutionary Spiritualists," such as Mün-
ster and the Munsterites, were not interested in establishing
a "Christian logic of history" through the concordance of the
principal events of church history with the succession of biblical figures and visions;[130] rather, they sought the immediate conversion of history into eschatology.

        The man who was most responsible for integrating
this prophetic-symbolic exegetical method with a fully-developed practical, "experiential," theology was Friedrich Adolph
Lampe (1683-1729).   Goebel spoke of him as "the greatest
theologian in the German Reformed Church since the Reformation, and the most influential in the eighteenth century. "[131]
While the first half of his statement may be disputed, the
latter cannot.   Though he has received comparatively little
attention in the history of Christian doctrine, he was the
most representative theologian of "Reformed Pietistic Orthodoxy" in Germany.   He was born at Detmold at a time when
several of the German Reformed synods, finding their parochial
life rent by rationalism from without and Labadist separatism
from within, were considering "how the irresponsible ignorance, which is found to be so thoroughgoing in the congregations of our land, may be met. "[132] The same synod sought
to meet this situation by requiring week-day catechizing, in
addition to the existing Sunday catechizing, and improved
home and school instruction.   The Synod of Cleve, where
Labadist schism had destroyed several congregations, complained in 1693 about the "fallen Christianity in the last times"

---

*God is not understood in terms of formal being but by His
activity among men.

and of the neglect of private catechizing (in 1697, this Synod even ordered private catechizing "where feasible" instead of the regular weekly preaching). [133] The Duisburg consistory complained of the "coarse, irresponsible, even damnable ignorance of God's Word by most laymen, even the elderly," and the General Synod of 1686 proclaimed that

> The Synod has with great regret considered and taken to heart the unfortunate position of the Church of God, which is plagued by revealed enemies, but is also inwardly distraught by atheists, wickedness, and indifference ... [134]

Lampe's advocacy of churchly piety (in opposition to Labadism) while a pastor at Duisburg reflected the tendency of the General Synod of the Lower Rhine to underplay the polemical defense of scholastic orthodoxiam by emphasizing "the study of piety."[135]

Lampe studied at Bremen (1698-1702) and at the University of Franeker (1702-3), where he became associated with the "earnest" Cocceians, Vitringa and Roell, who distinguished themselves from the non-pietistic (Groene)[136] Cocceians of Leiden. His conversion, which began under their influence, is described in his hymn Lob des Herrn Jesu, wherein he describes his penitential struggle (Busskampf) and rebirth (Wiedergeburt) as a lifelong process characterized by an eschatological dynamism.

> I yielded my heart to you, so unpure as it was,
> Will you consume it? I gave it willingly; I want
> to see it completely crushed and destroyed, so
> that You can finally erect your sanctuary therein...
>
> I search for You day and night,
> Until I in glory may behold you closely;
> Your beauty has so charmed me on earth. [137]

What is more striking in Lampe is not the trace of the canticles theme, but rather his repeated emphasis upon visual imagery to signify the continual breaking-in of the kingdom of Christ in nature and history.

Lampe seems to imply that the Labadists were at fault for seeking to attain a "pure" church within history. Man cannot convert history into eschatology; he is a witness to and a participant in the transformation of nature and his-

tory by the kingdom of Christ. The key to the Heilsgeschichte is the symbolic-prophetic interpretation of Scripture,
which is the antecipata historia. [138] Lampe writes in his
most important work, Geheimnis des Gnadenbundes,

> Where will the depth of the wisdom of God be more
> fully opened than when the various ways whereby
> God has ruled in His Church are investigated and
> compared with one another?--How orderly one step
> follows the other?--How the delightful arrangement
> plays (or, sparkles) not in a great disparity, since
> the antecedent is always a step of the future and
> that which follows is always a new and developing
> image of the past?[139]

Note the close relation he maintains between Word, nature,
and history.

> Since new discoveries in nature are daily made
> (through field glasses), what is it to wonder that
> new discoveries also take place through the in-
> creasing diligence in the examination of the godly
> Word and the promised growth in the knowledge of
> the last times (Dan. 12:4; Ex. 47:4) is always
> further enhanced toward being fulfilled?[140]

The model which was provided rational theology by the new
science had its counterpart in pietistic, prophetic theology
as the symbolic-prophetic exegetical method. All possible
events of profane history have meaning in terms of the fulfillment of prophecy (which means that more room is required in his commentaries for annotations than for the Scriptural text itself). [141]

From 1720-27, Lampe was professor of dogmatics and
church history at Utrecht, and from 1727 until his death he
served as pastor of St. Ansgar's and as professor in the
gymnasium in Bremen. [142] From these schools there proceeded a large number of men who disseminated his views
throughout the church. In his major work (Geheimnis des
Gnadenbundes, Bremen, 1712), he presents the heads of doctrine of Reformed theology from the standpoint of their practical implications for the Christian life. The first volume
treats the "nature of the covenant of grace" from the Cocceian viewpoint, and the following volumes trace the church
in history in terms of the threefold economy of the covenant
of grace under the promise (Vol. 2), the law (Vols. 3 and

4), and the gospel (Vols. 5 and 6). [143] Other popular works
included his catechisms (Milch der Wahrheit, nach Anleitung
des Heidelberger Katechismus; Einleitung zu dem Geheimnis
des Gnadenbundes; Erste Wahrheitsmilch für Sauglinge am
Alter u. Verstand);[144] his treatise on the Lord's Supper (Die
Heilige Brautschmuck der Hochzeit-Gäste des Lammes an
seiner Bundestafel, Bremen, 1710); his commentaries on
John; and the Delineatio Theologiae Activae (1727), a study
in ethics based upon the federal theology. [145] Let us com-
ment upon his interpretation of some salient points of Reformed doctrine, with reference to Scripture, the divine covenant, Christology, election, the church, and, most important, his doctrine of the order of salvation, which gave to
Cocceianism a peculiarly pietistic turn with its application of
the Heilsgeschichte to the inner life of the individual.

As a Cocceian, Lampe was, above all, a biblical theologian, and confessional writings, including the Heidelberg
Catechism, were clearly subordinated to Scripture. His use
of the symbolic-prophetic method of exegesis was accompanied by the conviction that all of Scripture stood under divine
inspiration and thus its data may not be criticized. [146]
Though he admitted the possibility that "certain errors may
have crept in through the carelessness of editors," a point
which was frequently stressed by the Leiden Cocceians, "yet
has divine Providence repeatedly kept watch that, when all
the different readings are grasped, still not a single basic
truth of the Gospel suffered damage because of it. "[147] Like
Vitringa, he sought to demonstrate the "prototypical" meaning of the biblical figures, and he found no less than twenty-
five parallels between Adam and Christ. [148] The Old Testament is of service to the sinner in revealing how "from the
foundation of the world man could be brought to fellowship
with God through an appointed Mediator." As with Vitringa,
Christ's earthly life is given a comparatively brief treatment. [149] He agrees with Cocceius in interpreting the fourth
commandment as a "purely ceremonial commandment," but
the implication is that the meaning of the Sabbath is greater,
not less, for the Christian: "The Lord seeks an inwardly
spiritual service. "[150]

Lampe's use of the federal theme is to be attributed
to its value in introducing the temporal idea of "economy. "[151]
He retained Cocceius' distinction between the covenant of
works and of grace, with the accent upon the latter. However, according to Schrenk, Lampe's major emphasis is upon

> ... the full asceticism, the affection, the 'good of
> the covenant' to subjective inner light, the manner
> of speech concerning the steps to sanctification,
> the fulness of detail in the description of the final
> glory, which makes the meager description of the
> kingdom of glory by Cocceius stand out striking-
> ly. [152]

There is an individualistic emphasis expressed in his tendency to interpret the covenant of grace primarily in terms of
personal rebirth rather than in Cocceius' sense as the faith
(fides) of the community (foedus). Ritschl contrasts Cocceius
with Untereyck and Lampe at this point, suggesting that

> Cocceius' doctrine of the kingdom of God is ex-
> pressed in terms of the 'bride of Christ,' namely
> that the sanctified Christians are not only the pil-
> lars of the church, but are also the jewels of the
> kingdom of Christ on earth. [153]

Yet, it might also be emphasized that there is an anti-in-
dividualistic emphasis in his affirmation that the believer is
a witness to and a participant in the transformation of nature
and history by the kingdom of Christ, which is discovered
through the symbolic-prophetic exegetical method. [154]

    In discussing the first "side" in the covenant, which
is the trinitarian God, Lampe (in a way that recalls Calvin)
says that God can no longer be recognized in nature as He
ought because of man's sin, and therefore one must "take a
magnifying glass for help," which is "the bright crystal of
the covenant of grace."[155] For Calvin, Scripture functions
as a pair of spectacles which enables us to see for the first
time our proper relationship to God;[156] for Lampe, it is the
Heilsplan which is revealed to man in Scripture in terms of
the economy of the covenant of grace. The Son, as the
Guarantor and Angel of the covenant, makes the atonement
for sin which is required by the Father, and the Spirit "medi-
ates the fellowship of sinners with the reconciling Son and the
reconciled Father."[157] Here is a kind of temporal order in
the work of the Persons of the Trinity which is absent in
Calvin. [158] Also, he held that "the satisfaction of Christ was
sufficient for the entire human race, but its actual purpose
applied only to the elect."[159] Calvin, unlike the Synod of
Dort,[160] sought to preserve the tension between the universality of Christ's work and the fact that not all believe in
Him: "For Christ is made known and held out to the sight

of all, but the elect alone are those whose eyes God opens,
that they may seek Him by faith. "[161] Thus, Lampe is closer to Calvin at this point.   In discussing the prophet-priest-
king scheme, Lampe places unusual emphasis upon its efficacy both in the sense of "instructing" and "affecting" as an
example for the believer:

> The history of our Saviour hands over a beautiful
> example whereby the new man is built not by God
> alone, but every believer must also be diligent to
> promote the growth and completion of salvation in
> himself; such is without all doubt. [162]

The second party in the covenant is fallen man:
"Come here sinner, this is a covenant for you! God wants
to be the first party; should you not wish to be the second?"[163] The fall, which he speaks of as "misery"[164] (in
the language of the Catechism), is placed within the developmental scheme of the Heilsgeschichte.   Fallen man is a "not
yet ripened fruit" and a "child who chokes in his blood. "[165]
The natural order of man is inverted in his fallen condition,
for the soul, the nobler part, no longer controls the body
(again, this is reminiscent of Calvin).[166]   Further, all acts
of the will are to be superseded by the understanding, though
the situation is reversed in fallen man.[167] It is the understanding which is wholly corrupt and has become the slave
of the dispositions.   However, grace for penitence was set
aside for man "according to the elapsing time of grace. "[168]
The dispersion of the Jews is regarded as an historical vindication of the fact that "whoever now remains a sinner
[will suffer] eternal punishment as a mirror of His justice. "[169] His temporal orientation leads him to speak of
"steps" in divine condemnation, for "he has the most to fear
who has the most light and has diverted the most means of
grace into corruption, " whereas those who had not accumu-
lated so much grace are brought as "a dead hound to God's
feet. "[170] The covenant belongs to him who, "in the reception of faith ... seeks as a poor beggar everything outside
himself with the Lord in His covenant. "[171]

Unlike the decretal theology of Bezan orthodoxy, Lampe
stands with Calvin and the authors of the Catechism in relating election to soteriology.   The "Elector" is the "highly-
praised Three-in-One" (hochgelobte Dreyeinheit) who

> ... by His free choice has determined to redeem
> men from sin according to the treasure of Christ,

by His own Person, to praise His glorious grace.
172

Like Calvin and unlike the Catechism, he teaches double predestination as two specific decrees, not mere fore-knowledge;
but he opposes the supralapsarians for their assumption that
God, in His eternal counsel, regards man as a sinful creature. 173 With his typological use of Scripture, he shows
that God, in the unfolding of His counsel from the beginning
of the world, has been choosing some and passing over others
for membership in His eternal kingdom. 174 In opposing the
Arminians' and rationalists' objections that the doctrine cir-
cumscribes the grace of God, Lampe emphasizes, in accordance with the Catechism, 175 that election should be considered under the aspect of trust.

> [The doctrine of election] also serves to impart a
> true and substantial trust for the people of God al-
> though the difficulties which it presents to reason
> can not yet be fully dispelled in our fragmented
> knowledge. 176

In God's time, this mystery of the covenant will also be
made transparent.

He seeks to mitigate the harshness of the doctrine of
double predestination by affirming that: (1) "a beginner on
the road of life" must not probe too deeply into the question;
(2) while in progress, one can never say categorically that
he is not among the elect, for "God can allow His grace to
appear to gravest sinners even in the last hour"; (3) our
ability to detect signs of election in others is not trustworthy,
for in this life "one must begin from below" in the school of
Christ; (4) God does not "send an angel from heaven" to
assure us of our election, for He wills that we should strive
with patience for eternal life by means of good works; and
(5) "whoever lives under the use of the means of grace hears
the summons of the Lord ... "177 Similarly, Calvin discussed assurance in the context of our "inward calling" with
respect to the visible structures of the church. 178

Lampe's use of Scripture finds its most unique dogmatic implication in his interpretation of the order of salvation (Heilsordnung), whereby the history of redemption is related to the inner life of the individual. Lampe envisions an
analogy between the seven days of creation and the seven
steps whereby godly grace unfolds itself by degrees in the life

of the elect.

The first step is the "powerful appeal," which Lampe distinguishes from the "general" call in the following manner.

> The general call is the outward presentation which God makes through the preaching of the Gospel, whereby all who hear it are summoned rationally and conclusively in order that they may attain the salvation acquired through Christ. [179]

This "general" call remains "fruitless" for most men, but it serves as a preparation for the elect, to whom the "powerful" or "effectual" call is addressed. This is

> ... that divine work of grace from God and His Spirit through which the elected sinners are not only summoned and persuaded under the presentation of the Word, but are also moved to consider rationally and powerfully, and with earnest, the transformation of their condition. [180]

The gift of grace is so conveyed by the Holy Spirit that "the will is permitted to receive no other truth than that which is first recognized as holy and good in the light of the understanding." [181] There is no established duration between the general and the effectual call; it commonly occurs within the "blossoming years of youth," as in Lampe's own case. Since man is no "block of stone," "God draws, and wishes that we at the same time let ourselves be pulled." [182]

The second stage is faith, which precedes regeneration because it is the appropriate image to use when speaking of the entry into the covenant of grace. [183] Saving faith is defined as

> ... that work of grace of God and His Spirit, through which the will of sinners called according to His purpose is inclined rationally and powerfully, in order that Christians may receive according to the sign of the Gospel alone and completely a perfect Saviour. [184]

He again uses the image of the beggar, who must release his "apparent good" to receive the gift of grace in preaching. [185] The image of the "ladder of faith" is also introduced, which is most fully explained in his "observations and additions" to d'Outrein's Golden Jewel, a Dutch pietistic commentary on the Catechism.[186] Just as a fugitive in peril of life who, in sighting a fortress, hastens "with ardent longing" to its shelter, so also he who takes shelter with the Lord Jesus as his "Lord Protector" passes from the "weaker faith" of "beholding from afar" to the "stronger faith" of actual possession.[187] In his Balm of Gilead, Lampe distinguishes two steps: first, the act of taking shelter in Christ, and second, the actual trust in Christ.[188] Lampe, with his developmental point of view, defends the weaker faith as real faith, though it is quantitatively less efficacious than stronger faith.

With Question 26 of the Catechism in mind, Lampe distinguishes between faith and assurance.[189] In explaining the question "What do you believe when you say 'I believe in God the Father Almighty, maker of heaven and earth'?", Ursinus had written, "To believe God and to believe in God are two very different things. The first expresses historical faith; the latter, true faith or confidence."[190] Lampe revised this by saying that the appeal to Christ belongs to faith, but assurance pertains to actual trust.[191] The latter is the fruit of faith, which appears in the lives of the elect. Snijders notes that the background for this discussion is the conventicle-piety of earnest Christians, like those whom Lampe gathered at Bremen, whom Lampe regarded as the true people of the Lord.[192]

The third stage in the order of salvation is regeneration, that

> work of grace by God and His Spirit whereby the elected sinner powerfully and all at once is transferred to the good and is actually brought from the situation of a sinner into the situation of grace.[193]

Schmidt, in his study of Luther and Spener,[194] charged that the latter replaced the forensic metaphor of justification with the biological metaphor of regeneration, though he formally retained the official Lutheran doctrine. If Lampe is to be charged with depreciating the doctrine of justification, it is by his decision to award regeneration temporal antecedence to it.[195] Lampe had a temporal distinction in mind when he wrote that regeneration

> ... is the narrow door, indeed the eye of a needle, through which one must enter by force to life, who

wants to save his soul. [196]

Though justification is the fourth stage, he wishes to make clear that it is

> not at the same time a duty, but a pure good, be-
> cause the sinner neither can nor should bring any-
> thing for it, and the Lord alone will have the honor
> that Jehovah is our righteousness. [197]

By it, the elect are absolved "not only in the order of heaven, but also in their own assurance. "[198] Lampe finds a description of this fourth stage in Question 60 of the Catechism:[199]
the imputation of Christ's righteousness is a benefit which is accepted "with a believing heart. "[200]

Sanctification, which is fifth, is that gift of the covenantal God wherein

> the regenerate and justified covenantal-comrade is
> continually transformed and is made further con-
> formable unto all good. [201]

Wendel notes that Calvin had made no special distinction be-
tween regeneration and sanctification--they are different images used to describe the lifelong process of repentance.[202]
A temporal distinction is made by Lampe, who interpreted regeneration as the new birth (an event antecedent to justifi-
cation).   In this stage, the believer is "set apart" for a spiritual battle to be waged against the world, sin, and the devil and his angels. [203]   Calvin had said that the rigor of the law, apart from grace, is not its principal use; rather, its principal use is as the guide and stimulus toward righteousness for the Christian. [204]   Lampe wrote that

> In sanctification we can be brought very near to
> the goal if we only want earnestly to receive the
> means at hand.   Between the position of grace and
> of glorification there is no third position.   Where
> the position of grace ceases, there the position of
> glorification begins. [205]

The highest step within the stage of sanctification is evangeli-
cal "fullness" (Vollkommenheit), wherein "the Spirit of Christ works so powerfully within the believer that they already realize the beginning of full obedience in His Person. "[206]

The consequence of sanctification is "sealing," the sixth step, which is

> ... the last work of grace by God and especially by the Holy Spirit, whereby the sanctified covenant-comrade is perpetually established in the position of grace, and, by his confirmation, receives an assurance in his soul for the awakening of a living hope. [207]

When the elect are received into grace by the work of the Spirit, "it is impossible that they can become lost; rather, they are upheld without failing."[208] In this, he appeals to the decree of the Synod of Dort,[209] which "shines as a costly pearl" and is a comfort to the Christian amid temptations, difficulties, illness, and death. The sealing is a "pure gift of the covenant of grace; not a duty."[210]

His earthly course being completed, the believer at last reaches the final (seventh) state, glorification, "the last work of grace of the trinitarian God," whereby

> ... the soul of the true covenant-comrade will be restored in full possession of the acquired highest bliss with Christ first at the day of death and hereafter at the day of the general resurrection and judgment, when the entire nature of man will be restored according to body and soul. [211]

There is no "spiritual sleep" of the soul after death as the Psychopannychists taught.[212] He has the rationalists in mind when he answers that he does not know where the place of bliss is located. It is the Raumlichkeit in which Christ has entered with His glorified body and where the believer who has completed the steps toward bliss attains the highest perfection of a "wise" (vernunftiges) creature.[213] However, even the glorified believer will still remain an "ABC student" beside the matchless wisdom of God.[214] Lampe at times colors this discussion with the imagery of bride mysticism, reminiscent of medieval mysticism--especially in his reference to the Ja-Worts of faith.

> It is no trifling thing when a bride gives her bridegroom the Ja-Wort. And the Holy Spirit also considers His work as a spiritual betrothal. (Hosea 2:19ff., and II Cor. 11:2).[215]

The Reformers' doctrine of forensic justification has become
one phase in the ordo salutis which takes place in the covenant of grace between God and man.

Lampe's extraordinary emphasis upon this order of
salvation led him to emphasize not only the distinction between the church militant on earth and the church triumphant
in glory, but also between the "inward" and the "outward"
church. [216] The latter refers to the general membership of
the church on earth, while the former refers to those earnest
Christians with whom he met in conventicles (and who were
to assist in the reformation of the general church). There
is a Donatist tendency in his conviction that the unregenerate
pastor or teacher is unable to present the "inner" or "effectual" call, [217] yet he castigates the Labadists for making a
judgment which belongs only to the Lord. [218] However, this
does not prevent members from seeking an established church
served by a converted minister. He sought to enhance
church discipline at Duisburg and Bremen by undertaking
house visitations and by preaching practical sermons, which
were accompanied by appeals for conversion. Calvin, the
Catechism, and the Palatinate Liturgy had related discipline
to the Lord's Supper, for discipline served to protect the integrity of sacrament and church from the faithless. [219] This
moral dimension was so emphasized by Lampe that the sacraments tend less to be common means of grace than signs of
the "covenantal seal" which are awarded to the believers. [220]
He finds this seal to be typologically represented in the Old
Testament in the rainbow and in circumcision. [221] Further,
the edification of the church proceeds not only from the ministry, as with Calvin, [222] but also from those earnest, con-
venticle-affiliated Christians.

He castigated the utopianism of the Labadists since
he recognized that the church is inevitably composed of wheat
and tares. [223] However Lampe was in fundamental agreement with them that "the millenium was imminent, and that
Christ's kingdom would soon be established on earth, at
which time Rome would fall. "[224] As Schrenk has shown, [225]
Cocceius had moved toward the conquest of anti-chiliasm
among the orthodox in the church by means of his idea of the
"fulfilled time of the church"; with Vitringa and Lampe, the
doctrine of the approaching reign of Christ on earth for a
thousand years, which had heretofore been "overwhelmingly
separatist, " became acceptable within the church tradition.
The application of the figure seven is applied to the state of
glory both within the order of salvation for the individual be-

liever and within the macrocosmic economy of the Heilsgeschichte. The Gnadenbund is divided into the following
periods which pertain to the history of the church--or king-
dom--in the world since the birth of Christ: the time of the
apostles to the death of John, the persecutions until Constan-
tine the Great, the time of freedom until the coming of the
"anti-Christendom,"[226] the period of the Waldensians, the
Reformation, the time of the Protestant church until the beginning of the eighteenth century, and the approaching millenium, when the Anti-Christ at Rome will be overthrown.[227]

        Thus, Lampe's theology represents the late pietistic
meshing of the precisianism of Teelinck, Udemans, and,
above all, Voetius with the heilsgeschichtlich theology of Cocceius and Vitringa. The former defined the Christian life,
which was based upon the new birth, in terms of an exalted
emphasis upon Calvin's third use of the law (and the third
section of the Catechism), with the result that the works
which were the marks of spirituality, in accordance with the
syllogismus practicus,[228] came to be defined in terms of a
prescribed course of spiritual exercises. The latter contributed the dynamic, eschatological-oriented Heilsordnung,
based upon the symbolic-prophetic interpretation of Scripture,
with the result that the periodization of history became the
basis for the detailed structuring of the order of salvation
within the life of the elect.

        At Herborn, Olevianus' concern for the promotion of
early piety in children had led him to prepare a homiletical
catechism which would in effect be a simplified doctrinal exposition in question-and-answer form,[229] and Zepper's emphasis upon catechetical comprehension rather than memorization was a source of the later pietistic emphasis upon the
response of the individual.[230] His Politica Ecclesiastica
(1595) provided a pattern for Voetius, despite his Aristotelian-
ism--an indication of the adaptability of his views, by his
followers, to those of Cocceius.[231] Here too, the practical
orientation of theology had been accompanied by Count Johann's promotion of the "Protestant union politics" of the late
sixteenth century and by opposition to the onslaughts of Aristotelian and Cartesian scholasticism. With this background,
the theology of Lampe was warmly received at Herborn in
the early eighteenth century, and a compendium of the writings of Lampe and Vitringa was the principal theological textbook in use at the Academy.[232]

        The reception of Reformed Pietism at Herborn had

momentarily been threatened by the attempted introduction of pietistic separatism by Heinrich Horch (1652-1729). Horch, who had been influenced by Untereyck at Bremen and who had defended Question 80[233] of the Catechism against the Jesuits, became pastor and professor of theology at Herborn. However, he was dismissed in 1697 in view of his extreme separatism, which included his advocacy of changing the worship service into a prayer meeting, opposition to the prevailing practices of administering the sacraments, and his preaching of the imminence of the eschaton. With Vitringa and Lampe, he taught the seven periods of the church, which would be consummated by the establishment of the kingdom of Christ on earth and its deliverance by Christ to the Father. [234]

However, Horch's dismissal by the Count of Nassau-Dillenburg was opposed by the city council, the guilds, and the congregation, and they promptly gained the support of the city magistrates to elevate the piety of the church by establishing conventicles in the homes of church members and private family worship services. [235] It was this action which, more than anything else, enabled Herborn to become the veritable center for Reformed Pietism by the time the Otterbeins appeared on the scene in the eighteenth century. [236] The Rhenish-Westphalian General Synod (1677) had ruled that separatism was partly to be met by more attention to catechization in order that "each member of the Synod thereafter should not only attend to the study of orthodoxy, but of piety, too."[237] With this in mind, the faculty of Herborn approved (in 1680) the publication of the first major work by a German Reformed Pietist, Wilhelm Dieterici's Der Wahre inwendige und suszwendige Christ, [238] which helped to establish the Herborn precedence of opposing separatism with the praxis pietatis, not with the old orthodoxy.

It was the Otterbeins, the influential, Herborn-trained pastor-theologians of the eighteenth century, whose theological writings, which have heretofore not been read by an English-speaking scholar, mediated this tradition during the height of the Enlightenment. These men, as spokesmen for the Reformed Church in Germany and America in the latter half of the eighteenth century, regarded themselves as the last defenders of the old faith against the massive inroads of rationalism in the life of the church.

Notes

1. "In Galileo, an independent natural basis for religion had begun to determine the biblical understanding of revelation."--John Dillenberger, Protestant Thought and Natural Science. (New York, 1960), 62.

2. Ibid., 66.

3. Quoted in Heinrich Schmid, Doctrinal Theology of the Evangelical Lutheran Church. (Minneapolis, 1961), 60.

4. This is discussed in chapter one of Orlando H. Wiebe, Johann Arndt; Precursor of Pietism (Ph. D. dissertation, State University of Iowa, 1965).

5. See the discussion of these men in Albrecht Ritschl, Geschichte des Pietismus, I (Bonn, 1880), 153-194.

6. Arminius, who had been charged with refuting errors of Coornhert, became convinced on the basis of Scripture that loyalty to the Reformed tradition required that the Bezan view be rejected. After his death in 1609, the five points of Remonstrance were composed by a group (led by Episcopius), which may have agreed with Arminius, but were not sufficiently argued with his persuasiveness and rootage in Scripture to convince most Reformed that Calvinism was not being compromised (the points were conditional predestination, universal atonement, saving faith, resistible grace, and uncertainty of perseverance). The principal attack against their position was the Counter-Remonstrance, largely influenced by the supralapsarian Gomarus (a student of Ursinus). When the issues were settled at Dort in 1618-19, a concept of unconditional, single predestination which was neither clearly supra- nor infralapsarian, limited atonement, total depravity, irresistible grace, and the perseverance of the saints were affirmed. --See Schaff, III, 550-97.

7. Ritschl, I, 101ff, and 130ff.

8. Graffmann, "Erklarung...," 71.

9. Beardslee, Reformed Dogmatics, 265.

10. Ibid.

11. Ibid.

12. Ibid., 274.

13. Ibid.

14. Ibid.

15. Ibid.

16. Ibid.

17. Ibid., 281.

18. Ibid.

19. Ibid., 292.

20. Ibid.

21. Ibid., 294.

22. Ibid., 319.

23. Ibid.

24. Ritschl, I, 118.

25. Ibid., 130ff; and Schrenk, op. cit., 67ff.

26. Charles McCoy, The Covenant Theology of Johannes Coc-
    ceius (Ph. D. dissertation, Yale, 1956), 148.

27. Ibid.

28. Josef Bohatec, Die cartesianische Scholastik in der
    Philosophie und reformierten Dogmatik des 17. Jhdts.
    (Leipzig, 1912), 87f.

29. Sys. Theology, II, 318; quoted by McCoy, 126.

30. Aph. prol., I, 3; quoted by McCoy, 128.

31. Preface to S. T., quoted in McCoy, loc. cit.

32. S. T., I, 4, 129.

33. Ibid.

34. Preface to Cocceius' Exposition of the Covenant of Grace..., quoted in McCoy, loc. cit.

35. Aphorismes, III, 9; quoted in McCoy, 141ff.

36. Ibid., 152.

37. Ibid., 157ff.

38. Ibid.

39. Ibid., 161.

40. S. T., XVII, 18; quoted in Heppe, Reformed Dogmatics, 232.

41. Graffmann, "Erklärung...," 72.

42. Ibid.

43. Ibid. This would lead to a new form of dicta probantis, whereby the testimony of Scripture is only received secondarily through the medium of the Catechism.

44. Ibid.

45. See discussion above, 6f.

46. Cocceius' Catechesis, quoted in Graffmann, 73.

47. Ibid.

48. Ibid.

49. Jurgen Moltmann, Zeitschrift für Kirchengeschichte, 71, (1960), 110-129.

50. Schrenk, op. cit., 334.

51. Cocceius' emphasis upon the successive, progressive stages of the covenantal history (Heilsgeschichte) is one which is foreign to Calvin and even to Bullinger, who made more preeminent use of the federal theme.

Cocceius' conceptual frame of reference, which is characterized by the ideas of "fruition," "perspicuity," and the "harmony" of Scripture as the "unum systema totius prophetiae ubique sei similis," has been placed by several interpreters (i. e. before Schrenk and Molt-mann, Wilhelm Bousset, who advanced this view in his Die Offenbarung Johannis, Göttingen, 1906, 333), in the camp of the late medieval apocalypticism and the historical interpretation of Joachim of Fiore (c. 1130-1202). --Moltmann, op. cit., 114, 123.

52. Bousset, op. cit., 333. The ban had been retained by the Voetian Pietists, who, with Augustine, had interpreted the millenium as the first thousand years of Christendom.

53. Schrenk, 333.

54. Bousset, 210ff.

55. Schrenk, 297.

56. See discussion in Chapter 1, Section a., in contrast with the non-organic quality of the Lutheran catechisms.

57. This is a question which Graffmann (69ff.) has raised though no definitive answer is offered.

58. Möller, 398.

59. Cocceius, Einleitung zu den prophet. Schriftung (Frank-furt, 1699), 243; quoted in Möller, 399.

60. Ibid., 402.

61. See Inst., 2, 15, and the Heidelberg Catechism, Q. 54.

62. Möller, 407.

63. Bohatec, op. cit.

64. The Cartesian position (cogito ergo sum) could be held along with or in opposition to the Copernican system.

65. Ibid., 87ff.

66. Ibid., see also Emil Weber, Reformation, Orthodoxie, u.

Rationalismus. I. 2. (Darmstadt, 1966), 290-356; and
Emanuel Hirsch, Geschichte der neuern evangelischen
Theologie, Band II, "Die neuen philosophischen u.
theologischen Anfänge in Deutschland." (Gütersloh,
1952).

67. Ibid.

68. Once more, as in medieval scholasticism, human reason
is potentially unlimited as a source of truth.

69. James Good, History of the Reformed Church of Germany, 1620-1890. (Reading, Pa., 1894), 367.

70. Bohatec, 51ff.

71. Ibid., 56.

72. Lentulus published Nova Renati Des Cartes Sapientia
facilliori quam antehac methodo detecta. (Herborn,
n. d.) Ibid., 57.

73. Clauberg replied with his Defensis Cartesiana (Amsterdam, 1648), Ibid.

74. Ernst Bizer, "Die reformierte Orthodoxie u. der Car-
tesianismus," in Zeitschrift für Theologie u. Kirche.
55. (1958), 342.

75. Ibid.

76. Praef., 209, quoted in Bizer, op. cit.

77. Ibid.

78. As Bizer shows (352ff.), Wittich remained orthodox on
the doctrine of justification, and was an infralapsarian
with regard to predestination.

79. Graffmann, "Erklärung...," 76.

80. Ibid.

81. Solomon Van Til (d. 1713) was a Dutch Cocceian who
wished to reconcile Cocceius' biblical theology with
the new science by introducing elements of scholasticism and Cartesian philosophy into theology--McCoy,

op. cit. , 324.

82. Graffmann, op. cit. , 77.

83. See Schaff, III, 311ff. , and Van Til, Homiliae Cate-
    cheticae.

84. Van Til, Commentary on the Heidelberg Catechism,
    quoted in Graffmann, 77.

85. Ibid.

86. Ibid. , 76.

87. Bohatec, 57.

88. See Max Wundt, Die deutsche Schulmetaphysik des 17.
    Jhdts. (Tübingen, 1939), 80ff.

89. Bohatec, 58.

90. David Dunn, et al. , A History of the Evangelical and
    Reformed Church. (Philadelphia, 1961), 14.

91. Ibid.

92. Friedrich Uhlhorn, Geschichte der deutsch-lutherischen
    Kirche. (vs. , Leipzig, 1911), I, 198; quoted in Theo-
    dore Tappert, Introduction to Pia Desideria, (Phila-
    delphia, 1964), 3.

93. Ibid. , 5.

94. Marie E. Richard, Philip Jacob Spener and His Work.
    (Philadelphia, 1897), 5.

95. Spener's dates were 1635-1705. He was pastor at Frank-
    furt, 1666-86.

96. Spener, Erbauliche Evangelisch- u. Epistolische Sonntags-
    Andachten. (Frankfurt, 1716), 638, quoted in Tappert,
    op. cit. , 13.

97. The first form was Latin for youth in school; the second
    was the German Mass for the general public; and, the
    third form, "which should be fashioned according to
    the right kind of evangelical order" (Ordnung) is for

"those who mean to be Christians in earnest, and confess the gospel with hand and mouth. " They must
"register their names and assemble alone in some
house to pray, to read, to baptize, to receive the
sacraments, and perform other Christian works. "
However, the crucial line is "In brief, if we had the
people and persons who in earnest coveted to be
Christians, the order and form could soon be made. "
Luther never thought he had them. The Homberg
Church Order had prematurely thought that it could
implement this third form, and that Luther would sanc-
tion it. --John Evjen, "Luther's Ideas Concerning Polity, " Lutheran Church Review. XIV. (1926), 217-19.

98. With Franke, the new birth became a dated event.

99. Schaff, I, 547.

100. See above, 96.

101. See above, 25 and 54.

102. Good, op. cit. , 76-92.

103. Dunn, op. cit. , 16.

104. Ibid.

105. Ibid.

106. Heppe (op. cit. , 118ff.) has attempted to trace the influ-
      ence of English Puritanism upon these men (for ex-
      ample, there are parallels between the casuistry of
      Udemans and that of Sibbes, Perkins, or Baxter).
      On the other hand, Stoeffler (The Rise of Evangelical
      Pietism, Leiden, 1965, 121ff.) has stressed the influ-
      ence of the indigenous traditions of Dutch mystical
      piety, as represented by the great Ruysbroek, Grote,
      Radewyn's Brethren of the Common Life, and such
      Spiritual Anabaptists as Hans Denck and Sebastian
      Frank.   There are certain resemblances between Ude-
      man's Jacob's Ladder, in which he described the de-
      velopment of the Christian life through various steps
      (i. e. these steps are humility and repentance, know-
      ledge of Christ, true faith in God (through Christ),
      true confession of faith, a godly (blessed) life, Chris-
      tian patience, spiritual joy through Christ, and per-

severance of the saints. --Ibid., 125). This is to be compared with Van Ruysbroek's "seven steps of the ladder of spiritual love. "

107. Ritschl, I, 153.

108. Stoeffler, 102ff.

109. Ritschl, I, 371ff.

110. Hurst, 344.

111. Ibid.

112. Alfred Adam, "Die Kirchengeschichtliche Rang der Nassauischen Union von 1817," in W. G. Steck, et. al., Um evangelische Einheit (Herborn, 1967), 119. Adam discusses the pietistic kingdom theology in his analysis of the protestantische Unionspolitik movement at Herborn.

113. The New Schaff-Herzog Religious Encyclopedia. XII (New York, 1910), 218ff.

114. Similar studies were also made of Galatians, Titus, and Romans. --Ibid.

115. Ibid.

116. Cocceius, Sa. Th. Kp. LXXXII, par. 7; quoted in Möller, op. cit., 415.

117. Ibid.

118. Ibid., 416ff.

119. Ibid.

120. Vitringa, Hypotyposis historiae et chronologiae, discussed in Möller, 417.

121. Ibid.

122. Vitringa, Typ. doctr. proph., II, Cp. I, par. 15; quoted in Möller, 417.

123. Vitringa, Hypotyposis, 7; op. cit.

124. He cites Herder as a link in this relation. With Herder, God reveals Himself not only in the Word, but also in history--a distinction between the sacred and the secular that is foreign either to Cocceius or Vitringa. -- See 432-440.

125. Ibid., 419.

126. Ibid.

127. Ibid., 420.

128. Calvin, (Inst., 2, 11), enumerated several such distinctions.

129. Ibid., Note Art. 17 of the Augustana.

130. For a discussion of this point, see Karl Löwith, Meaning in History (Chicago, 1964), 245.

131. Max Goebel, Geschichte des christlichen Lebens in der rheinischwestphalischen evangelische Kirche, (Coblenz, 1852-1862), II, 403, 432.

132. Quoted in Goebel, op. cit., 401.

133. Ibid.

134. Ibid., 402.

135. Ibid., 402ff.

136. These more "pure" Cocceians, were named after their principal spokesman, Henricius Groenewegen (d. 1692).

137. "Lob des Herrn Jesu," quoted in Goebel, 408-10.

138. This is a phrase used by another ernstige Cocceian, Van der Honert; cited in Möller, 128.

139. Ebd. IV, 124; quoted in Moltmann, 128.

140. Ibid.

141. Geheimnis des Gnadenbundes, (Bremen, Verlegts Nathanael Saurmann, 1748 ed. used), II, 49.

142. Karl Müller, "Lampe," The New Schaff-Herzog Religious Encyclopedia, VI, (New York, 1910), 405.

143. Ibid.

144. These catechetical works will be noted in relation to the Otterbeins.

145. Müller, loc. cit.

146. Lampe, Rudimenta Theologiae elenchticae, 14; quoted in Gerrit Snijders, Friedrich Adolph Lampe (Harderwijk, 1954), 161.

147. Lampe, Syntagma Dissertationum, II, 10 quoted in Snijders, 162.

148. Gnad. IV, cap. IV, par. XII.

149. Ibid., II, Cap. XIII, par. 1.

150. Ibid., III, (1758 ed.), 2, 989ff.

151. Stoeffler, op. cit., 170.

152. Schrenk, 303ff.

153. Ritschl, I, 371ff.

154. Ritschl neglects this prophetic aspect of Reformed Pietism with his intention to indict all Pietism as a revival of the a-social individualism inherent in medieval asceticism.

155. Ibid., I, 26ff.

156. Inst. 2, 16, 4. Calvin says "We are reconciled to him who already loved us, but with whom we were enemies on account of God."

157. Ibid., I, 53ff.

158. Snijders, 77.

159. Gnad., I (1651 ed.), 185.

160. The doctrine of limited atonement was one of the five

basic tenets of the Synod of Dort.

161. Comm. in Joh. 3:16, C.R. 75, 65; quoted in Paul Van
     Buren, Christ in our Place (Grand Rapids, 1957),
     102ff.

162. Gnad., IV, i, 171.

163. Ibid., I, 68.

164. Ibid., I, 79.

165. Ibid., I, 79.

166. Ibid., I, 89.

167. Compare Gnad. I, 89 with Inst. I, 20, 7.

168. Gnad., I, 98.

169. Ibid., I, 109.

170. Ibid., I, 100, 109.

171. Ibid., I, 728.

172. Ibid., I, 123.

173. Snijders, 84.

174. Ibid., 81.

175. In the Catechism, comfort is the felicitous mode in
     which the doctrine of election is presented, as "our
     only comfort in life and in death."--Question 1.

176. Gnad., I, 152.

177. Ibid., I, 157-9.

178. See Inst., IV, 1.

179. Ibid., I, 224.

180. Ibid., I, 232.

181. Ibid., I, cap. VII, par. XXV.

182. Ibid.

183. Snijders, 85.

184. Ibid., I, 273.

185. Ibid., I, 313.

186. D'Outrein, Het gouden kleinoot van de leere der waarheid die naar de godsaligheid is; vervattet in den Heidelbergischen Katechismus. (All editions after the Amsterdam edition of 1719 included the annotations of Lampe.)--James Tanis, Dutch Calvinistic Pietism in the Middle Colonies. (The Hague, 1967), 10.

187. Ibid., 136; quoted in Snijder, 86.

188. Lampe, Balsam aus Gilead, 103, 169ff; quoted in Snijder, loc. cit.

189. Ibid.

190. Ursinus, op. cit., 139.

191. Snijders, 87.

192. Ibid.

193. Gnad., I, 360.

194. Martin Schmidt, "Spener u. Luther," in Luther-Jahrbuch XXIV (Berlin, 1957), 102-29.

195. Inst., IV, 11, 11. Of course, Lampe took his cue from Calvin, who related faith to lifelong repentance, though it must be noted that Calvin regarded the latter as logically but not temporally distinct from justification: "Justifying grace is not separate from regeneration although these are distinct things."

196. Gnad., I, 409.

197. Ibid., I, cap. X, par. XXXI.

198. Ibid., I, 428.

199. Snijders, 89, Q. 60: "How art thou righteous before

God?"--Schaff, III, 326.

200. Ibid.; Lampe also uses the image of a "garment" in Gnad., I, cap. X, par. XXVI.

201. Gnad., I, 483.

202. Quoted in Wendel, op. cit., 242.

203. Snijders, 90.

204. See Inst., II, 7, 2.

205. Gnad., I, 535.

206. Gnad., I, cap. XI, par. XLVI.

207. Ibid., I, 582.

208. Ibid., I, 586.

209. Ibid., I, cap. XII, par. IX, and Snijders, 91.

210. Gnad., I, cap. XII, par. XXXII.

211. Ibid., I, 641.

212. Calvin, in his Psychopannychia, had said, "The soul, even when it is dead, has its immortality, the which we affirm ... "--quoted in Wendel, 174.

213. Gnad., I, 662, and Snijders, 92.

214. Gnad., I, 679.

215. Ibid., I, 732.

216. Ibid., II, 53.

217. Ibid., IV, 1, 800.

218. Ibid., IV, 1, 768, and Snijders, 95.

219. Thompson, op. cit., 42.

220. Snijders, 97.

221. Gnad., cap. II, par. XXXIII, and Snijders, 97.

222. Inst., IV, 3.

223. Goebel, op. cit., I, 417.

224. Good, op. cit., 391.

225. Schrenk, op. cit., 303ff.

226. The "anti-Christendom" refers to the medieval church.

227. From Gnad., IV, cap. X, par. XIV, and Synopsis his-
     toriae sacrae, 229; discussed in Snijders, 99.

228. The practical syllogism is: "whoever believes shall be
     saved; there are practical evidences (viz., my sanc-
     tified life) that I believe; therefore I shall be saved."
     --discussed in Conrad Cherry, The Theology of Jona-
     than Edwards (New York, 1966), 151-7.

229. This matter is discussed in James Tanis, "The Heidel-
     berg Catechism in the Hands of the Calvinistic Pie-
     tists" (unpublished article), 6. Tanis notes that the
     Catechism was too weighty for maximum success in
     the instruction of children which led to the growth of
     other catechisms derived from it, including Olevianus'
     Der Gnadenbund Gottes, which includes a "Bawren
     Catechismus" for use by fathers with their children.

230. Ibid., 7.

231. Tanis, Dutch Calvinistic Pietism..., 18n.

232. A. W. Drury, The Life of Otterbein. (Dayton, 1884),
     39.

233. Q. 80: "What difference is there between the Lord's
     Supper and the Popish Mass?"--Schaff, III, 335.

234. Schrenk, 302.

235. Good, 342.

236. James O. Bemesderfer, Pietism and Its Influence on
     the Evangelical United Brethren Church. (Harrisburg,
     1966), 50.

237. Records of the Rheinisch-Westphalian General Synod
      (1670), quoted in Good, 365.

238. Tanis, Dutch Calvinistic Pietism..., 18n.

PART II

THE OTTERBEINS

Chapter 3

A THEOLOGY OF THE CATECHISM
FOR A DAY OF CRISIS

Who were the Otterbeins? History has bequeathed us
with only a few scant church records which scarcely allow us
to become acquainted with them as living men. To be sure,
United Brethren historians have lavished admiration upon
Philip Wilhelm, the brother who ventured to colonial North
America and became instrumental in organizing the Church of
the United Brethren in Christ. However, if Americans are
to understand this leader of the German-American awakening,
they surely must come to terms with the tradition of German
Reformed church life from which he emerged. Previous historians have made cursory references to this background
while lamenting the fact that Philip Wilhelm Otterbein left
only a few letters and one sermon as a testimony to his life
work. [1] It was known that two of his brothers, who remained
pastors in the region of Herborn, Germany, had gained recognition by the publication of several volumes of sermons and
textbooks based upon the Heidelberg Catechism, that redoubt-
able bulwark of Reformed church life.

Oddly enough, denominational historians have largely[2]
ignored this substantial literary heritage, despite the fact
that it represents the theological tradition in which the American Otterbein was nurtured. A reading of these long-forgot-
ten German volumes enables the Otterbeins to come to life
as forceful, articulate spokesmen for the Reformed faith in
an age of rising secularism. Their works were of such importance for Philip Wilhelm that he spent great effort in distributing them among his German-American parishioners. [3]

In that day of disruption in church life, which was a
consequence of the German Enlightenment, the Otterbein home
kindled the flame of devotion to the time-honored religion of
the Catechism. Since the time of Olevianus (1536-1585), the
author of the Catechism who had taught at Herborn, heads of
families had been entrusted with the power of discipline in
the congregation--a measure which contrasted with the exclu-

sive, pastoral aristocracy which prevailed in Beza's Geneva. Accordingly, the inculcation of the Catechism was not only the duty of the minister but also of the parents in the home. This tendency was strengthened with the erosion of catechetical preaching in the German Reformed churches of the eighteenth century. Olevianus, who recognized that the Catechism was too weighty for maximum success in the instruction of children, had prepared a simplified version to be used by fathers with their children at home.[4] Hence, it was in the home that the Otterbein children received the love for the Catechism which would lead two of them to become its influential interpreters for the church of their day.

Six sons of Johann Daniel Otterbein grew to become pastors in the Reformed Church of Nassau-Dillenburg, including Georg (1731-1800), whom Drury notes "stood with the leading minds of Germany" and was "thoroughly convinced of the error of the spirit of his age."[5] Since he regarded the Heidelberg Catechism as the symbol of the faith which was being threatened by the rational theologians, Georg moved to bolster this faltering standard by publishing three large volumes of sermons on the Catechism which were preached during his long pastorate at Duisburg.[6]

His life in this cosmopolitan setting brought him into contact with the philosophical currents of the German Enlightenment. Prominent rational theologians with whom he was personally acquainted included Samuel Collenbusch (1724-1803) and the Hasenkamp brothers. Collenbusch, who had arrived at Duisburg as an alchemist, was introduced to the fashionable thought of Descartes. He became a leader of a select circle of theological liberals who were interested in relating Cartesian philosophical insights to problems of dogmatics. These men, led by J. G. Hasenkamp, regarded the highly-valued Reformed doctrines of Christ's vicarious atonement and predestination as outmoded dogmas, and they replaced the theology of the Heidelberg Catechism with an ethical religion founded upon the possibility of Christian perfection.[7] Their philanthropic activity included the founding of a missionary society at Barmen. Hasenkamp long sought to bring Otterbein into the circle, but despite his emphasis upon Christian practice, he refused to join in these endeavors because of their heterodox, universalistic presuppositions.

Otterbein remained convinced that the only virtue worthy of the name was that which took seriously the inability of unredeemed man to act morally. This was the point

of his chief divergence from the natural religion in vogue in
his day. Christian Wolff (1679-1754) of Halle had hoped to
demonstrate the rational basis of church dogma. The Creator, he reasoned, wished so to reveal His majesty that He
might be apprehended through the created order by natural
man. [8] An emphasis upon feeling and emotion--derived from
the Pietists--was combined with this rational theology by
Mosheim, Baumgarten, and the "Kantian" theologians in the
final third of the eighteenth century. For them, Christianity
was defined as a moral realm which exists independently
alongside natural science, and revelation was the disclosure
of what was potentially knowable through "moral" reason.
Under the influence of the Enlightenment, church administration was increasingly divorced from the rubrics of the historic church orders and confessions--chief of which was the
Heidelberg Catechism.

When Georg Otterbein wrote the preface of his first
volume of sermons on the Catechism at Duisburg in 1799,
he correctly perceived that, to stem the erosion of church
dogma, one had to come to grips with the intellectual heavy-
weights of the Enlightenment. And yet, his pages were written for the remnants of the faithful, not for the university
trained. This meant that his defense of the faith was a comfort for the faithful though it was scarcely taken seriously by
those intellects against whom it was directed. Otterbein observes that "our moralists now approvingly regard man as
healthy and speak much of the worth of man," but they fail
to remember that "natural man has been lost through the
fall" and that he can only be saved through "Jesus Christ,
the second Adam."[9] The moralists prescribe to natural man
the "diet of the healthy." They speak beautifully of duties
and obligations "but they fail to show from whence the power
of practice comes."[10] The result is that "pure morality appears only in books." It is nothing else than Kantian philosophy, which one is inspired to embrace "in order to advance
with his age, without being concerned what will be wrought
through it."[11] The gospel, he says, teaches that man's sick-
ness must be treated and that he must be "restored to
health" before the prescription can be given to him which belongs only to the healthy. If our physical health is held only
in "weak skeins" and is subject to "creeping plagues," how
much more does this condition pertain to our moral health!
In short, he urges that the word "enlightenment" be rein-
stated according to its traditional meaning, which was the
illumination of the elect by the Holy Spirit. He traces the
fault to the "inappropriate courtship" of philosophy by theology

which has led to the "abduction of Christianity. "

While Georg was waging his struggle in the cosmopolitan setting of Duisburg, a younger brother, Johann, was ne-
gotiating his way through the vagaries of sectarian Protestantism while serving as pastor in the relative isolation of
tiny Wittgenstein-Berleburg. This parish had become known
as a home for separatistic, radical Pietists. His problem
was to determine how this fervor might be channeled in the
direction of churchly piety. Separatism had always been an
implicit danger in the Pietists' propensity for conventicles,
which were ostensibly intended to be cell groups for the renewal of the church from within. The radical Pietists regarded all institutional churches, Catholic or Protestant, as
fallen, and the true church as spiritualized within the believer, to whom God reveals all truth. Many of the sectarians
who sought refuge at the friendly court of the Duke of Wittgenstein-Berleburg were devotees of Jakob Boehme (1575-1634).
He had taught that man is capable of regaining lost angelical
powers through a life of celibacy and union with the heavenly
wisdom ("Sophia"). Like the rational theologians, the radical Pietists, with their aim of divinizing man, rejected the
doctrines of imputed righteousness and predestination. Their
great literary production was the Berleburg Bible, an edition
of holy Scripture with extensive symbolic-prophetic annotations, which was published by J. M. Haug from 1730 to
1744.

Though radical Pietism resulted in permanent religious
organization in the Moravian and Brethren (Dunker) sects, [12]
many of its doctrinal deviations remained suspect even among
churchly Pietists in principalities of orthodox strength.
There is a resemblance between the order of salvation set
forth by the Otterbeins in their exposition of the Catechism
and the radical Pietists' view that becoming a Christian was
a process of letting Christ take mystical shape ("Gestalt") in
the soul. However, the Otterbeins' order of salvation was
carefully presented within the categories of Reformed doctrine
and with only a subordinate appeal to mystical categories.
This meant there could be no unequivocal elevation of "private" revelation over the authority of the written Word of
Scripture.

Faced with the opposition of Enlightenment theologians
and radical Pietists, the Otterbeins assumed the considerable
role of being spokesmen for the church and its historic confessions in an exceedingly precarious age. Before tracing

the history of the Heidelberg Catechism, Georg Otterbein observed that it "still has its friends," though its enemies were
clearly more visible. [13] By the latter half of the eighteenth
century, it had been displaced as the principal symbol of
Reformed church life in many parts of Hesse and Nassau,
but Steubing reports that, after 1750, it was still being ex-
posited with the approval of the consistory at Herborn. [14]
Who were its friends, upon whom the Otterbeins relied in
defense of it? Who were its enemies, and how did they succeed in undermining it?

At Herborn, the Reformed university where the Otterbeins received their theological training, there was an anti-
scholastic tradition of catechizing which favored comprehension rather than rote memorization of the Catechism. As an
aid in understanding the questions and answers, the Catechism was included in the several editions of the Herborn
hymnal, which made the comforting doctrine of the Catechism
accessible to the faithful in times of political oppression and
rationalistic skepticism. With its decline as a church confession during the Enlightenment, the Catechism became the
personal credo of the pietistic defenders of the faith, who
popularized a unique mode of catechetical exposition in which
the sequence of questions and answers represented a fixed,
temporal order of salvation. Following the lead of Cocceius,
Lampe, and Stähelin, the Otterbeins transformed the Heidelberg Catechism into a series of "spiritual steps" which were
designed to unlock the truth of Scripture and lead one to
heaven. A pilgrim's progress in this order of salvation may
be gauged by visible marks, which indicate whether he remains "afflicted" and "anxious" or whether he is "partly
secure" or "fully persuaded." It was the Swiss Pietist,
Christoph Stähelin, whose Catechetical House Treasure made
the fullest use of the mystical theme of the "ladder of para-
dise" (Scala paradisis) in interpreting the Catechism:

> Here, dear reader, you have, as it were, a ladder
> to heaven with three rungs. If you would use it to
> reach heaven, then you must step on each of the
> three rungs and not step over any one of them. [15]

The earnest Christian proceeds by these three steps, which
correspond to the three divisions of the Catechism. This
theme is partly derived from The Seven Steps of the Ladder
of Spiritual Love by the medieval Flemish mystic, Jan van
Ruysbroeck, for whom the ladder was Christ himself and its
rungs were humility, the knowledge of Christ, faith, confes-

sion, godliness, patience, spiritual joy, and perfection. [16]

When Georg Otterbein counted himself among the friends of the Catechism, he was the last to lead a small remnant of the faithful to withstand the active forces of the German Enlightenment. His hope was "to augment their comfort and Joy" amid the apostasy of the day. [17] Like Lampe, he wished to adapt the content of doctrine according to the levels of individual students, for "... these first truths are [not] nourishment for children. It is still milk which nourishes them. "[18] The authority of the Catechism rests upon its biblical witness, but the mode in which doctrine is presented is "certainly not unpsychological"--which seems to be a negative way for Otterbein to say, as did Lampe, that the objective presentation of "saving knowledge" in the Catechism is matched by the conduciveness of the questions for the subjective appropriation of salvation by the will. He defined in some detail what it is that is "not unpsychological" about the Catechism, which makes it so appealing to the mind and will. "It [the Catechism] follows the going forth of the Holy Spirit, which convicts of sin, of righteousness, and of the judgment. "[19] After rendering this estimate of the first section of the Catechism, he then exaltantly refers to the second and third sections by declaring

> How beautiful it is to learn to know the order itself,... what we originally were, what we have become through the fall, and what we shall again become through the fully gracious design of God. [20]

The implications of his "theology of the Catechism" are subtle yet unmistakable. The Reformers had hoped that the evangelical catechism would protect the objective character of the church and the consensus of Christian doctrine from any private excursus into Scripture. The same document, interpreted as an "order of salvation" (Heilsordnung), could become the basis for an atomistic view of salvation. [21] When he discussed the third section of the Catechism, it became something more than an aid for quickening the priesthood of believers who were created by the Word (the treasury of grace). The intention was to mold Spirit-filled persons who themselves become the true treasure of the church. The corporate ministry of Word and sacrament, for which Calvin and the authors of the Catechism had provided, was in part displaced by the appeal to each man to ascend the order of salvation contained within the Catechism.

When Otterbein explained the objective work of grace
by appealing to its "comprehensibleness," whereby man is
directed to his own inner experience, he aspired to make use
of "clear and certain" propositions for the defense of super-
natural revelation. He was addressing an audience which
was already conditioned by such terms. Thus, he informed
his readers that they would find in his sermons a collection
of "comprehensible truths" which are also the "most fundamental ones ... which are worthy of the name Christian."[22]
Since he sought to bring the "comfort and joy" of salvation
which the natural reason cannot provide, such terms as "comprehension" and "clarity" are used to show the efficacy of
doctrine. He was interested in the inherent rationality of the
"order of salvation" only as it furthered this end.

Such "rational" terminology has led to the charge that
the catastrophe of Protestant theology after the Reformation
was that it lost its object, revelation, by speaking of religion
from a manward point of view.[23] Older orthodoxy had taught
that the problem of "religion" should not be considered at
all.[24] However, by pointing to the problems posed by the
study of world religions and natural religion, Otterbein was
attempting to present his study of the Catechism in the light
of relevant issues of the day. His day not only witnessed
the demise of rigid Protestant "orthodoxy" and "scholasticism," which earlier Pietism had opposed. It had also
brought the realization of the fears that had led conservative
theologians to uphold the scholastic formulas so firmly:
much eighteenth-century Christianity really lost contact with
the historic faith. By prefacing his vindication of the Catechism with a discussion of "religion," Otterbein did relate
man to God's revelation in an "independent" form, apart from
his existence as the "possession of Christ" (Question 1).
However, he was always explicit that it is the duty of reason
to accept revelation--it is not the duty of reason to inquire
into all fields, including the doctrines of the Catechism.

Because of his concern that "the length of the answers
to the questions of the Heidelberg Catechism may cause diffi-
culty for the reader,"[25] Otterbein produced a substantial textbook on the Catechism for use in schools and catechetical
classes.[26] Like Ursinus, he listed sub-questions under each
question and answer in the Catechism in order to explain the
hidden logic behind the expression of the text and to render
discernible, in a simplified fashion, the thought. By this
analytical procedure, he sought to revive evangelical catechizing at a time when many youths in the Reformed churches of

the lower Rhine were being confirmed without a knowledge of
the Catechism--especially when the rationalist catechisms began to displace it. [27] The introduction to his textbook is
composed of sections on "Religion," "Scripture," "God," and
"Man," which are intended to orient beginning students in the
study of the Catechism. Before each of these sections, he
has prefaced a definitive statement of the subject, which is
followed by a series of analytical questions and answers, interspersed with biblical verses, that are intended to induce
the student to comprehend the meaning of the statement.
Memorization of the questions and answers need not be vacuous but are vital to the comprehension of the meaning of the
"order of salvation," provided the instruction is accompanied
by a mature, regenerate teacher. Otterbein still acknowledged the priority of content over form, but in a day when
the Catechism was being completely displaced, he discovered
that the "order of salvation," which is at the heart of the
Catechism, can be located by an analysis of the structural
order of the questions and answers.

Otterbein's tireless efforts to render the Catechism
efficacious for all levels of understanding, "according to psychology and experience,"[28] were guided by one pre-eminent
objective: "... to promote righteous living and to render un-
forgettable that the Christian religion is a knowledge of the
truth for godliness."[29] This statement is perhaps the most
succinct definition of the faith, to which the Catechism points,
that Otterbein gives. Whether used in preaching or in teaching, the "order of salvation," to which the Catechism points,
is a wholly practical, not a speculative, knowledge. "One
cannot begin too early ... to learn to know God" in this
vital way. [30] For Otterbein, this "knowledge of the truth for
godliness," or again, this "way of salvation," was a prede-
termined, immutable order which must be made comprehensible and efficacious for the individual by adapting it to his
particular level. The phrase that he preferred to use when
speaking of the heart of the Christian faith is the "true
Christianity," which is the "pearl of unending worth, that is
sought with great solicitude."[31] This "true Christianity" is
equated with the answer to Question 1 ("That is my only
trust in life and in death, that I am not my own, but that I
belong to my faithful Saviour Jesus Christ.")[32]

Though Otterbein refers to the proclamation of the
finished work of Christ, as contained in Question 1, he proceeds at once to speak of the Christian life in terms of "the
earnest steps, either short or long, which must be taken by

you and me, and can only once be done. "[33]   "An endless
eternity depends on these [steps]. "[34]

> Only through careful efforts, courageous battles
> and steadfast perseverance can one reach the de-
> sired goal. Not all who run there win the prize.[35]

He asked his readers, "Has the great transformation passed
you by, which makes us Christians-in-deed?"[36]   And the appeal follows, "Have you made the heartfelt decision which
consists solely in living for Him who has died for us?"[37]
"This is the way the [believer] goes ... and he abides therein. "[38]   This theology shifts the nature of Question 1 from
the classic Reformed theology of mystical union and election
to a theology which emphasizes decision, efforts, and in der
Tat Christianity. As we shall see,[39] the doctrinal implications of this shift become apparent in Otterbein's treatment
of the individual questions of the Catechism.

The filter through which Otterbein saw the Catechism
is illumined by Barth's observation that the emphasis on
"praxis" in the eighteenth century reflected the conviction
that the folly of the religious wars was to be attributed to
the fact that men had only a theoretical understanding of the
Christian credos.[40]   This is true whether "praxis" is seen
in terms of the Pietists' reference to the inner work of the
Spirit, which was not without outward legislation and fashion-
ing, or the rationalists' reference to the outward work of the
moral man, which was not without the language of the inner
renewal of the heart. There was a sense that life had been
rendered helpless by dialectical subtlety, the "unfruitful theologizing" which had robbed truths of faith of their true content. The consequences of the eighteenth-century reaction
against this tendency was the "moralization" or "bourgoise-
ification" of theology.[41]

Otterbein's adherence to the Catechism led him to
temper somewhat this ethos of his age. Though he spoke of
the essence of "true Christianity" as being "a knowledge of
the truth for godliness" or "the way of sanctification, " he
was careful to relate the "way to holiness" to the possession
of the Redeemer and His benefits, which is consistent with
Calvin and the Catechism.[42]   These benefits "bear the name
Christian" by virtue of "Jesus Christ, who has taught them
and has embodied them all. "[43]   "By this name, these benefits are distinguished from those of natural religion, " which
refers to "the honor of God according to the knowledge which

we have received from God through reason, nature, or creation. "[44] "Natural religion is not sufficient for salvation" because of "the fall of man, which leaves us in doubt concerning the most important truths. "[45] In contrast, the Christian
religion teaches us to recognize God in Christ "principally
from the godly revelation in holy Scripture. "[46]

Nevertheless, Otterbein's emphasis was clearly upon
"praxis" as is indicated by his assertion that "the true "Christianity is a matter of experience. "[47] This statement reflects
the tendency of Reformed Pietism in Germany from the days
of Untereyck, a century earlier. The old Reformed covenant
theology is retained, but what becomes important is the subjective, inward "good of the covenant for me. " Thus, it is
not surprising that the quasi-mysticism of Johann Arndt, the
early Lutheran Pietist, was acknowledged among the Reformed
Pietists. According to Arndt, "true Christianity" does not
result from hearing the Word alone; the outer Word is instrumental in producing it, but it effectually proceeds only from
the "inner ground of the heart. "[48] The image "new birth"
here gives a stronger expression to the character of the new
being of the Christian as life. [49] In the hands of the Reformed Pietists, the "new birth" which is at the heart of
"true Christianity" is given a legalistic shape which is lacking in Arndt. To Georg Otterbein, the "pearl" which is
"true Christianity" is to learn to know "the beautiful order
of salvation itself ... and what we should again be according
to the gracious purpose of God. "[50] In order to be reborn
as a true Christian the only recourse is the "order of salvation, " contained within the Catechism, which the believer
must ascend in stairstep fashion by the grace of God.

The ultimate authority for this "order of salvation"
set forth in the Catechism is the Bible. As Tanis has explained, the doctrine of Scripture in the Catechism is "implicit rather than explicit" in that it "did not busy itself with
the problems of how God inspired the biblical text but with
the more immediate and relevant concern of the way in which
the Bible inspired man. "[51] Scripture was Otterbein's point
of departure for developing theology "on the framework which
the Heidelberger provided. "[52] He wrote that "The Bible is
the source, and the Catechism points out the order which is
derived from this source. "[53] He showed familiarity with the
historical study of Scripture that had been developed by the
Reformed theologian Cocceius, for he writes "If one circum-
spectly compares Scripture with Scripture, and distinguishes
time and circumstances, its meaning soon will become

clear. "[54] In asserting that "Scripture explains itself through itself, "[55] Otterbein sought to encourage the faithful, who were buffeted by the rationalists' efforts to explain biblical faith in terms of human reason. Nevertheless, he also emphasized an "intelligible reading of the Bible," which leads him to criticize the practice of allowing children to learn to read from it "since they may read more than they can assimilate. "[56] Rather, Scripture texts should be learned in association with "the intelligible study of the Catechism" in order to "bring children unconsciously into the recollection of Scripture that their joy might be increased. "[57]

Otterbein indicated that we can be convinced of the "godliness of holy Scripture" only by revelation, for "no one can reveal and teach [these truths] except God. "[58] Thus, he did not say that the infallibility of the Bible is a truth self-evident to all, but that it is an infallible truth that only God can reveal the secrets of Scripture. However, there are "external" evidences in Scripture which serve to establish its credibility to all, such as the fulfillment of prophecy, the miracles, and the beneficial effects of the teaching of Scripture upon mankind. [59] The ultimate test whereby we are "assured of the godliness of holy Scripture for ourselves" is "when one has experienced its power," which "secures the most reliable assurance. "[60]

This firsthand experience of the truth of Scripture is attained when the Bible is recognized as the source of the order which is set forth in the Catechism. The "truths" of Scripture which are to be experienced refer to the fixed sequence of God's redemptive acts and to the spiritual steps whose completion, under God's grace, is necessary for the attainment of salvation. For the Otterbeins, the Catechism was regarded less as the means of preparing catechumens for admission to the Lord's Supper and to the life of the visible church as an expression of the Word of God, and more as the "heavenly guide" whereby an individual might attain salvation by progressive stages. They saw the Catechism as the only sure guide for leading one out of the labyrinth of eighteenth century rationalism.

Notes

1.   See A. W. Drury, Life of Otterbein. (Dayton: Otterbein Press, 1898).

2. The only denominational historian to deal with this material is H. B. Stehmann, who translated a small portion of G. G. Otterbein's instruction on the Catechism for the 1874 issues of the Religious Telescope, the United Brethren denominational periodical.

3. A record of the copies he distributed in North America is found in the preface of the second German edition of these works. In addition, a volume on the Catechism by J. D. Otterbein was reprinted at Lancaster, Pennsylvania, in 1790.

4. Olevianus' Bawren Katechismus. (Herborn, 1587).

5. Drury, Life, 33.

6. G. G. Otterbein, Predigten über den Heidelbergischen Katechismus. 2 vols. in 1. (Duisburg: Helwing, 1800; Lemgo: Meyer, 1803).

7. J. W. Cuno, "History of the Otterbein Family," in The Monthly Itinerant (Harrisburg, February, 1880); IX, No. 10, tr. H. B. Stehmann.

8. John Dillenberger, Protestant Thought and Natural Science. (New York: Doubleday, 1960), 168.

9. G. G. Otterbein, "Vorrede" to Predigten..., I, 8.

10. Ibid.

11. Ibid.

12. See Donald Durnbaugh, The Believers' Church. Chicago, 1970).

13. "Vorrede" to Predigten..., I, 8.

14. John Herm. Steubing, Nassau Chronicle u. Vade Mecum, 191.

15. Stähelin's Catechetischer Hauss-Schatz, oder Erklärung des Heidelbergischen Katechismus. 3 Auff. Basel, 1737, 27-29. tr. in James Tanis, "The Heidelberg Catechism in the Hands of the Calvinistic Pietists," (unpub. art.), 16.

16. Ibid., 14.

17. "Vorrede" to Predigten, I, 37.

18. Ibid.

19. Ibid., I, 40.

20. Ibid., I, 40ff.

21. However, the German Enlightenment had already, to a
    large extent, removed the possibility of the corporate,
    confessional church.

22. Ibid., I, 43.

23. Karl Barth, Church Dogmatics, I, 2 (Edinburgh: T. &
    T. Clark, 1956), tr. G. W. Bromiley, 293.

24. As Barth notes, Calvin could "quietly incorporate this
    problem into his discussion" in Inst. 1, 2, 1. --Ibid.,
    293ff.

25. G. G. Otterbein, Unterweisung nach dem Heidelbergi-
    schen Catechismus. (Frankfurt: Zülicher, n. d. --
    1788?), 2.

26. Ibid.

27. Heinrich Graffmann, "Erklärung des H. K. in Predigt u.
    Unterricht des 16. bis 18. Jhdts.", in Handbuch zum
    Heidelberger Katechismus. (Duisburg: Brendow,
    1963), 66.

28. Predigten, I, vi.

29. Ibid., I, vii.

30. Ibid., I, viii.

31. Ibid.

32. Ibid., I, ix.

33. Ibid.

34. Ibid.

35. Ibid.

36. Ibid.

37. Ibid.

38. Ibid. , I, xi.

39. See chapters four through six.

40. Barth, Die Protestantische Theologie im 19. Jhdts. (Zürich: Zollikon, 1947), 72ff.

41. Ibid.

42. See Calvin, Inst. , 3, 1, 1.

43. Predigten, I, 4.

44. Ibid.

45. Unterweisung, 4.

46. Ibid.

47. Predigten, I, 44.

48. Johann Arndt, True Christianity, (Philadelphia: Smith, English, and Company, 1869), I, ch. 36.

49. Orlando Wiebe, Johann Arndt: Precursor of Pietism (Ph. D. Dissertation, unpublished; State University of Iowa, 1965), 146.

50. Predigten, I, 40.

51. Tanis, 9.

52. Ibid. , 12.

53. Predigten, I, 45.

54. Ibid.

55. Ibid.

56. G. G. Otterbein, Lesebuch für deutsche Schulkinder. (Philadelphia: Karl Cist, 1795), 2.

57. Ibid.

58. Ibid.

59. Unterweisung, 6ff.

60. Predigten, I, 8.

Chapter 4

THE PILGRIMAGE OF FAITH

It has been suggested that Protestant scholasticism, which found its final synthesis in such symbols as the Helvetic Consensus Formula (1675) and in the Genevan orthodoxy of Francis Turretin (d. 1687),[1] sought to surround the ideals of the Reformation with a systematic teaching which would preserve them. However, its consolidation was followed by its immediate eclipse.[2] For example, Turretin's integration of elements of the covenant theology with high Calvinism did not seem to modify the flavor with any non-scholastic, biblical emphasis, nor with the warmth of personal religion found in the Heidelberg Catechism.[3]

When the Otterbeins attempted to bring Christian doctrine and piety out of disrepute, the shape which they gave to the traditions of Calvin and of the authors of the Catechism was distinctly a product of the pietistic theology they had learned at home and at Herborn. By noting how the Otterbeins spoke of God and man, we shall attempt to discover whether late pietistic theology, in its battle against the secularism of the day, became a viable alternative to a bankrupt Protestant scholasticism.

A matter of chief concern in their exposition of the Catechism is whether they took seriously the assumption made in Question 1--the reality that "Christ is already there,"[4] and that the gospel is first and foremost the proclamation of the objective faith which becomes the indispensable basis for a theology of subjective faith. Recent interpreters of the Catechism[5] have agreed that Question 1 does not merely summarize in advance the several matters taken up in the ensuing questions. When it asks "What is your only comfort in life and in death?" and answers with the affirmation "That I, with body and soul, both in life and in death, and not my own, but belong to my faithful Saviour Jesus Christ...," we are given an unequivocal proclamation of objective faith. However, the focus of attention quickly shifts to considerations of subjec-

tive faith in Question 2, which states that the three things
necessary for the knowledge of this "comfort" are an awareness of man's misery, his redemption, and his need for
gratitude. The mainstream of interpretation, from Ursinus
to Barth, has held that this enumeration of saving facts,
which are found in Questions 2 to 129, are inseparable from
the confession implicit in Question 1. The subsequent questions indicate that this trust is rational, in the sense of intelligible, and that this comfort and trust has the character
of knowledge.

However, when Georg Otterbein begins his exposition
of the Catechism, he uses Paul's admonition for men to "desire the reasonable, pure, milk of the Word" (I Peter 2:1)
as his text. [6] The reason for his choice of this text becomes
apparent when we remember his theological training at Herborn. Friedrich Lampe, whose works Otterbein had studied,
in his important dogmatic work entitled The Milk of Truth, [7]
described how a person desiring salvation could appropriate
the "secret" of God's covenant of grace. It occurred to
Otterbein that the weakness of scholastic catechizing was that
it appealed only to the intellect. Why, he insisted, could not
doctrinal instruction address man as a whole--appealing not
only to his comprehension but even to the fundamental re-
ordering of his total life? He thought that he could discern
an unmistakable order within the structure of the Catechism
which, if followed, could produce the "imperishable seed of
the new birth. "[8] Here we find a clear shift in the direction
of a theology of "religious consciousness," although it was
still presented within the context of the objective proclamation of grace.

In speaking of this "order of salvation" (Heilsordnung)
which is rooted in Scripture and delineated in the Catechism,
Otterbein was indebted to another Reformed dogmatician,
Cocceius, who had first broken from the deductive methodology of Protestant scholasticism in a rather thorough-going
way. His device was to speak of revelation as a series of
covenants in which God redemptively related himself to men
through history. [9] However, when Otterbein tells us how
these acts can become efficacious for mankind, he brings
repentance and faith into a prescriptive temporal order to be
experienced by the believer. We may recall that Calvin, in
Book III of the Institutes, proceeds from faith to repentance,
and justification is not discussed until later. [10] Otterbein,
taking his cue from Question 2, begins with repentance and,
unlike Calvin, makes clear that this sequence is intended to

be chronological for human experience as well as logical for human thought. In his catechizing, Otterbein is preeminently interested in the psychological condition of his readers, in order that they might be guided through these ordered steps of the spiritual life. For Calvin, repentance is lifelong, but justification, the basis for objective faith, is complete at the outset of the Christian life.

We are left with the probability that the Otterbeins fundamentally altered the confessional nature of the Catechism--and it had been primarily regarded as a confession of faith in the Reformed tradition since the seventeenth century. It would seem that in the latter part of the eighteenth century, that age of enlightened men who thought they had been freed from the shackles of tradition, the Catechism might better serve as a prescriptive guide to the sequence of saving facts which men could voluntarily and individually appropriate to themselves. Let us examine some implications of this rather significant shift in the meaning of salvation.

a. Questions One and Two: The Description
   of the Mature Christian

"The Catechism," observes Georg Otterbein, "breathes the spirit of true Christianity" with "its intention to commend to the pilgrim the Christian religion as the true trust, the most certain counsel, and the best guide on the trouble-laden way to eternity."[11]

The person who follows the guide to salvation which the Catechism provides is a pilgrim, and the Catechism is "the way" in which "we will abide, that has the word of eternal life."[12] "The order which our Catechism has chosen is in accordance with the movement of thought of our souls."[13] This order "follows the Spirit of Truth, which first convinces one of sin, then of righteousness and judgment."[14]

The central affirmation that "I belong to Jesus Christ," which explains the meaning of "comfort" in Question 1, is understood by Georg Otterbein not as the objective foundation for faith but as the ultimate possibility that can be attained by the person who completes the pilgrimage through the several steps of the spiritual life. Hence, he admonishes his readers to pay attention to the condition of their own hearts. "What is your only comfort in life and in death?" asks Otterbein.

> This question assumes [the need for] consideration
> and reflection on its condition, its stipulation, con-
> cerning time and eternity,...it presupposes that
> we are thoroughly happy here below.... The ques-
> tioner wants to know what kind of notion of comfort
> the answerer has...what kind of hope and expecta-
> tion after death he has?[15]

The affirmation, asserts Otterbein, does not proclaim that I
belong to this Lord in my present state of anxiety.   Instead,
it is only the confession of "a true, persuaded, living Christian...who has sought and found rest for his soul."[16]   It is
the expression of the highest attainment of the Christian life.
Otterbein implores the reader to "make the attempt" and ascend the ladder of salvation.   Only then will you "experience
that which is the true and only trust in life and in death."[17]
"How will it help you if you repeat these words without understanding and conviction?"[18]   He recognizes that each man
belongs to God,[19] but through sin each is now separated from
God and thereby must heed the divine call by following the
plan.

How does Otterbein know that this order prescribed by
the Heidelberg Catechism is the only correct guide to salvation?   "The Christian religion," he observes, "is to be distinguished from all other known religions" because this plan
is set forth at the beginning of the Catechism (Question 2)
"in all its richness and affection."[20]   This path is known to
be true since it has the characteristics of true religion: it
gives the rationale for communion with God which is both
rooted in Scripture and verified by experience.   The Catechism is not valued as a textbook of correct, propositional
knowledge of religion; instead, it is a roadmap which provides the wayfarer with trustworthy landmarks on his pilgrimage to salvation.

Further, its validity is proved by the fact that it
bears the marks of being none other than the manifestation
of the predestined will of God.   Although the authors of the
Catechism did not speak of "double" predestination, as did
Calvin,[21] it is well known that they made use of the word
"comfort" as the felicitous mode for presenting the doctrine
of election.   The most profound sign of our election and our
certification as members of the true church (Question 54) is
our "believing fellowship with Christ."[22]   Unfortunately,
Protestant scholasticism after Beza sundered the decrees
from the theology of "our God" in covenant.[23]   Philip Wilhelm

Otterbein probably had the scholastic view of predestination
in mind when, after being accused of denying the doctrine,
he confessed:

> To tell the truth I cannot side with Calvin in this
> case. I believe that God is love and that he de-
> sires the welfare of all his creatures. I may be
> permitted to explain myself more clearly. I be-
> lieve in election, but cannot persuade myself that
> God has absolutely and without condition predestined
> some men to perdition. [24]

However, the Otterbeins did not side with those eighteenth-century Arminians who anchored the concept of predestination in faith and experience but reduced the decision
of faith simply to a human, rational possibility. [25] When Johann Otterbein visited each day the prison cell of a condemned murderer to present to him the saving plan of the
Catechism, he engaged in a patient, psychological probing of
the convict's heart. His goal was not to urge the man to
make a rational decision for faith, but to determine whether
there were any signs of the operation of the Spirit as a result of his presentation of the order of salvation. For example,

> On October 10 (1785) I asked him, 'How is it with
> you now?... Are you assured of the grace of God
> through Jesus, or do you need to search for it
> with greater earnestness?'[26]

The Otterbeins wrestled with "the problem" of inte-
grating head and heart, intellect and will, more than anyone
else in their tradition. Concerning his need for conversion,
Johann Otterbein said to the convict, "Previously you had
your Catechism only in your head; I hope the truth itself will
become sensible [fühlbar] in your heart."[27] The Great
Awakening in America did split head from heart, with the result that Unitarianism, rationalism, and propositionalism became the antagonists of revivalism, and vice versa. In the
ensuing fray, both parties often lost sight of the priority of
grace. The "new measures" theology of the nineteenth-century Finneyite revivalism often viewed salvation not so much
as the miracle of grace as the right use of appointed means.
Although this consequence may have been implicit in the Otterbeins' systematizing of the teachings of the Catechism in
terms of their ordo salutis, it was restrained by their high
view of grace.

b. Section One: Man's Misery As the First
   Stage in the Order of Salvation

When the pilgrim begins his sojourn from unfaith to
faith, according to the plan of the Heidelberg Catechism, he
must first come to terms with his miserable condition from
the law of God (Question 3). The man who perceives his
guilt here is not the believer, to whom the good news of comfort (Question 1) has already come. It is the self-knowledge
of natural man, which is the prerequisite first step in his
pilgrimage toward salvation. "Whoever does not know his
faults, sins, and needs, and so long as he does not know
them, will not lay them aside," writes Georg Otterbein, "and
his house of hope is built upon sand."[28] The knowledge of
sin is the chronological starting point in "the way in which
we receive the grace of Christ."[29] The order which the
Catechism presents is matched by the "disorder in our souls
and bodies" which is the fruit of sin.[30] It is not those who
are clinging to the one hope in life and in death who also
know that they are such as break God's law.[31] For the Reformers, law and gospel is distinguished for purposes of
theological clarity.[32] They would not have condoned the notion that we are first schooled by the law, and then freed by
the gospel.

Having made this criticism, we might do well to recall that, as the Otterbeins wrote their expositions, they had
in mind antagonists from two sides. On the one hand, there
were the rationalist pastors of their day who had rejected the
Catechism because of its embarrassing admonition that "I am
by nature prone to hate God and my neighbor" (Question 5).
On the other hand, there was also the strong remembrance
of the scholastic catechizers, who had vacuously proclaimed
the doctrine of comfort as an intellectual proposition which
operated mechanically upon parishioners.

In accordance with Question 7, Georg Otterbein explains the fall as an historical event which, through physical
inheritance, became the basis for the subsequent sin of humanity.[33] However, his main interest lies in speaking of
particular human sins in the observable realm of moral conduct.[34] The regenerate man is one whom the trained pastor
can clearly distinguish, on the psychological level, from the
natural man. When the signs of grace are lacking, as in
the case of the condemned convict whom Johann Otterbein
was counseling, the demand for introspection is unflinching:

> Read your Catechism and study it well (Questions
> 6-9). From this original sin arise countless daily
> or actual sins, which manifest themselves in our
> thoughts, words, and deeds. Stand sentinel upon
> your thoughts before your heart for merely a day;
> make a note immediately of every thought that
> arises; in the evening compare both the good and
> the evil ones with the Word of God....You would
> be terrified and amazed, and you would cry out:
> My sins outnumber the hairs of my head....Study,
> therefore, watch and see where your sins origi-
> nate. [35]

He then turns to a second source of misery, in addition to
the felt effects of sin: "that which is caused by the punishment of sin."[36]

> Read your Catechism (Questions 10-11)....Do you
> not tremble at this terrible, menacing judgment of
> God, the holy and righteous Judge?...Endeavor to
> understand and feel your wretchedness; try to com-
> prehend the direct and indirect punishment which
> is a consequence of your sins....[37]

When he asks the convict to read Question 8, the declaration
of the universal sinfulness of man, he says

> ... do not read it with a view of becoming pious
> and holy--that will come at the proper time; but
> read it in order that you may learn to feel and un-
> derstand your miserable sinfulness and your utter
> inability to accomplish any good. [38]

He acknowledges that this repentance which comes from such
spiritual anxiety is the work of the Holy Spirit.

> Poor sinner! How sadly you stand in need of this
> salve--the light of the Holy Spirit. I pray God,
> for your sake, to apply it....Make haste, repent,
> be diligent in good works before the evening of life
> is at hand. [39]

Having begun the experience of conscious rebirth, through
anxious self-appraisal, contrition, and repentance, the pilgrim is now ready to continue his precise ascent of the steps
of the spiritual life toward the goal of experimental godliness.

c. Section Two: Man's Redemption As the
    Second Stage in the Order of Salvation

The section of the Catechism which deals with Christ's
work as Mediator (Questions 12-19) lends itself quite well to
the Otterbeins' propensity to catechize by means of a fixed
ordo salutis. First, the need for the Mediator to be both
true God and true man is demonstrated, and only afterward
(Question 18) is this Mediator identified as "our Lord Jesus
Christ" who is known "from the holy gospel" (Question 19).
Only in the power of His divinity can the Mediator restore
righteousness and life to us. Georg Otterbein treats this
section in two parts, so that the sinner might comprehend
the possibility of salvation in Christ as a prerequisite for its
actualization in and for him. [40] The convicted sinner first
must "know the value of salvation" and, on this basis, he
"follows the call of grace and comes to Christ."[41] Only then
has he "tasted the comfort of the gospel."[42] "According to
this order God's crown of life awaits...."[43] To Reformed
Pietists, such as the Otterbeins, the giving of this promise
of redemption is to be distinguished from its fulfillment--a
matter of hope to which they gave an apocalyptic interpretation.

We know from Ursinus' comments on these questions
that the discussion of the Mediator in the Catechism was
fashioned in the context of the covenantal theology which had
been prominent in the Reformed tradition from the time of
Zwingli and Calvin. [44] Ursinus introduced the notion of the
twofold "covenant of nature" and the "special covenant" with
the elect. [45] This covenantal tradition was mediated through
Cocceius, Vitringa, and Lampe to the Otterbeins, all of whom
shared the view that the kingdom is the inheritance which
Christ has earned for the elect. [46] Although the Otterbeins
recognize that all men are under the sign of the covenant established by Christ, their real interest lies in the experimental discovery and encouragement of signs of grace within
those to whom this covenant applies. [47] In contrast to the
rigid confessionalism of Protestant orthodoxy, Georg Otterbein makes clear that this saving work of grace visits men
regardless of the church tradition to which they belong.

> Who then will become holy?... That will publicly be
> revealed on the great judgment day, when the world
> ruler, who is unsectarian, judges without regard to
> person, and makes a separation, placing the sheep
> on his right and the rams on his left. [48]

In speaking of saving faith, whereby men are redemptively related to Christ, the Catechism affirms with Calvin
that "certain knowledge" (Question 1) is the decisive factor.
However, to offset the intellectualizing tendency which appeared early in the Reformed tradition, it added that true
faith was also a "hearty trust. " Corresponding to the types
of men, which range from the unconverted to those under
conviction to the reborn, so Georg Otterbein also distinguishes types of faith. There is a historical (intellectual)
faith, a temporal faith, a miraculous faith (given to demon-
strations of miracles), and the true saving faith. The latter
"trusts firmly upon God's promises,...and remains in quiet
resignation [Gelassenheit] in all God's ways. "[49]

        Here Otterbein introduces a theme which is not found
in Calvin nor in the authors of the Catechism. By describing "hearty trust" in terms of "resignation" [Gelassenheit],
he uses a term which is distinctive of South German Anabaptism. Hans Denck (c.1500-1527) had preached "yieldedness"
to God's will in self-surrender as the basis for the imitatio
Christi. Gelassenheit leads to progressive "divinization and
inner lordship over all that is creaturely. "[50] There was
considerable interchange between Anabaptism and Pietism in
the Reformed sectors of Germany during the eighteenth century. The devotional classic of the Mennonites, both in Europe and in America, was the anonymous Geistliches Lüst-
gärtlein, which was published at Herborn in 1787. Friedmann, an Anabaptist scholar, expresses amazement that this
work could have been published on the press of a Reformed
academy, [51] but this fact only reflects the continuation of the
irenic tradition of pietistic ecumenism at Count Johann's
school. In this work, which is reminiscent of Arndt's Para-
diesgärtlein and Tersteegen's Geistliches Blumengärtlein, the
progressive resignation of the soul is described as it proceeds through "experiences of spiritual elevation and peace
as if walking through a beautiful flower garden. "[52] However,
the Otterbeins never carried this theme to its full implication by saying that one attains the "comfort" of Question 1 by
escaping his creatureliness, in Neo-Platonic fashion. For
them, the pilgrim clearly remains finite and confined to his
worldly calling while on earth. The dogmatic structure of
the Catechism was capable of no other interpretation on that
point. They also emphasized the cognitive aspect of true
faith, for "without knowledge [of the plan of salvation] no belief can take place. "[53] "That which should work upon the
heart must be made intelligible to the understanding. "[54]
Hence the distinctly pedagogical mode in which Otterbein pre-

sents the call for trustful commitment.

Another question which is pertinent to the pilgrim being redeemed is how much doctrinal knowledge should he be
given to attain maturity as a Christian? The canon within
the Catechism is the Apostles' Creed (Questions 22 and 23),
which introduces the Catechism's doctrine of God (Question
25). In his commentary on these questions, Ursinus had re-
verted to a rather complicated scholastic technique by propos-
ing definitions of the nature and unity of God, by analyzing
the terms "Essence," "Person," and "Trinity," and by refuting anti-Trinitarian objections. [55] However, the Catechism
itself avoids such procedures and limits its discussion to the
acts of God "as He has revealed Himself in His Word." [56]

Drawing upon his Cocceian heritage, Georg Otterbein
concerns himself with the givenness of God as revealed in
Scripture and Catechism, which he prefers to the knowledge
of God which is available "from our reason and from nature"
(Aristotelianism). [57] As a Pietist, the notable feature in his
discussion of the Trinity is the way he easily shifts to an
anthropological frame of reference by applying the doctrine
to "our lives ... which are a school; not with respect to our
entire destiny, but rather in the beginning." [58] Thus, the
true measure of the doctrine is its experimental efficacy, and
the route to the knowledge of God is the knowledge of ourselves: "We can understand very little of the secret of God
the Father and Christ, except for that which we see in the
redemption of a sinner." [59] His doctrine of God also has a
pronounced pneumatic emphasis, for it is the Holy Spirit who
"qualifies us for the salvation which Christ has earned." [60]
The clearest knowledge of God is attained by the Spirit's activity in "renewing the image of God in man, sanctifying, and
leading us on a smooth road, that we might certainly come
to the end of our goal." [61] This perfection of the image of
God in man is analogous to the state of glorification, which
seals the restoration of the broken covenant of grace.

The experimental efficacy of doctrine remains the
norm when Georg Otterbein turns to the meaning of Creation
and Providence (Questions 26-28). In Question 26, the words
"I believe" precede the statement on Creation, and Georg Otterbein emphasizes this use of the singular because "every
mature Christian must make this confession for himself." [62]
The believer is reminded that "this earth is the place of battle, discipline, and preparation for a better life" and that
"one enters the kingdom of God through trials." [63] There is

a confident certainty in these lines, which stems from the affirmation in Question 26 that the Lord whom we confess is none other than the omnipotent Creator and Preserver of the universe, the Father of our Lord Christ. The trustworthiness of Providence serves as a guarantee for those who are "on the way" to salvation. Here Otterbein's indebtedness to the prophetic theme from Vitringa and Lampe becomes apparent. Lampe had written

> ... since one daily makes new discoveries in nature (through binoculars), what wonder is it that, through increased diligence in the examination of the Godly Word, new discoveries appear and the promised growth in the knowledge of the last times appears?[64]

Otterbein observes that

> This beautiful order of the things of this world, the course of the sun, the moon, and stars, the succession of the years, the ordering of every creature according to his nature,... the harmonious union between cause and effect, ends and means, ...[attest] that He leads all things by His powerful Word.... Everything waits upon God, and He nourishes each thing according to its appointed time.... Accordingly, the prophecies and their fulfilment also emanate from the truth and certainty of the Providence of God.[65]

Both nature and history are correlated with Scripture in the confident expectation of the believer.

The pilgrim has now passed through the knowledge of his misery (Questions 2-11), which is the first step, then the comprehension of the necessity of Christ (Questions 12-18) and the source of this knowledge in the gospel, as summarized in the Apostles' Creed (Questions 19-25). He reaches the fruition of the second step in his pilgrimage when he realizes that this Lord of the universe (Questions 26-28) is also the Saviour of mankind (Questions 29-64).

In its doctrine of redemption, the Catechism retains Calvin's teaching concerning the threefold office of Christ, as prophet, priest, and king. Georg Otterbein places as much emphasis upon the office of the Christian, who not only confesses Christ but also "gives unmistakable signs of assurance

that he knows Christ for himself. "[66]   Also like Calvin, the
Catechism speaks of union with Christ as an active union
which enables me to be a "living sacrifice" for Him. [67]
Georg Otterbein's continuous search for the practical test of
doctrine is encouraged by the Catechism's frequent queries
"What benefit do you receive from this...?"[68]   The benefit
of the Incarnation is that Christ became the "Mediator between two estranged parties," and the practical test of the
doctrine is for the sinner to contrast the "holy origin and
birth of Jesus Christ" with "our impure and unholy birth. "[69]
The practical test for the doctrine of Christ's atoning death
and descent into hell is our success, by God's grace, in killing and burying the old sinful man. [70]   The ultimate test of
even so lofty a doctrine as the Ascension, which has to do
with Christ's (and our) heavenly flesh, is its practical efficacy in the spiritual exercises of the Christian life.   At each
point, the Catechism's emphasis upon the unique work of
Christ is contrasted by Otterbein with his stress upon Christ's
example as the prototype for the believer to emulate. [71]

A critical issue throughout the Reformed tradition is
the relation of righteousness and law. [72]   Though the Otterbeins wish to affirm that "one can contribute nothing toward
justification by merit, "[73] their covenantal terminology led
them to speak at times of faith as a condition for justification.   "God has promised [the Christian] all this [holiness
and righteousness] upon His oath," writes Johann Otterbein,
and "you [the Christian] in return have given yourselves to
God upon your oaths.... "[74]   There is also their tendency to
structure conversion into a fixed and necessary order of
steps which begins saving faith at the stage of legal preparation itself.   Georg Otterbein refers to the whole "order of
salvation" (Heilsordnung) as the "way of sanctification. "[75]
Their insistence upon the completion of these steps for salvation made justification one temporal stage in the process of
the total renovation of man, and what was decisive was the
completion of the renovation.   However, it was left to their
spiritual descendants, the United Brethren and Evangelical
leaders of the nineteenth century, to stress entire sanctification to such an extent that justification in itself has no saving
effect apart from it. [76]

Notes

1.   See John W. Beardslee, III, Theological Development at
     Geneva under Francis and Jean-Alphonse Turretin

(1648-1737).   (Ph. D. Dissertation, Yale University,
1957).

2. Ibid. , 698ff.

3. Ibid.

4. Karl Barth, Church Dogmatics, I, 2.   (Edinburgh, 1956),
    9f.

5. See Karl Barth, The Heidelberg Catechism for Today.
    (Richmond, Virginia, 1964), 28ff; Heinrich Ott, Theol-
    ogy and Preaching.   (Philadelphia, 1961), 34; Gott-
    fried Locher, "Das Vornehmste Stuck der Dankbar-
    keit," Evangelische Theologie, I, 1957, V. 12, 565;
    quoted in Ott, loc. cit.

6. P. H. K. , I, 53; all Scripture references are translations
    from the Otterbeins' German texts.

7. Friedrich Lampe, Milch der Wahrheit nach Anleitung des
    Heidelberger Katechismus zu Nutzen der lernbegierigen
    Jugend aufgesetzt... (Herzfeld and Frankfurt edition
    used, 1746).   See also Graffmann, "Der Unterricht
    ...," op. cit. , 46.

8. P. H. K. , I, 56.

9. Graffmann, op. cit. , 43.

10. See John Calvin, Institutes of the Christian Religion,
     Book III, Chapter 11.

11. P. H. K. , I, 77.

12. Ibid.

13. Ibid.

14. Ibid.

15. Ibid. , I, 80.

16. Ibid. , I, 82ff.

17. Ibid. , I, 83.

18. Ibid.

19. Ibid. , I, 84.

20. Ibid. , I, 101.

21. See Corpus Reformatorum, I, 74; also, Thompson, loc.
    cit.

22. Thompson, op. cit. , 44.

23. Beardslee, Reformed Dogmatics, 19.

24. Philip Wilhelm Otterbein, "Letter Sent to Deputies in
    Holland from Baltimore, June 15, 1788"; in Core,
    op. cit. , 100.

25. See Dillenberger and Welch, op. cit. , 91; "Defined in this
    way, the decree means no more than that God has de-
    clared that whoever accepts Christ will be saved and
    whoever does not will be excluded" (a "description of
    a general situation"). --Ibid.

26. J. D. O. , op. cit. , 107.

27. Ibid. , 111ff.

28. P. H. K. , I, 107.

29. Ibid.

30. Ibid. , I, 110.

31. This is the view of Barth, The Heidelberg Catechism for
    Today, 32.

32. Ibid.

33. P. H. K. , I, 141ff.

34. Ibid. , I, 147ff.

35. J. D. Otterbein, op. cit. , 218.

36. Ibid.

37. Ibid. , 219.

38. Ibid.

39. Ibid.

40. Barth wishes to regard this section as an unbroken unit,
    based on the affirmation in Question 18 that this Me-
    diator is "Our Lord Jesus Christ. " He is uncomfort-
    able with the fact that the Catechism, in this section,
    moves from "possibility" to "reality, " and not the re-
    verse. --Barth, The Heidelberg Catechism for Today,
    137ff.

41. P. H. K. , I, 208.

42. Ibid.

43. Ibid. , I, 209.

44. See Ursinus, op. cit. , 96; Calvin, Institutes, 2, 9-11;
    and Barth, Church Dogmatics, II, 2 (1960), 58.

45. Ursinus introduced the foedus naturae, later called the
    foedus operum by Polanus, and the foedus speciale,
    the eternal covenant with the elect. These evolved
    from his combining the covenant theme with the prim-
    itive lex naturae, which stemmed from Melanchthon.
    See Barth, Church Dogmatics, II, 2, (1960), 59.

46. Ibid. , also, Jürgen Moltmann, Theology of Hope (New
    York, 1967), translated by James Keitch, 70; Schrenk,
    op. cit. , 291ff.

47. See P. H. K. , I, 281. Barth notes that Cocceian "his-
    toricism in theology always involves psychologism, "
    especially among pietistic Cocceians, for whom moral
    precisionism (derived from Voetius) was a dominant
    factor in the covenant. --Barth, Church Dogmatics, II,
    2, 58.

48. P. H. K. , I, 240.

49. Ibid. , I, 249.

50. Hans Denck, Whether God is the Cause of Evil (1526),
    91; quoted in George H. Williams, The Radical Refor-
    mation. (New York, 1962), 157.

51. Robert Friedmann, Mennonite Piety through the Centuries. (Goshen, 1949), 210.

52. Ibid., 208. Another contemporary Mennonite work undoubtedly known at Herborn during the Otterbeins' day was the Wahrer Christen... geistliche Himmelsleiter... nebst angehangter Historia des Passions (n.d.).

53. P.H.K., I, 250ff.

54. Ibid., I, 45.

55. Ursinus, op. cit., 121-138.

56. Philip Schaff, The Creeds of Christendom, III. (Grand Rapids, 1966), 315.

57. G. G. Otterbein, U.H.C., 74.

58. P.H.K., I, 282.

59. Ibid., I, 283.

60. Ibid.

61. Ibid.

62. Ibid., I, 300.

63. Ibid., I, 304.

64. Lampe, Gnadenbund, IV, 124; quoted by Moltmann, op. cit., 128.

65. P.H.K., I, 332.

66. Ibid., I, 410. This affirmation is a response to Question 34.

67. Ibid., I, 378ff.

68. (Underlining mine.) See also Q. 36, concerning Christ's "holy conception and birth," Q. 43, concerning Christ's "sacrifice and death," Q. 45, concerning Christ's resurrection, and Q. 49, concerning His ascension.

69. P.H.K., I, 429.

70. Ibid., I, 463ff.

71. The theme of Nachfolgi Christi was well-known at Herborn because of the Mennonite literature then in circulation there.

72. Questions 59-64.

73. P.H.K., I, 655.

74. Ibid., I, 234.

75. G. G. Otterbein, U.H.C., vii.

76. Philip Wilhelm Otterbein was co-founder, with the Mennonite Martin Boehm, of the Church of the United Brethren in Christ. However, the Lutheran Jakob Albrecht (Albright), founder of the Evangelical Association, experienced conversion under the influence of Adam Riegel, a U.B. lay preacher. Hence, there was a measure of continuity in these two traditions from the outset. --See Raymond Albright, A History of the Evangelical Church. (Harrisburg, 1956), 34ff.
    Bishop W. W. Orwig of the Evangelical Association expressed his views on Christian perfection in 1856 as follows: "Those who profess religion have been summoned to seek sanctification and have been assured that, if they did not obtain [entire] sanctification, then they would not be able to see the Lord. Someone may wonder what my opinion may be concerning the fate of those who die without entire sanctification. That is clear: They will inevitably be lost. A partially sanctified person will be as little come to heaven as one who is altogether impure. Then will all the justified, who have not obtained entire sanctification, be lost? Undoubtedly!"--W. W. Orwig, "The Necessity of Entire Sanctification," quoted in Ralph Kendall Schwab, The History of the Doctrine of Christian Perfection in the Evangelical Association. (Menasha, Wisconsin, 1922), 40.
    For a fuller discussion of this development, see William Henry Naumann, Theology and German-American Evangelicalism; the Role of Theology in the Church of the United Brethren in Christ and the Evangelical Association. (Unpublished Ph.D. Dissertation, Yale University, 1966), University Microfilms, No. 66-13, 920.

Chapter 5

KINGDOM AND CHURCH:
THE IDENTITY OF THE PILGRIM

How should we identify this pilgrim whom the Otterbeins have been addressing, and whose sojourn has now
brought him to the stage of redemption, which corresponds
to Part Two of the Heidelberg Catechism? Is he the churchman who, according to Calvin and the authors of the Catechism, was to become a lifelong disciple to the Word of God
through the visible means of grace found in the institutional
church? Or, was he a member of a new kingdom of believers which was gradually supplanting the old, fallen institutional church? The Otterbeins' exposition of Questions 50
to 58 and 65 to 85, which is the source for our inquiry, is
unmistakably inclined toward the latter view, although the
shift in emphasis is frequently held in check by their loyalty
as pastors to Catechism and church.

When the pilgrim passes from his misery to the
promise of redemption, he is empowered to live in hope of
the fulfillment of the promise, which was given a thorough-
going eschatological interpretation by the Otterbeins. Georg
Otterbein exhorts his readers to "reflect every day upon the
majestic appearance of Jesus Christ, and watch, for we know
not the day nor the hour, when the Son of Man will come. "[1]

In the first Confession of Faith adopted by the United
Brethren in 1789, in which five Reformed pastors and two
Mennonites participated, the second article of the Creed is
rehearsed with emphasis upon Christ's coming again, at the
last day, to judge the "quick and the dead. "[2] Yet, it noticeably omits any mention of the Church in its discussion of the
Holy Spirit. It is not until 1815, with the growth of diver-
gent practices within the fellowship, that the General Conference called for believers to receive "order and church discipline, " lest "the spirit of love and charity ... be lost. "[3]
With Lampe, the Otterbeins had taught that "the Millenium
was imminent, and that Christ's Kingdom would soon be set
up on earth. "[4] Philip Wilhelm Otterbein, who left only a

few literary fragments, stated his position on the Millenium
with considerable detail.   He noted that "Christians are divided" on the issue, although

> They generally believe--and that is my opinion too
> --that there is in prospect a more glorious state
> of the church than has ever been; and this we call
> the millenium.   Some of them believe that Christ
> will personally reign in his church on earth a
> thousand years; but the best and most precious
> divines do not believe that.   And in this I agree
> with them. [5]

Otterbein was not siding with the anti-chiliasm of
Voetius and Johannes à Marck, who had related Revelation
20:1-7 to the first thousand years of Christendom and had excluded a future millenium. [6] He believed that there will be
a "more glorious state of the church," viewed as a fellowship of visible saints, though "it is wise to be cautious in
all about forming opinions upon all subjects [that is, the setting of dates] that the Scriptures do not decide."[7] The future
millenium will appear, but "before this happy time the Antichrist, the man of sin, will appear" (II Thessalonians 2:3f.)
and

> ... in his time Christians will be persecuted--the
> Antichrist will persecute them--in a manner they
> have never been persecuted from the foundation of
> the world.   It appears from revelation...that be-
> fore the millenium begins the seven vials of the
> wrath of God will be poured out, and the scattered
> Jews will be, must be gathered, and the fulness
> of the Gentiles brought in, before the millenium
> can be accomplished in its full extent. [8]

This is not merely esoteric speculation, for "it is certain
that these great events will come, and they seem to be at
hand." These prophecies will be fulfilled, and they are being fulfilled from day to day, and you may live to see great
things."[9] In light of the urgency of the matter, believers
are admonished to "hear what Christ says" and to "make our
calling and election sure."[10]

How important is this millenial doctrine to the pilgrim
who is climbing the steps of the spiritual life?   Although it
may be argued that Philip Wilhelm Otterbein "did not make
the millenial teaching the central part of his gospel preach-

ing, "[11] care should be taken to note the extent to which
eschatological thinking, which was central to Cocceius and
Lampe, penetrated the Otterbeins' theology. Their future
orientation was also informed by the dimension of hope, for
which Calvin and the Catechism had provided with their emphasis upon the ascension and the glorified rule of Christ.
This influence undergirded the dynamism of their order of
spiritual steps (Heilsordnung), wherein the fundamental image
for the Christian life was the errand on which the believer
was sent as a pilgrim. The visible means of grace in the
institutional church serves to "make our calling and election
sure." The historical consummation of this pilgrimage for
the whole body of believers will be the millenial glorification
of the saints on earth, not the premillenial appearance of
Christ.

Since the Otterbeins' ecclesiology appears in relation
to this eschatological outlook, let us examine their kingdom
theology by noting: (a) its origin; (b) its present status; and
(c) its appointed end.

(a)   Georg Otterbein holds with Questions 50 to 52 of
the Catechism, as also with Calvin, [12] that the kingdom of
Christ is the meaning and power behind the history of redemption.   Christ, as spiritual Head of His Church, is the
real identity of the "hand" which governs all things (Questions 27 and 28), and "through Him the Father governs all
things" (Question 50).   The Incarnation represents Christ's
personal assault upon the "kingdom of Satan" over mankind,
whose rule is the "judgment of divine abandonment" of man
because of sin. [13]

The Otterbeins picture this cosmic conflict against a
background of Scriptural interpretation which is akin to the
symbolic-prophetic exegesis used by the pietistic followers
of Cocceius.   Vitringa's exegetical meditations, which were
studied by the Otterbeins at Herborn, included expositions of
the patriarchs and other Old Testament figures as "types" of
Christ.   A popular version of these studies was published by
Johann Jakob Rambach (1693-1735), a student of Vitringa who
was also a professor of theology at the Lutheran University
of Giessen and a chief figure overlapping Lutheran and Reformed Pietism. [14]   This work was widely read by later generations of United Brethren and Evangelicals and was reis-
sued in 1886 in America by the press of the Evangelical Association. [15]   In his study of the life of Jacob, Rambach notes
that the ladder of heaven (Himmelsleiter) "is the means of

uniting heaven and earth, " and "so is Christ the means between God and man, heaven and earth. "[16] This ladder, being Christ Himself, was also a "way on which one on earth
could ascend into heaven"--an allusion to John 14:6. "There
are various stages on this ladder whereby Christ descended
from heaven to earth and whereby ascended from earth to
heaven. "[17] In this description Christ's priestly office is
subordinated to His role as the regal Guide to heaven whom
we are to follow, step by step, if we are to be reconciled
to God, "who stands over this ladder. "[18]

> As Christ Himself, our Saviour, to whom we look
> and through whom we become holy, had to humble
> Himself so deeply before He could be exalted to
> the right hand of God, so will we poor creatures
> ... not demand to change His order and to find an
> easier way to heaven. Rather, the Christian will
> remain with His order. Whoever humbles Himself
> and climbs down with Christ will be raised with
> Him. [19]

Rambach concludes that in this image of the ladder "we must
recognize clearly and certainly [klar und deutlich--the trade-
mark of the rational theologians!] that Jacob's dream was a
vision of Jesus Christ as the only way to life. "[20]

Georg Otterbein refers the step-by-step progression
of the believer, which corresponds to the descent and ascent
of Christ, to the tripartite structure of the Heidelberg Catechism. "How beautiful is its order, " he writes.[21] "Other
orders may be more systematic, but this is the most comprehensible and fruitful for the understanding. "[22] In describing "how Christ has won the victories of the kingdom for
us, "[23] Georg Otterbein, like Vitringa and Rambach, appeals
to the typological interpretation of the "scepter of Judah, "
which is found in Jacob's farewell address to his sons in
Genesis 49:10. Calvin, too, had foreseen a promise of
Christ in this passage, but he had tempered his rendition
with a warning against those apocalyptic-minded Christians
who, "with a pious diligence to set forth the glory of Christ,
have betrayed excess of fervor. "[24] In relating Christ's
birth (Questions 35 and 36), Otterbein argues that the scepter
had passed from the kingdom of Judah when the time had
fully come for the Son to appear (an allusion to Galatians
4:5). In speaking of Christ's suffering and death (Questions
37-39), he wants to show that the Jesus who appeared before
Pilate was the Messiah by an appeal to prophetic history.

> One knows from history, when the Roman Caesar
> Tiberius has ruled, when Pontius Pilate has been
> his governor in Judes, which was also the time of
> the life of Jesus on earth, and the time of His suf-
> fering and death--that thus the scepter has depart-
> ed, and had already noticeably departed from Judah
> --thus the time of the Messiah should come. 25

In His exaltation, Christ is pictured as holding the scepter
of Judah over the kingdoms of the earth and drawing men to
Him. 26

Otterbein omits some of the details of Rambach's typological exegesis, such as the champion who comes to "bind
his foal to the vine and his ass' colt to the choice vine" (Genesis 49:11)--a reference to the blessings which the elect in
the kingdom of Christ shall enjoy. 27 Rambach also regards
the washing of clothes in the blood of grapes (Genesis 49:
11b) as a description of how Christ, being clothed with human nature, reconciled the elect with God and purified them
"as a garment" in His blood. 28 "His eyes shall be red as
wine" (Genesis 49:12) is perceived to be a picture of Christ
in the exalted majesty of His kingly office. 29

Thus, the Otterbeins described the basis for the kingdom of the elect in terminology which was reminiscent of
this symbolic-prophetic school of exegesis, which considerably exceeds the typological interpretations of Calvin.

(b) In describing the present status of the kingdom,
the Otterbeins speak in terms of "the benefits we now receive from this glory of Christ, our Head" through the gifts
of the Spirit (Question 51). Christ exercises direct Lordship
as Head of His Church and as general Providence in world
history as well. Calvin had spoken of the Church participating in the kingdom of Christ by being made "to sit in heavenly places with the triumphant Christ in His kingdom. "30 By
virtue of this participation the Church can engage in the task
of extending the kingdom upon earth. The "benefits" we receive indicate that our participation in the new humanity of
the glorified Christ lies at the heart of the eschatology in
Calvin and in the Catechism. This kingdom may now "be in
some measure beheld" by considering "those who in a manner have the kingdom of God within them. ... "31

It is important to observe the essential difference be-

tween Calvin's views on the kingdom and those of the Otterbeins. There is a dynamic tension in Calvin's thought between the present completeness and incompleteness of the
kingdom. It is complete insofar as it refers to Christ Himself and His gospel, but insofar as it is also the society of
the godly, it is characterized by growth until the advent of
Christ. [32] Then the kingdom which is realized in Christ will
be "transferred to the whole body of the Church. "[33] The
historical Church, as outlined in Book IV, is related to the
Body of Christ and the kingdom of Christ "partly by the
preaching of the Word and partly by the secret power of the
Spirit" in conjunction, [34] for the Spirit "so pierces" to the
hearts of men that "both must be joined together in order
that the kingdom of God may be established. "[35] This growth
of the Church in history through Word and Spirit is in "union
with Christ. " Meditation on the future life is a vital part of
the exercise of daily faith. In the period between the resurrection and the consummation Christ has given Himself to us
in a "looking glass," for

> We, who have not yet reached that great height,
> behold the image of God as it is presented to us
> in the Word, in the Sacraments, and in fine, in
> the whole service of the Church. [36]

Hence, "God manifests Himself so familiarly in the order of
the Church that the heavens, so to speak, are opened to
us. "[37] This renovation of order is necessary since

> ... the perfection of order which the prophets had
> everywhere promised would exist at the coming of
> Christ, cannot exist unless God assembles under
> His government those men who had gone astray. [38]

However, the Church within history can never be correlated with the kingdom. Since the kingdom of Christ is
only begun in it, it remains ambiguous and its perfection is
deferred until "Christ shall once come that He may restore
all things. "[39] It is for this reason that Calvin said the kingdom operates through the Sacerdotium as well as the Regnum
of Christ, for it is through His mediation and death that all
things are restored. [40]

Philip Wilhelm Otterbein once preached a sermon on
Christ's Incarnation which is the only complete sermon by
the American brother that is available to us. [41] What is
striking in it is the different mode in which it presents the

kingdom theme. Whereas Calvin had maintained a dynamic
tension between its completeness and incompleteness, Otterbein forms a complete dichotomy between the objective and
the subjective aspects of Christ's kingdom work. Once again,
his intention is to extract what is experimentally efficacious
from the doctrine. Christ suffered, he said, so that "through
death He might destroy him who had the power.... "[42] "Yet,
with all of that, the matter of our salvation is not fully concluded. "[43] "Christ has not nearly concluded His work of
salvation upon the cross," though "as our Mediator, Christ
did accomplish all that His heavenly Father had assigned Him
to do in and through His humanity, as well as the things
prophesied of Him by the prophets and Moses. "[44] His work
remains inconclusive because "... if Christ accomplished
everything, why then does the devil still have his kingdom in
all of us ever since birth?"[45] The external ministry of
Word, sacraments, and church discipline are without effect
unless they are accompanied by an earnest quest for complete righteousness of life, which means holiness.

> In the degree to which a man is subject to the
> power of Satan and sin, to that degree also he is
> subject to wrath, curse, and damnation, He is in
> all respects in an unhappy situation. Hence, who-
> ever builds his salvation on Christ in a way that
> is merely outside himself, so that all the while he
> remains in his sin, is building on a foundation of
> sand. No matter what such a person may know
> or hope about salvation and redemption, it will
> merely be a dream and empty imagination. [46]

Christ's work, and His continued mediation as exalted head
of the Church, has objective validity only in that it has reconciled God to man. Of crucial importance is the practical
necessity for Christ now to reconcile us individually to God
by creating in us lives of holiness.

> But has not Christ given His life for our redemp-
> tion? This remains true. It is true that Christ
> has through death paid the redemption price for
> our sins and also reconciled God to us. With re-
> gard to God our salvation is fully accomplished.
> And when Christ also reconciles us to God, then
> redemption is fully accomplished on our side as
> well. [47]

In Calvin and in Question 51 of the <u>Catechism</u>, Christ's reign over church and world in His kingdom is as Man, and His new humanity nourishes believers in their life in His kingdom through Word and sacrament. The pledge of our redemption is the promise that Christ stands in our place before His Father, that "we have our flesh in heaven" as a sign that "He will also take us, His members, up to Himself," and that by the power of His Spirit we do not seek what is within us, but "what is above" (Question 49). However, Otterbein regards Christ's work as "merely the groundwork" for our salvation. [48] The Spirit is not primarily the "counterpledge by whose power we seek what is above," as the Catechism affirms. By His power we seek what is within us: "... the really great mystery, Christ in us. "[49] This different emphasis[50] indicates Otterbein's adoption of Arndt's theme that "The kingdom of God is within you, "[51] and discipline serves to reshape the inner life according to the principle of "Christ in us." It is in this context that he elaborates the idea of spiritual rebirth.

Christ's objective work in "reconciling the Father to us" affects us only in that it "also gave a picture of that which He must do in us, that He must destroy the kingdom of Satan in us just as He has destroyed this kingdom outside of us. "[52] "Christ has through His suffering given us Himself as an example," whereupon "the really great mystery, Christ in us," may be enlivened. [53]

> Whoever fights under the discipline of the Holy Spirit is led to victory finally by grace. And this is the work of redemption, Christ in us. The marks by which it can be recognized are a loss of the desire or tendency toward sin, a ceasing of sin itself. The fruits of it are holiness, a new human being, and a process of life which goes on steadfastly toward perfection. [54]

Though God offers His promise of salvation to sinners, "nothing impure can enter the New Jerusalem." Hence, only those who are completely renovated by the kingdom within are fully accepted by God. "A heart unbroken [is] the kingdom of Satan within us. "[55]

The Otterbeins appeared confident that the final "glorious" age of the church was soon to appear, and thus the goal of the pilgrim must be the perfection of the kingdom within him in order to hasten its realization within history, which would close with the appearance of Christ as Judge.

Only in this way can he look toward that final day with hope
rather than fear. "To the extent that Christ rids us of our
sin, to that extent also are we redeemed through Him. And
wherever sin ceases in us, damnation also ceases."[56] Or
again, "If there is no Christ in us, there is also no Christ
for us."[57] This completion of our redemption does not con-
sist in looking up and ahead to the exalted Head. Rather,
Christ must "come inside us and destroy the kingdom of sin,
penetrating us spirit, soul, and body with His light and
life."[58] "You must travel this way if on that day you want
to find mercy."[59]

The relation of faith and practice becomes a crucial
factor in delineating the Otterbeins' kingdom theology. Although they frequently speak of both while seldom relating
the two, it is possible to draw some judgments about their
relationship.

In the first place, it is clear that the presence of
this "kingdom within" must always be accompanied by visible
manifestations. The death of the old man in repentance,
which is the inward work of the Spirit, finds its outward expression in the penitential struggle (Busskampf) of the penitent. Its progress can be charted by the sensitive pastor in
private counseling, characterized by psychological probing,
as in the case of Johann Otterbein and the condemned murderer. The moment of rebirth (Wiedergeburt) finds outward expression in the peace and joy of the believer and in his freedom from daily sins.

Second, the Otterbeins' ecclesiology, on the one hand,
shifted toward the idea of an invisible church by emphasizing
true heart religion found in individuals, which transcends visible, historical expressions and is universal and spiritual.
It is the invisible church amid the actual church. Yet, on
the other hand, to the extent that the regenerate became identified by outward marks, the emphasis upon the invisible became the definitive norm for the visible church.[60] To the
extent that believers become visible to one another, by their
fitness to partake of the Lord's Supper as the sign and seal
of their rebirth and by their participation in conventicles,
the Otterbeins identify the kingdom of Christ with the fellowship of visible believers, and the kingdom of Satan with the
unregenerate world, which may include the visible structures
of the Reformation churches.[61]

This tendency calls to mind the pattern of radical disjunction between the two worlds which characterized Anabaptism, with which the Otterbeins were acquainted.[62] By emphasizing that those who have the "kingdom within" are known by visible marks, the Otterbeins imply a clearly defined separation of the two worlds. Separation from the world (Absonderung) is synonymous with killing the old man within, and "to the extent that Christ rids us of our sin, to that extent also are we redeemed through Him."[63] In contrast, the Reformers--notably Luther's "two kingdom" ethic with its dialectical tension--held that true believers are not visible even to each other, but rather one believes that where they are present the marks of the true church also are present.[64]

The Otterbeins' interest in seeking visible marks of regeneration in men, while also maintaining that the true church is the universal, spiritual company of those in whom Christ dwells, are ideals which came into conflict in Philip Wilhelm Otterbein's ecumenism. He was led to participate in the "unsectarian" meetings of the United Brethren in the hope that, the more Pietism grew, the more the church would become one. However, the attempt to give visible expression to this spiritual fellowship resulted in a new ecclesiastical institution.

Although there was evidence of Anabaptist influence in the Otterbeins' ecclesiology, perhaps a more important influence was what Barth has called the emergence of the new, voluntary form of association which became a characteristic of eighteenth-century man. With the demise of the old "obligatory" institutions, which were embodied in the structure of the corpus Christianum, the need arose "to find the proper, true, living, invisible community" and "to discover, work, and build that proper community...within, beyond, and beside the old institutions."[65] It is an expression of the age's "absolute will for form," which indicates that "the meaning of a societas, as distinct from an ordo, is Gesellschaft"--"an association of companions who meet by their own free choice, independently of the old institutions."[66] This means, for Barth, that an "entirely new way of distinguishing between the lower and higher orders of men" has come into being. In the case of the Otterbeins and in the United Brethren movement, men of different families, classes, or ecclesiastical traditions can become brethren as members of a "sacred circle of common views and common aims."[67]

Georg Otterbein reflected these emphases in his ecclesiology while interpreting Questions 53 to 56 of the Cate-

chism, which present the doctrine of the Holy Spirit (Question 53) as an introduction to the doctrine of the Church
(Questions 54-56). With regard to the Spirit, he makes a
distinction between the "extraordinary" gifts of the Spirit,
such as the works of the prophets and apostles, and the "or-
dinary" gifts, which reflect the activity of the Spirit in "leading sinners to holiness."[68] He looks to the last days of the
new covenant, the time of the millenial kingdom on earth, as
the "time when far richer gifts of the Spirit are promised."[69]
This present age "will not inherit the kingdom of God" because it is "of the flesh and without the Spirit."[70] The
Spirit, he says, is only received in identity with the Word,
but union with Christ through Word and Spirit is not discussed in the context of the institutional church. Rather, it
is the result of the individual's appropriation of the order of
salvation in the Catechism. Only by this appropriation is
one entitled to membership in the universal, spiritual company of those in whom Christ dwells. This outlook becomes
all the more clear when we recall that, at the Otterbeins'
time, the Catechism was primarily taught by pious parents
in the home from "house-book" editions.

In the lofty doctrine of the Church in Question 54, the
Spirit upholds the Communio sanctorum on earth in defiance
of its human weakness. For Georg Otterbein, the dominant
image is not the eschatological tension between the church
militant and the church triumphant. Instead, it is the disjunction between the "outward" and the "inward" church.[71]
The former has reference to "those who confess Christ out-
wardly with the mouth." The latter concerns those who also
confess Him "with their lives, who believe in Him inwardly
in and of the heart as true practical Christians [Thatchris-
ten]."[72] This is a typical expression of the Otterbeins' tendency to speak of a true inward church which nevertheless
becomes visible to believers, though not to the world.

For Calvin, the eschatological tension between the institutional church and the kingdom of Christ, or between the
church in its visible and invisible aspects, indicates that the
church within history can never be correlated with the kingdom.[73] For Georg Otterbein, the outward church, which
contains "good and bad, righteous and hypocrites, as the
threshing floor on which wheat and chaff are both found,"
tends to stand in disjunction with the "Holy Catholic Church"
of Question 54, which is identified as the "inward church"
or the "kingdom within."[74] It is true that the "outward, visible church" is the place where "the pure proclamation of the

Word of God ... and the service of the sacraments according to the instruction of Christ" is recognized. [75] However, this merely indicates that where the external structure is found, there are always called "believers who constitute the inward, invisible, and true church."[76] To the extent that believers become identifiable to one another by their striving toward holiness, as well as through their participation in small groups, then known as "conventicles," the emphasis upon the "inward church" or the "kingdom within" became the new definition of the visible church in distinction from the Reformed churches of the day. This indicates that the "class meeting" concept was not unique to Methodism! The metaphor of the Body of Christ was retained, but the up-building of the Body resulted from the help of the members who, having the kingdom of Christ within them, were engaged in the quest for holiness. "The kingdom does not come with outward appearance, but rather it is inward."[77] One does not become a member of the inward church only by "being baptized and attending public worship."[78] "That is not sufficient evidence that one is a true Christian."[79] Only those who "demonstrate the power of godliness," in terms of the Heilsordnung, are full members of the spiritual priesthood.[80]

Georg Otterbein's interpretation of the sacraments, as found in Questions 65 to 85, is also influenced by his methodology: they function as seals which culminate the pilgrimage of faith. Question 65 points to this interpretation when it indicates that faith comes by preaching while the sacraments confirm faith after it is already present. Especially in the case of the Lord's Supper, the sacrament "seals" the promise of the gospel for us (Question 66). The demand is for self-examination and introspection focusing upon one's fitness to approach the Lord's Table, which detracts from the Eucharistic character of the sacrament. [81] Calvin had wished to protect the integrity of the institutional church as "Mother" of the faithful and as the realm where God is re-ordering His Creation in anticipation of the parousia, when Christ's kingdom will be established in perfect order (integritas ordinis). [82] With Otterbein, the point of reference is always the conversion (Wiedergeburt) of the individual when he speaks of Word and Spirit creating faith through preaching and confirming faith by the use of the sacraments. In all cases, the sacraments were reserved for those who passed beyond the first stage in the plan of salvation. [83] Only those who had advanced to the knowledge of man's redemption could partake of the sacraments in an invisible as well as a visible way. [84]

Hence, Georg Otterbein regards baptism as only a
seal of the covenant with the believer, which is probably
more closely akin to the Anabaptist outlook than to that of
Questions 69 to 74 of the Heidelberg Catechism, which also
spoke of the action of the sacrament in itself. For Ursinus, [85]
baptism is the sacrament of entrance into the church (sacramentum introitus), by virtue of the fact that children of
Christian parents are regarded as heirs of the covenant of
grace. By this sacrament, they begin to be engrafted into
Christ's Body and share in His benefits of forgiveness and
renewal (Question 70). However, Otterbein applies his rubric that "the holy Scripture distinguishes the visible and the
invisible. "[86] The latter refers to the "inward bath of rebirth."[87] The Catechism wished to hold both that baptism
is a sign and seal of faith and that it is appropriate for in-
fants because of the universality of the promise and the need
to distinguish children of believers from others. We must
also remember the practical consideration--that the long-
standing state church concept required the defense of infant
baptism. Although the Otterbeins dutifully defended infant
baptism, Philip Wilhelm Otterbein increasingly became open
to different modes during his association with Mennonites and
others in the United Brethren movement. When speaking of
infant baptism, the Otterbeins' always stressed, "what will
you do with your baptism?" While addressing the condemned
convict, Johann Otterbein asks

> Have you then kept your covenant of baptism? No,
> you have not. You have broken the covenant; like
> the prodigal son, you have literally squandered all
> the gifts which follow the sacred rights of baptism.
> You have served sin, the world, and the devil....
> What is your present condition? How are you pre-
> pared to die? Think about it seriously. [88]

When thinking of the apostolic order of repentance and baptism, it is a seal. When thinking of infant baptism, only
those who "demonstrate the power of godliness" by virtue of
their conversion, not their baptism, are full members of the
spiritual priesthood.

Likewise, the visible/invisible rubric is applicable in
Georg Otterbein's interpretation of the Lord's Supper, in accordance with Questions 75 to 80. The reality to which the
signs point is the Christ whose kingdom is immanent within

the hearts of believers. Again, Otterbein renders formal
adherence to the doctrine of the Catechism. In the Supper
we not only receive the promise that Christ's "body was offered and broken on the cross for me and His blood was shed
for me, as certainly as I see with my own eyes the bread...
and the cup" (Question 75). [89] What is more, I receive this
promise because "Christ Himself feeds and nourishes my soul
to everlasting life, as certainly as I receive... and taste"
(Question 75). [90] The more often the sacrament is observed,
the more the believer participates in Christ's benefits and is
"united more and more to His sacred Body by the Holy Spirit,
who dwells both in Christ and in us, that although He is in
heaven, and we on earth, we are nevertheless flesh of His
flesh and bone of His bone" (Question 76). This assertion
left confusion with regard to the role of the communion elements, since their meaning as signs of God's descent to man
are obliterated. [91] We have here a doctrine of Christ's spiritual (not physical) real presence, which is to be distinguished
from the view of Luther, on the one hand, and that of Zwingli,
on the other.

The Otterbeins were not really interested in precisely
how Christ was present in the Supper. They vastly limited
the role of the elements by regarding them primarily as the
outward signs and seals of an invisible, immanent kingdom
of Christ within the believer. The believer must "always be
spiritually united with Christ, not just when he partakes of
the Supper...." [92] The denominational tradition long followed
the Otterbeins' lead on this issue, thus devaluing the sacrament itself as a means of grace. Instead, preaching and
small group sharing take on a kind of sacramental quality of
their own.

The Catechism relates church discipline to the Lord's
Supper in order to uphold the integrity of the sacrament and
of the church as a whole. [93] Hence, discipline becomes a
crucial issue for the Christian life. Both Calvin[94] and
Ursinus[95] also recognized that the church, despite man's
best efforts, remains imperfect within history, for it stands
in an eschatological tension with the kingdom of Christ that
will be revealed at the last day. Even with Voetius, [96] it
was assumed that there would be tares among the wheat at
the Table. However, the Otterbeins, while disavowing separatism, nevertheless try to give a definitive explication of
the worthy and the unworthy communicant, in order that the
godless could be readily identified and excluded. The Lord's
Supper is not for children, nor the unworthy, nor the dead,

but for those who "prove themselves" that they are on pilgrimage to salvation.[97] Only those who

> ... find themselves penitent, humble, faithful, sincere, without hypocrisy, full of good convictions and resolutions for the future, can and should draw near. The Lord calls them.[98]

In short, the Lord's Supper is not a converting ordinance; it is only for visible saints. Although the unregenerate may "have the appearance of godliness" before the world, their lack of the power of godliness should be evident to believers.[99] Fitness to participate in the Supper is so crucial for the Otterbeins because it is a sign and seal of the rebirth, whereby believers become visible to one another. This view was to find its culmination in the "love feasts" which always concluded the "big meetings" in the early period of the United Brethren in America.

When the Otterbeins spoke of the "keys of the kingdom" (Questions 83 to 85), which are preaching and the administration of discipline, they were more mindful of promoting the "kingdom within" than of perserving intact the parochial traditions of preaching from manuscripts, worshipping by liturgy, and maintaining general social respectability devoid of inward piety. They were ever concerned with upbuilding the fellowship of individual pilgrims in faith who would become the basis for the approaching spiritual church on earth. Their use of small groups (conventicles) for earnest Christians, while not intending to be substitutes for regular church attendance, still tended to set apart the true Christians and hence become the definitive norm for the visible church. The prayer and Bible study groups for true believers, which Horch had introduced at Herborn in 1690, were also fostered by Philip Wilhelm Otterbein in his first parish at Ockersdorf--an innovation which, as Spayth records, "surprised his friends and astonished his hearers."[100] This experimentation with small groups, which is enjoying a current rebirth in American Christianity,[101] was later renewed by Otterbein in his parishes in America.

The filter through which the Otterbeins read the ecclesiology of the Catechism was the eighteenth-century propensity for forming voluntary associations in place of the old "obligatory" institutions.[102] Yet, this outlook did not result in a break with the existing church so long as true believers remained at heart invisible, though they could become identifiable to another through holy living.

(c)   The Otterbeins' kingdom theology found its origin
in their typological interpretation of "how Christ has won the
victories of the kingdom for us" and its present status in
the "kingdom of Christ within" the believer.   What concerns
us now is its appointed end, which is the Millenium and the
subsequent return of Christ in the last judgment.

Although the Otterbeins were unwilling to set God's
timetable for Him, they were sure that it was coming soon.
Their belief in the imminence of the Millenium, when Christ's
kingdom would be established upon earth through His saints,
was encouraged by the presence of unbelief and persecution,
for immediately "before this happy time the Antichrist, the
man of sin, will appear."[103]   "We seldom meet men in
Christ in our time," notes Philip Wilhelm Otterbein, for "the
time we live in is truly dangerous, it is the final hour of
which the Apocalypse prophecies."[104]   Since "these prophecies are fulfilling from day to day," believers are admonished
to "be ready ... and that is the best thing we can do--make
our calling and election sure."[105]

Calvin had repudiated the radical eschatology of the
Anabaptists as a false temporalizing of the Christian hope.
He preferred instead the Augustinian view which interpreted
the Millenium as a period of church history, from the epiph-
any to the parousia.[106]   He rejected the view that the Millenium was to be a future historical period of one thousand
years because "... such a limitation of the kingdom would
jeopardize not only the heavenly transfiguration of the pious
but also that of their exalted Head."[107]   The millenial kingdom described in Revelation 20 was regarded as the rule of
Christ over regenerate souls before the resurrection of the
flesh at the second coming.[108]

This view contrasts with Philip Wilhelm Otterbein's
assertion that the Millenium is the approaching "more glorious state of the church" which is preceded by the persecution of the Antichrist.   In 1804, he wrote to his nephew in
Germany that

> The times will get even worse and which of us will
> see them?   Only those who keep the commandments
> and faith in our Lord Jesus Christ; in America we
> still live at peace, but who is to know for how long?

The judgment of God is spreading and will reach
every corner of the earth. [109]

We find here no hint of Jonathan Edwards' conviction
that the kingdom of God is to begin in America. [110] Piety
and patriotism do not seem to be mixed.   The coming age
of the spiritual church is an event that will stand in radical
disjunction to the present age of the church in history.   The
principal new departure in the biblicism of Cocceius and
Vitringa, which the Otterbeins inherited, was the emergence
within the church tradition of "a concern for the historical
future in the idea of the millenium. "[111] Vitringa and his
student Bengel had believed that exegesis should "subserve
the purpose of a mathematical calculation of the Last-Day
and chronology of the end-event. "[112] The Otterbeins no-
where resorted to this technique.   With their subjective ten-
dencies, they perceived in the history of their own age, in
the moral deprivation of the unregenerate and the moral at-
tainments of the regenerate, the controlling factor in the interpretation of the Apocalypse.   This moral interpretation
makes the place of a realistic eschatology in their thought
difficult to evaluate.   Although Philip Wilhelm Otterbein spoke
of the Millenium as an approaching new age of the church
within history, its arrival was directly related to the nurture
of the personal "kingdom within" those who were following
the Heilsordnung, which was accompanied by outward, visible
marks.

When dealing with "the return of Christ to judge" in
Question 52, Georg Otterbein does not distinguish between the
judgment as a future event consummating world history and
as the existential event confronting each man at death. [113] In
either case, it becomes the final judgment of the success of
the pilgrim's sojourn on earth.   He writes,

> Stand still in this state of mind, my reader.   How
> will you fare in courage?   You, whoever you may
> be,... must appear before the Judge.   The day and
> the hour can certainly not be stated.... Take care
> that you are suited for it by a holy pilgrimage and
> by a godly existence. [114]

Men will then discover that justification is not imputed to
them unless they "fit themselves [in this life] for justification" by "growing up rightly and continuing to grow" that they
might "hold themselves ready for the hour [of judgment]. "[115]
This conditional understanding of justification is akin to the

synergism found in Melanchthon and Wesley.

In reflecting upon the "resurrection of the body" and the "life everlasting" (Questions 57 and 58), Georg Otterbein related soteriology to personal immortality. "The earthly life is only a certain foretaste of the whole."[116]

Whether the goal being considered was the coming millenial church after the fall of Antichrist, the last judgment, or personal immortality, the focus was always the present moment. Now is the time for the believer to realize the success of Christ's redemption by entering upon a pilgrimage of holiness which would bring the kingdom of Christ to fruition within him and within history. This emphasis upon the existential demands of grace in the present moment was to be a hallmark of Evangelical and United Brethren theology, as expressed in its missionary, philanthropic, and educational pursuits in the nineteenth and twentieth centuries. The motive underlying this diverse range of pursuits lies deeply embedded in the experiential kingdom theology of the Otterbeins.

Notes

1. G. G. Otterbein, P. H. K. , I, 179.

2. Disciplines of the United Brethren in Christ, Part I, 1814-1841, ed. by A. W. Drury. (Dayton, Ohio, United Brethren Publishing House, 1895), 1-3. See also James O. Bemesderfer, Pietism and its Influence upon the Evangelical United Brethren Church. (Harrisburg; Published by the Author, 1966), 74.

3. The Discipline of the Evangelical United Brethren Church. (Harrisburg and Dayton: The Board of Publication, 1959), 10.

4. James Good, History of the Reformed Church of Germany, 1620-1890. (Reading, 1894), 391.

5. P. W. Otterbein, "Letter Concerning the Millenium" (n. d.), Core, 102.

6. See the discussion of these men in Tanis, Dutch Calvinistic Pietism..., 133ff.

7. Core, 102 (enclosure mine).

8. Ibid.

9. Ibid.

10. Ibid.

11. Bemesderfer, 76.

12. Calvin's Commentary on Phil. 3:21; Corpus Reformatorum
    80, 56; quoted in Quistorp, op. cit., 48.

13. P. W. Otterbein, Die Heilbrigende Menschwerdung, Core,
    81, 84.

14. Johann Jakob Rambach, Christus in Mose, oder Ein-
    hundert Betrachtungen über die vorhehmsten Weissa-
    gungen u. Vorbilder auf Christum in den funf Büchern
    Moses. (Cleveland, 1886). I located this edition of
    Rambach in the E. U. B. Archives at Dayton, Ohio.
    It was first printed in 1727. Rambach was an appro-
    priate devotional source for Evangelicals, with Al-
    bright's Lutheran background.

15. Ibid.

16. Ibid., 106.

17. Ibid.

18. Ibid., 108.

19. Ibid., 107.

20. Ibid., 109 (enclosure mine).

21. G. G. Otterbein, P. H. K., I, 40ff.

22. Ibid., I, 141.

23. This is Rambach's phrase, op. cit., 167.

24. Calvin, C. O. T. C., Genesis II, 452.

25. G. G. Otterbein, P. H. K., I, 449.

26. Ibid., I, 537.

27. Rambach, 160.

28. Ibid., 167-172.

29. Psalm 53:1-10, Revelation 5:6, Mark 3:5, and Revelation 3:16 are cited as proof texts. --Ibid., 174ff.

30. See T. F. Torrance, Kingdom and Church. (Edinburgh, 1956), 91.

31. Calvin's Commentary on Isaiah 42:25; quoted in Torrance, 96; Calvin speaks of the "Regnum Dei" when he refers to God's eternal majesty, and the "Regnum Christi" with reference to the reign of Christ over the world until His parousia. See also John M. Tonkin, The Church and the Secular Order in Reformation Thought. (N.Y., 1971).

32. See Calvin's Commentary on Hebrews 2:17, Corpus Reformatorum 83, 91ff.; discussed in Torrance, 115.

33. Calvin's Commentary on Hebrews 2:11, Corpus Reformatorum 83, 28ff.; and 2:13, Corpus Reformatorum 83, 31; Torrance, 116.

34. Calvin's Commentary on Luke 11:10, Corpus Reformatorum, 73, 197; Ibid., 98.

35. Ibid.

36. Calvin's Commentary on Matthew 13:16, Corpus Reformatorum, 73, 362.

37. Calvin's Commentary on Psalm 27:8, Corpus Reformatorum, 36, 426.

38. Calvin's Commentary on Mark 15:43, Corpus Reformatorum, 73, 788.

39. Calvin's Commentary on Acts 3:21, Corpus Reformatorum, 76, 73.

40. Ibid.

41. Philip Wilhelm Otterbein, Die Heilbrigende Menschwerdung u. Der Herliche Sieg Jesu Christi Deu Teufel u. Tod (1760), Core, 77-90.

42. Ibid., 83.

43. Ibid.

44. Ibid.

45. Ibid.

46. Ibid., 84.

47. Ibid.

48. Ibid.

49. Ibid.

50. For Calvin, discipline serves to refashion the whole life of the church in all its members after the image of Christ's new humanity in anticipation of the condition of glory at His advent. --See Torrance, 155.

51. Johann Arndt, True Christianity. (Philadelphia, 1869); See also Friedmann, op. cit., 20.

52. P. W. Otterbein, Die Heilbrigende Menschwerdung, 85.

53. Ibid.

54. Ibid., 85.

55. Ibid.

56. Ibid., 86.

57. Ibid., 87.

58. Ibid.

59. Ibid., 89.

60. See also Dale Brown, The Problem of Subjectivism in Pietism (unpublished Ph. D. Dissertation, Northwestern University, 1962).

61. For Luther, these visible structures have "sacred secularity" because they stand in dialectical tension with the "Geistliches Regiment. "--See William Lazareth,

"Luther's Two-Kingdom Ethic Reconsidered," in Paul Empie and James McCord, Marburg Revisited. (Minneapolis, 1966).

62. See Tonkin, op. cit., Chapter 4.

63. P. W. Otterbein, Die Heilbrigende Menschwerdung, 86.

64. Paul Althaus, The Theology of Martin Luther. (Philadelphia, 1966), tr. by Robert C. Schultz, 294-322; see also Wendel, 291-312.

65. Karl Barth, Protestant Thought from Rousseau to Ritschl. tr. by Brian Cozens. (New York, 1959), 41.

66. Ibid.

67. Ibid.

68. P. H. K., I, 572.

69. Ibid., I, 573.

70. Ibid., I, 581.

71. Ibid., I, 588.

72. Ibid.

73. See Calvin's Commentary on Acts 3:21; Corpus Reformatorum, 76, 73.

74. G. G. Otterbein, P. H. K., I, 593.

75. Ibid., I, 597.

76. Ibid., I, 597ff.

77. Ibid., I, 594.

78. Ibid., I, 605.

79. Ibid.

80. Ibid.

81. Thompson, op. cit., 48.

82. Calvin, Institutes, IV, i, 4; and Commentary on Mat-
    thew 25:31.

83. G. G. Otterbein, P. H. K. , I, 700.

84. Ibid. , I, 706ff. : The visible [sacrament] can easily
    bring to our minds the invisible, because of the simi-
    larity it has with it, and because of the relation which
    God has established between them. Both names are
    often confused in holy Scripture, as also their charac-
    teristics. The words of institution and the attached
    promise of God gives the assurance of God to the
    faithful that the promised grace is for him, for him-
    self, and his faith can be placed wholly upon it.

85. See Corpus Doctrinae Orthodoxae sive Catecheticarum
    explicationum D. Zachariae Ursini. (Heidelberg,
    1612), 423; quoted in Thompson, 38. See also Calvin
    on Acts 3:25.

86. G. G. Otterbein, P. H. K. , I, 743.

87. Ibid. , I, 731.

88. J. D. Otterbein, J. K. B. , 234.

89. G. G. Otterbein, P. H. K. , II, 4.

90. Ibid. , II, 9ff.

91. Calvin's Genevan Catechism, L. C. C. , XXII, 31; quoted
    by Thompson, op. cit. , 50.

92. G. G. Otterbein, P. H. K. , II, 17.

93. See the discussion of these questions in Thompson, op.
    cit. , 42ff.

94. Calvin, Institutes, IV, 12.

95. Ursinus' Corpus doctrinaw Orthodoxae, 491-528; cited in
    Thompson, op. cit. , 43.

96. Voetius, Proeve van de kraght der godsaligheydt, 287ff. ;
    cited in Tanis, op. cit. , 142.

97. G. G. Otterbein, P. H. K. , II, 61.

98. Ibid., II, 64.

99. Ibid.

100. Spayth, op. cit., 17 (See above, chapter 3).

101. See Thomas Oden, Beyond Revolution; A Response to the Underground Church. (Philadelphia: Westminster Press, 1970).

102. Barth, Protestant Thought, 41.

103. P. W. Otterbein, "Letter Concerning the Millenium," Core, 102.

104. G. G. Otterbein, P. H. K., I, 573.

105. Ibid.

106. Calvin's Commentary on Phil. 3:21, Corpus Reformatorum 80, 56; cited in Quistorp, 48; Quistorp (150, 193) notes that this spiritualizing tendency of Calvin also derives from Augustine, who to an extent combines Greek spirituality with biblical realism.

107. Institutes, III, 25, 5.

108. Quistorp calls this "plainly a spiritualizing" exegesis of Revelation 20:5ff. --Quistorp, op. cit., 161.

109. P. W. Otterbein, "A Letter sent from Baltimore to a Nephew in Heinsburg, June 21, 1804. "--Core, 103.

110. See Jaust, Clarence H. and Thomas H. Johnson, eds., Jonathan Edwards. (New York, 1962), 410ff.

111. James P. Martin, The Last Judgment in Protestant Theology from Cocceius to Ritschl. (Grand Rapids, Michigan: Eerdmans, 1963), 67.

112. Ibid., 66.

113. P. H. K., I, 547.

114. Ibid.

115. Ibid., I, 557 (enclosure mine).

116. Ibid. , I, 630.

Chapter 6

GRATITUDE: THE APOTHEOSIS OF THE PILGRIM

Having negotiated the steps of repentance and faith, the pilgrim who is struggling to actualize the "kingdom within" reaches the third and final stage in his sojourn when he "demonstrates the power of godliness."[1] "True Christianity," writes Georg Otterbein,

> is a matter of experience. It does not consist in words, but in power, in event, and in deed.... True faith is living and active through love; and love is the fulfilment of the law.[2]

Only when he makes visible the kingdom within him does he become a full member of the spiritual priesthood.

In considering the Otterbeins' interpretation of ethics, which is based upon Section III of the Heidelberg Catechism (Questions 86-129), our attention is turned to a problem peculiar to Reformed theology. This is the so-called "practical syllogism" (syllogismus practicus), which is derived from an emphasis upon the obligations rather than the consolations of grace as expressed in terms of thankful and responsive love. The syllogism may be stated as follows: whoever believes shall be saved; there are practical evidences (viz., my sanctified life) that I believe; therefore I shall be saved.[3]

That this is a problem implicit in Calvin is attested by the following observations. The moral law can only be spontaneously obeyed as it "finds its place among believers in whose hearts the Spirit of God already lives and reigns."[4] This is Calvin's "third and principal use" of the law, "which pertains more closely to the proper purpose of the law."[5] "Even though they [the believers] have the law written and engraved upon their hearts by the finger of God," they still may profit from the law because by it they are "aroused to obedience" and to good works.[6] The rigor of the law does not remain, for

> God, having turned his gaze from his servants'
> works, which always deserve reproof rather than
> praise, embraces his servants in Christ, and with
> faith alone intervening, reconciles them to himself
> without the help of works. [7]

Yet, its claim does remain, and good works performed after
a man is justified do have a certain value--though, once
again, no credit is to be given man for such works.

> Of his own fatherly generosity and loving-kindness,
> and without considering their worth, he raises
> works to this place of honor, so that he attributes
> some value to them. [8]

"But," you may interrupt, "does this not revive the
corpse of work's righteousness, which Luther had put to
rest?" Calvin still insisted that man deserves no credit because: (1) such good works are invariably the gift of God's
grace;[9] (2) even good works after justification retain in them
the taint of sinfulness, and God accepts them, not because of
their worth, but because He imputes to them the righteousness of Christ;[10] and (3) even if man could fulfill the entire
law, his successful efforts would deserve no credit because
he would only have given God what he owed Him, which is
his duty. [11]   At the same time, one may gain the assurance
of election through good works, for the ability of the saint
to take up his cross manifests a clear proof of the grace
with which God has endowed the believer. [12]   Or again, Calvin states that good deeds, while having no merit in themselves, do help saints-in-the-making recognize that they are
called of God. [13]

When the Catechism's Question 86 states that "we may
be assured of our faith by the fruits thereof," it is affirming
that "it is as I live as an elect man that I am assured of my
election."[14]   Here, as with Calvin, the works a man does do
not bind God to accept him.   He remains totally dependent
upon God's gracious promises in the gospel.   Practice is
never divorced from faith; it is faith itself "testifying to the
reality of itself and its object."[15]   Wherever faith and practice are divorced, it has been disastrous for our heritage.
Creedalism and moralism become inherent dangers wherever
head and heart are split and the unity of faith and practice
is forgotten.

Eighteenth-century theology tended to ignore this rich

interaction of faith and practice.   It reflected the fear that
the folly of party strife in the clash between theological antagonists was due to the fact that man had only a theoretical
understanding of the confessional statements of faith--an "unfruitful theologizing" which led to the widespread tendency to
"moralize" or "bourgeois-ify" (verbürglichen) theology. [16]

        Johann Otterbein at times appears to be overcome by
the logical implication of the practical syllogism.   "True
thankfulness to God," he notes, requires "conversion to God
and holy conduct manifested in good works. "[17]   Although
such works are necessary, he is aware that they can only
"result from true faith and accomplish the glory of God. "[18]
"No one should deceive himself with his own good works. "[19]
Yet, in the course of his psychological probing of the condemned convict, the testimony of works comes to be regarded
as the primary testimony to faith.

        I have explained the two divisions of the Catechism.
        ... I have shown to you what is necessary for man
        to do before he is truly able to be thankful to God
        and to render Him due honor.   Do you see, then,
        of what you are still in need?[20]

He then refers to practice as a "second conversion. "   In our
"first conversion we have only been purified from the external, repulsive manifestations of sin and dead works. "[21]   It
has enabled us to take up our true task, which is "to follow
this progressive grace in the purification of the heart, by
continual repentance and by searching after holiness throughout the entire period of our lives. "[22]   The first steps of repentance and faith are only "the garment of salvation, " writes
Philip Wilhelm Otterbein, for "whoever stands in grace will
keep on going. "[23]   "Growth is a mark of the state of grace
and stabilizes the heart.   The higher a degree of godly life
a man reaches in this time, the firmer will be his hope for
the future. "[24]   "The more holy here, the more glorious
there. "[25]

        Johann Otterbein sought to come to terms with the di-
mensions of the problem of faith and works by resorting to
a rather subtle distinction.   The pilgrim who has arrived at
the third stage "would most certainly grow weary, if not
finally succumb" were he "obliged to fulfil the demands of
the divine law according to the requirements of God. "[26]
Since God's requirements exceed what is possible for man--
even regenerate man--to perform, he adopts the following

solution:

> Because God knows how feeble are all the efforts
> of mankind to perform any good, he therefore, for
> Christ's sake, is very gracious to the poor sinner,
> and does not demand a literal, but an evangelical
> obedience, according to the covenant of grace. [27]

He distinguishes between "legal" and "evangelical" obedience,
or between that which emanates from the law and must be
done by man on his own and that which emanates from faith
and must be done by the power of the Holy Spirit. He finds
support for this distinction in Question 114, which asserts
that although those who have been converted to God cannot
keep His commandments perfectly, yet "with earnest purpose
they begin to live, not according to some but according to
all the commandments of God. "[28] It is the testimony of
evangelical obedience which is the chief witness to faith. [29]
Evangelical obedience does not encourage the believer to seek
merit only in his own good deeds. Rather,

> The more that such a one, who possesses true
> faith and has received grace through Christ, de-
> sires to exercise continual repentance and true holi-
> ness, the more he engages in the love and praise
> of God, and the sooner will he perceive how ill-
> adapted and unfitted he is of his own accord to ac-
> complish any good; and that all good must be ac-
> complished through the grace of God in Christ, by
> means of the Holy Spirit in him. [30]

The necessity of works serves to enhance the believer's humility, for he learns that "his inseparable weaknesses are a
great burden to him, and incite him to seek more earnestly
the forgiveness of his sins and righteousness through Christ. "[31]

Because good works are not merely the marks of true
faith, but also the conditio sine qua non, holy living is
brought into a living relationship with the doctrine of the
Catechism.

> The truth must demonstrate its power, and then
> one has a well-founded hope of eternal life; and if
> brought unfailingly to the end of his faith, namely,
> the salvation of his soul. This hope produces
> trust, and one is clearly already made holy in this
> life. One is made content with all God's ways and

is thankful from the heart. The way of holiness
leads quite certainly to eternal life. [32]

This is the way to the restoration of the lost image of God
in man, that God might be glorified in us. [33] "Through a
godly pilgrimage the ignorance of the men of the world is
muted, the wicked must be shamed, or perhaps even moved
to desire God if they are brought to self-examination, and
thus the godly pilgrimage of the Christian becomes manifest. "[34] The believer is then recognized as a member of
the "kingdom of the almighty King" and he "lives under His
scepter in joy. "[35] "Such a thing also must take place in the
correct order so that the way, whereupon the Christian trav-
els to salvation becomes a holy way. It is the way Christ
has traveled before.... no one who has sojourned on this way
has regretted it. "[36]

The distinction between the visible and invisible aspects of the Christian life is also apparent in Georg Otterbein's discussion of the law. Although the ceremonial and
juridical law of the Old Testament is no longer applicable to
the Christian, the positive law of the Decalogue remains valid
both for the external conduct and for the inner life and motive of man. He observes that the Decalogue pertains to the
first step in the order of salvation since "first we can learn
to recognize our misery from it. "[37] After receiving the
promise of redemption in the second step, it also pertains
to the believer in the third step since the law "can and should
serve as a guiding principle of our holiness. "[38] The social
dimension of holy living is dependent upon the personal dimension, for "Where there is no love for God, there is also
no true love for the neighbor. "[39] This priority is to be
maintained because "the law is spiritual,... which means that
there are no empty, external deeds either commanded or
prohibited. Instead, they are to be looked upon from the
heart. God requires not only an outward, but also an inward
obedience, as the ten commandments clearly teach. "[40]

The works of love for neighbor, which result from
continued repentance after faith has begun, are more than
the effect of faith; they are the actualization of faith in practice. This Christian practice is presented with an element
of Voetian precisionism, for "whenever a chief virtue is commanded and a chief vice is prohibited, everything is to be
comprehended under it and belongs to it as a type or genus. "[41]
Georg Otterbein uniformly begins his sermons on the Decalogue by presenting "the words of the commandment," then

"the commentary of our Catechism upon it," and finally his
traditional personal appeal for his readers to comprehend
and apprehend in practice the doctrine being presented.[42]
Only when a believer has become a priest to his neighbor,
by virtue of his conversion, does he prove or make manifest
his baptism. Otterbein distinguishes the gift of faith from
practice by asking, "... is it not one thing when Pharaoh
takes Joseph from prison?"[43] The act of pardon makes possible the life of faith as a new vocation, as "when Pharaoh
enrobes [Joseph] in kingly apparel and set him as a prince
over the whole land of Egypt."[44]

Through practice the Christian moves toward the culmination of the final stage of his pilgrimage, which is Christian perfection. Although Question 115 teaches that perfection is only fully attained after this life, it is to be sought
continually. "If we follow Christ's leading we will more and
more be renewed in the image of God."[45]

Perfection is described by the Otterbeins on the one
hand as sinlessness and purity of intention. For Philip Wilhelm Otterbein, the obligations of grace lead him to conclude
that "He who denies the possibility of living without sin denies God, and deserves no other answer than the one the
Saviour gave the Sadducees--'Ye do err, not knowing the
Scriptures, nor the power of God (Matthew 22:29)'."[46]
Georg Otterbein defines sin as "whatever does not proceed
from faith."[47] The diligence of man remains dependent upon
the power of God. As the Otterbeins probed their parishioners for proofs of progress toward sinlessness, they did not
regard their own experience as the only or normative possibility, for, as Philip Wilhelm Otterbein confessed, "I have
never preached that a person must be converted in a moment...."[48]

> God acts according to his free and unlimited power
> and wisdom, calling one directly, another indirect-
> ly; pulling some at once fully from destruction as
> a brand from the burning, while with others the
> work proceeds more slowly.[49]

The need for separation from the world (Absonderung) was an
important corollary of the doctrine of sinlessness. This
other-worldly asceticism was accompanied by an emphasis
upon adiaphora, for play and idleness was associated with the
decadent times of "these last days."[50]

On the other hand, love of God and neighbor is the
positive expression of the striving toward perfection. While
we remain in the world, "we are not to afflict, injure, or
oppress one another; rather, we are to serve, to benefit
others, and to help."[51] Unlike earlier Anabaptism, obedience to Christ must always take place within the established
orders of society. "The Lord wills that you be subject to
all human orders," wrote Georg Otterbein, "not only to the
highest authority, but also to the lesser authorities, the em-
ployers whom you serve."[52] It is within these orders that
obedience (Nachfolge) takes place.[53] Although the opposition
from the adherents of the German Aufklärung frequently
caused the Otterbeins' readers to suffer persecution for their
faith, they were admonished to "be content," for "God is
good."[54] They were laboring with the awareness that "The
time is short, and what you accomplish in it is important."[55]

The Otterbeins had an overwhelming interest in spell-
ing out in terms of human experience the effects of the work
of Christ. When they admonish the believer to "prove yourself daily," this practice is to be judged primarily in terms
of motive rather than in terms of the actual consequences of
the action.[56] In conversion, man is not counted righteous
before God unless he is freed from daily sins by the purification of his motives. "Proving" himself is the outworking
of these pure intentions. The transformation of man in
Christ must withstand empirical description if it is to be at
all valid. "Examine yourself," writes Georg Otterbein, "to
determine whether you have become better or worse."[57]
The paradoxical subtlety of simul iustus et peccator is over-
looked with his emphasis upon Nachfolge, which is elaborated
in terms of psychological stages and states. The relation
between "Christ in us" and following Christ as our prototype
is not free from ambiguity. However, Philip Wilhelm Otterbein explains the relation as follows.

> Christ through His suffering has given us a picture
> of that which He must do in us, that He must de-
> stroy the kingdom of Satan within us, just as He
> has destroyed this kingdom outside of us. He has
> given Himself to us as an example.... And this is
> the work of redemption, Christ in us.[58]

"Christ in us" does not indicate a quietism which stands opposed to the obligations of gratitude. Instead, it is viewed
as the culmination of the lifelong task of repentance. It can
only be truly said that Christ and His kingdom are "in us"

when pure motives within have issued in outer manifestations
of love of God and neighbor.   Greater emphasis is placed
upon the motive rather than upon either the quality or quan-
tity of the value which is produced as a consequence of the
action.

Among the chief works of piety which characterize
living faith is prayer.   When Johann Otterbein reflects upon
the doctrine of prayer in Questions 116 to 129 of the Catechism, it is once again Christ the Exemplar and not Christ
the High Priest that is the controlling theme.   "In these efforts, the believer looks to Christ as His precious predeces-
sor; to the Holy Spirit, the rightful teacher of prayer,... and
to the Christ who has suffered like him with unspeakable
groans. "[59]

The Otterbeins were convinced that their empirical
description of the transformation of man in Christ according
to the plan of the Catechism cohered with the order presented
in Scripture.   Georg Otterbein's attempt to document this relationship led to the publication of his exposition of Romans
12--Geist des Wahren Christenthums nach Paulus.[60]   This attempt to square his empirical description with Scripture led
him to impose a temporally progressive pattern upon this
chapter.

> The true Christian treasures and honors every ker-
> nel of knowledge [in Scripture], not in order to be-
> come a more prodigious intellect..., but to direct
> his knowledge into deeds.   He learns diligently in
> order to improve himself continually.[61]

In Romans

> Paul has concentrated everything upon... the spirit
> of true Christianity... as the basis, the motive of
> Christian action, and the view and the goal upon
> which the eye of the Christian is to be directed.[62]

> This twelfth chapter of the letter of the apostle
> Paul to the Romans is one of the richest in all
> Scripture.   It contains the entirety of practical
> Christianity in a brief outline.   In this mirror one
> must consider himself, if one wants to see one's
> true nature and what the Christian can and should
> become.   With this consideration, one either finds
> the basis for being ashamed of himself or else it

must urge him on. [62a]

In his exposition of Romans 12:1, Georg Otterbein focuses upon the Christian's "rational, spiritual service of God" to document his case.   The "service of God" is more than church attendance and corporate worship.   "If we are to honor God with our whole lives, then we need to consider the meaning of 'rational'... with cognitive reflection on the future. "[63]   Calvin simply noted that "By calling it a reasonable service which God commands, Paul dismisses all that we attempt contrary to the rule of His Word as foolish, insipid, and rashly undertaken. "[64]   For Otterbein, "rational" is susceptible to an analysis of defined stages and states in Christian experience.

> The rational soul is preeminently operative....
> Sound reason must sanction its [activities].   It
> teaches us that... we are not to order this and that
> deed after Him... but rather we must endeavor to
> please Him at all times and all places. [65]

When Paul "beseeches us by the mercy of God" this suggests that Christ "takes his abode with Christians in a pilgrimage. "[66] He translates "Be not conformed to this world" (Romans 12:2) as "Do not sojourn according to the course of this world" with its "ungodly conditions and lusts. "[67]   "World" is not viewed primarily as the temporal state of fallen mankind in which he is obliged to remain while simultaneously being made righteous in Christ.   It refers to a range of human character and conduct to be shunned and it is also explained in terms of its opposite--the renewal of the mind.

> ... through precise examination and proof one is
> placed in the position to know the good, to judge,
> to distinguish, and to hold to it, and to treasure
> it highly... by examining and exercising it. [68]

"Following Christ, " he concludes, "is the way to perfection. "[69]   This is also the theme in the preface to the exegetical meditation entitled Das Leben Enochs (Duisburg, 1778), when he writes that

> Enoch walked with God [Genesis 5:22].   Our whole
> attention is upon this worthy description of the life
> of an exemplary, pious man who presented the witness to his time that he had pleased God.... The
> way which Enoch walked is also for you, dear

reader, if you wish to reach the goal. Consider
him. The Christian should learn to treasure the
extraordinary worth of this life of pilgrimage here
below. [70]

Although the Otterbeins' tend to interpret Christ and
other Biblical figures as types of Christ in terms of a moral
ideal, they remain insistent that it is not God-consciousness
but the power of God's grace which enables the Christian to
achieve the Christ-ideal. The new life of the believer manifests the "comfort" (Question 1) of forgiveness and regeneration. Georg Otterbein's criticism of the Kantian pastors,
who occupied many Reformed pulpits in his day, rested on
his conviction that Christ is not an external model designed
for our imitation. Rather, our relation to Him is intimate
and personal because His love has penetrated and shaped our
lives. Johann Otterbein concluded his instruction to the condemned convict with an admonition.

No one will be able to avail himself of the assurance of salvation unless he follows the prescribed
order of salvation in the Catechism; and yet the
first question of the Catechism, in that it presup-
poses something previous, is really secondary--it
is a consequence growing out of this prescribed
plan. And it is highly proper that the Catechism
should begin with this question, for everyone can
see at a glance what he can expect if he follows
the teachings and embraces the order of salvation
as contained in this precious book. [71]

According to the Otterbeins' Heilsordnung theology,
Christianity in a given parish was measured in terms of the
number and quality of genuine Christians present there. It
was with the activities of Philip Wilhelm Otterbein in the
American colonies--and expecially his role in the organization of the Church of the United Brethren in Christ--that this
theology found institutional embodiment.

Notes

1. G. G. Otterbein, P. H. K. , I, 44.

2. Ibid.

3. This is the formulation of the syllogism given in Conrad

Cherry, The Theology of Jonathan Edwards: A Reappraisal. (New York, 1966), 152.

4. Calvin, Institutes, II, 7, 12.

5. Ibid.

6. Ibid.

7. Ibid.

8. Institutes, III, 17, 3.

9. See Institutes, III, 15, 7: "... our regeneration is entirely and without exception from God. "

10. See Institutes, III, 7, 8: "His [God's] blessing alone finds a way, even through all hindrances, to bring all things to a happy and favorable outcome for us. "

11. See Institutes, III, 15, 3: "For to the Lord we have given nothing unrequired but have only carried out services owed, for which no thanks are due. "

12. Institutes, III, 8, 4: "Therefore Peter likewise teaches that our faith is proved by tribulations as gold is tested in a fiery furnace. "

13. Institutes, III, 14, 9: "... from the fruits of their [the saints'] calling they merely regard themselves as having been chosen by the Lord. "

14. See Barth's commentary, op. cit. , 335ff.

15. Ibid.

16. Karl Barth, Die Protestantische Theologie im 19. Jhdt. (Zürich, 1947), 72ff.

17. J. D. Otterbein, J. K. B. , 211.

18. Ibid.

19. Ibid.

20. Ibid. , 239.

21. Ibid., 213 (enclosure mine).

22. Ibid.

23. P. W. Otterbein, Die Heilbrigende Menschwerdung, 90.

24. Ibid.

25. Ibid.

26. J. D. Otterbein, J. K. B., 214.

27. Ibid.

28. Ibid.

29. Ibid.

30. Ibid.

31. Ibid., 215.

32. G. G. Otterbein, P. H. K., II, 96ff.

33. Ibid., II, 102, 104.

34. Ibid., II, 106.

35. Ibid., 110.

36. Ibid., 117.

37. Ibid., 154.

38. Ibid.

39. Ibid.

40. Ibid.

41. Ibid.

42. For example, in his sermon on the second commandment, the first two divisions are entitled "Die Worte des Gesetzgebers," and "Die Erlauterung unsers Katechismi daruber."--Ibid., 175.

43. P. W. Otterbein, "Letter Concerning Sanctification, Justification, and Church Discipline," (n. d.), Core, 101.

44. Ibid.

45. G. G. Otterbein, P. H. K., II, 422ff.

46. P. W. Otterbein, "Letter Concerning Sanctification, Justification, and Church Discipline," 101.

47. G. G. Otterbein, L. D. S., 44.

48. P. W. Otterbein, "Letter Concerning Sanctification, Justification, and Church Discipline," 101.

49. Ibid.

50. G. G. Otterbein, L. D. S., 47.

51. Ibid., 48.

52. Ibid., 43.

53. Ibid., 18.

54. Ibid., 33.

55. Ibid., 62.

56. Ibid., 65.

57. Ibid.

58. P. W. Otterbein, Die Heilbrigende Menschwerdung, 84ff.

59. J. D. Otterbein, J. K. B., 215.

60. G. G. Otterbein, G. W. C. (Frankfurt u. Leipzig: 1792).

61. Ibid., "Vorrede," vii.

62. Ibid., xiii.   62a. Ibid., 8.

63. Ibid., 13.

64. C. N. T. C. on Romans 12:1, 264f.

65. G. G. Otterbein, G. W. C. , 14.

66. Ibid. , 18ff.

67. Ibid. , 33.

68. Ibid. , 81.

69. Ibid. , 77.

70. G. G. Otterbein, Das Leben Enochs.   (Duisburg, 1778),
    "Vorrede, " iii, iv, viii.

71. J. D. Otterbein, J. K. B. , 215.

PART III

PHILIP WILHELM OTTERBEIN
AND THE AMERICAN EXPERIENCE

Chapter 7

OTTERBEIN AND THE RISE OF
GERMAN-AMERICAN EVANGELICALISM

a. Otterbein As an Evangelical Pastor in Pennsylvania

The relevance of the theological tradition of the Otterbeins for Americans lies in its role in nurturing the German
Reformed people of the Middle Colonies in the latter half of
the eighteenth century and as a determinative factor in the
rise of the United Brethren movement toward the close of the
century. Thus, this tradition became a factor in the development of the broader tradition of American evangelical Protestantism. This tradition, as represented by the published
writings of the Otterbeins and by the varied pastoral activities of Philip Wilhelm Otterbein (1726-1813), was obscured
amid the pervasive and leveling impact of the revivals, and
with the rise of denominationalism. As Tanis has observed,[1]
the many-sidedness of Pietism makes ambiguous the common
epithet that Frelinghuysen was the "Father of American Pietism." While Frelinghuysen was the leading spirit of the
Dutch Reformed people of colonial New Jersey and New York,
it was Philip Wilhelm Otterbein, pastor of leading colonial
German Reformed congregations (at Lancaster and later at
Baltimore) who occupied a similar position among his churchmen. Though his own literary production was meager, he
distributed the volumes of sermons on the Catechism by his
brothers in Germany and also implemented their theological
proposals in his own pastoral work.

Herborn, where he served as preceptor from 1748 to
1752, had been invigorated in his day by streams of Pietism
emanating from the Netherlands. It retained its loyalty to
the Reformed confessions, notably the Heidelberg Catechism,
during the Enlightenment, though its doctrinal position, as
represented in the writings of the Otterbeins, reflected the
pietistic theology. The Herborn of the Otterbeins' day sought
to invigorate this confessional standard and to extend its influence by the use of pietistic ideas and methods. Evidence
of this missionary concern is the school's enthusiastic re-

sponse to Michael Schlatter's appeal for volunteers to serve the German Reformed immigrants of the Middle Colonies.

In 1752, Philip Wilhelm Otterbein, with five fellow students, was ordained and left his preceptorship and his congregation at Ockersdorf for Amsterdam, where he took the oath of allegiance to the symbols of the Dutch Reformed Church[2] and then departed for the new world. Otterbein had been reprimanded by his parishioners for holding conventicles[3] at Ockersdorf, in an effort to enlist regenerate laymen to assist in reforming the church. He undoubtedly agreed with his brother at Burbach, Johann Otterbein, when the latter complained in 1770 to the counselor of his consistory as follows:

> Turn where you please, a distressing sight presents itself. Have we any news from anyone, it surely relates to his depravity. But, it cannot be otherwise. Those who live in the cities, as well as those in the country, are too extravagant, both in eating and in dressing ... There is no great dissimilarity between the present and Noah's time ... There is enough complaint, but it all refers to bodily necessity, and no one attempts to supply this want through the agency of an active Christianity ... I find so few imitating the life of Jesus--but on the contrary see nothing but worldliness, luxury, coldness, and pride; yet all expect to obtain salvation-- I cannot help thinking that the duties of a pastor are surely perplexing....[4]

This confusion describes the frustration of these latter-day Pietists. Rather than allowing his zeal to wane, Philip Wilhelm Otterbein determined to find his ministry on the foreign field.

Reformed families from the Palatinate, who had been migrating to Pennsylvania since 1709, were received as brethren by the Dutch in New York and New Jersey. The German Reformed people in Pennsylvania had asked the Synod of South Holland to assume responsibility for them, and this relationship began with the ordination of John Philip Boehm by the Dutch of New York in 1729,[5] and continued until 1793. In 1743, the Synod denied the Germans' request for a coetus with a degree of autonomy under Dutch supervision, and proposed instead that they, together with the Dutch Reformed people of Bucks County, unite with the Presbyterians of the

Philadelphia Synod in the colonies. Unlike the other parties,
the Germans balked, largely because of their fear that they
would lose their Catechism, as had frequently happened in
Germany. The revivalist parties (as represented by Frelinghuysen, Tennent, and their followers) were less rigid creed-
ally, worked well together, officiated at one another's
churches, and were less bound to the traditions of the mother countries. However, their presence created suspicion of
the proposed union on the part of the conservative Dutch Reformed people of New York. In 1751, the authorities in Holland were persuaded against the union as the result of an
anonymous report from the colonies that "neither now, nor
ever, can one be sure of ... the opinions of the Scotch pres-
bytery," meaning the Synod of Philadelphia, which, it was
charged, was "not only entirely independent, but without
forms of doctrine and liturgy."⁶ The Philadelphia Presbyterians, who were actually Old Siders, were incensed by
these charges, and replied that the Dutch and Germans could
keep their confessions, including the Catechism. However,
the die had been cast, and union was prevented.

The Holland authorities now determined not to abandon
their responsibilities to the Reformed people in the colonies,
and in 1747 Michael Schlatter presided over the organization
of a German coetus. It adhered to the church order adopted
by Boehm in 1725, which embodied the principles of polity
handed down by the Reformed synods of the Rhineland: provisions were made for a consistory, church discipline, catechizing of children, adherence to the Heidelberg Catechism,
and the proper administration of the temporal and spiritual
affairs of congregations. He was active in the organization
of congregations and in procuring funds in Europe for the
work in America, including a large sum raised among the
English for the foundation of charity schools among the Germans. However, published statements from the English sup-
porters of the program led the Germans to spurn the foreign
charity in the fear that the project, with its political over-
tones, would prepare the way for the establishment of Angli-
canism among them.

When Schlatter arrived in Pennsylvania with his six
young ministerial recruits in 1752, there were only four pastors to serve a German Reformed population of thirty thou-
sand.⁷ The problems they encountered stemmed from at
least two sources. On the one hand, the spartan demands of
frontier life and the immigrants' far-flung diaspora over the
vast frontiers would have made difficult the possibility of an

orderly parochial life, even if sufficient clergymen were
available. Thus, it is not surprising that there was frequently a sudden decline of interest in "religious matters" even
among those who had left their homelands in search of religious freedom. These Germans had been on the fringe of the
first Great Awakening, though Whitefield had made inroads into the Pennsylvania interior--especially among the Moravians
--in 1740. [8]

On the other hand, there was an active minority of
sectarian, mystical charismatics who continued to exert an
influence among the Pennsylvania Germans--especially those
of the Lancaster area--when Otterbein arrived. These sectarians were the children of the radical Pietists of the early
eighteenth century, with whom the Otterbeins had to cope in
Germany. [9] The most influential center of this sectarian ferment in colonial Pennsylvania was the Ephrata Community,
which attempted to proselytize the populace, including the
Reformed congregations, of Otterbein's day.

Otterbein became engulfed in parochial disorganization
and sectarian ferment when he accepted in 1752 the call to
become pastor of the Reformed congregation at Lancaster,
which at that time was a lively community of two thousand
and the home of the most substantial Reformed congregation
west of Philadelphia. This was a peak period in the history
of the Ephrata cloister, and their influence had frequently
penetrated the city of Lancaster. It was largely the popular
reception of the mystical tracts published at Ephrata that led
to Benjamin Franklin's decision to compete for the German
audience of the area by establishing his own German and English printing office in Lancaster. [10] The first issue of this
press was a circular letter of the Reformed coetus which set
forth the successful efforts of Schlatter's recent missionary-
recruiting tour. However, Franklin's Lancaster venture was
terminated in the early years of Otterbein's ministry there,
for the Germans of the area had become too heavily dependent upon the literature from Ephrata and from the Sauer
press at Germantown. Even Otterbein's library at this time
included a copy of the sectarians' Berleburg Bible, though he
never espoused the separatism and mystical extravagances of
the radical Pietists.

Otterbein began his labors at Lancaster with the handi-
cap that the church had been without a pastor for fully one-
half of its twenty-five year existence, and his immediate
predecessors, Vock and Schnorr, were unordained men who

had rent the congregation because of their pastoral negligence
and lack of proper ecclesiastical discipline. [11] Despite these
difficulties, the young Otterbein labored with sufficient success to enable the congregation to erect a stone church to replace the temporary log one. However, after serving his
appointed term of five years, he was anxious to withdraw
from the congregation because of his anguish over the indif-
ference of members of the congregation--a condition which
had been encouraged by the unsettling religious ferment of the
times and by the earlier lack of pastoral leadership. He demanded the exercise of "a just ecclesiastical discipline" and
"entire liberty of conscience" in the performance of his pastoral duties as the condition of his continuance, and this was
granted by the congregation. [12]

A review of Otterbein's Lancaster pastorate indicates
that it was here that he emerged as the leader of the evangelical or revivalist party within the German Reformed
Church. Among the papers of the church archives at Lancaster, there has been found a manuscript in the hand of Otterbein, which proposes that since

> For some time matters in our congregation have
> proceeded somewhat irregularly--especially among
> whose who reside outside of town [perhaps a refer-
> ence to sectarian influence of the Ephrata variety],
> we find it necessary to request that everyone who
> calls himself a member of our church and who is
> concerned to lead a Christian life, should come
> forward and subscribe his name to the following
> rules of order. [13]

These "rules of order" do not constitute innovations in themselves, for, as we have noted, a church covenant or order
had been drawn up by John Philip Boehm and adopted by his
congregation in Pennsylvania in 1725. Among Otterbein's
"rules" is the requirement that professors of Christianity
should subject themselves to a "becoming Christian church-
discipline. " To end disorder and to enable "that each member might be more fully known, " each person who desires to
receive the Lord's Supper shall, "previous to the preparation
service, upon a day appointed for that purpose, personally
appear before the minister, in order that an interview may
be held. "[14] The Catechism had regarded admission to and
exclusion from the Lord's Supper as the determinative issue
in the Christian life (Qs. 81 to 85), and the Otterbeins' exposition of these questions sought to explicate in detail the

marks of a worthy end of an unworthy communicant, in order
that the unrepentant could be readily identified and excluded.
Otterbein hoped to distinguish the worthy from the unworthy
participants, so that the Supper might "seal" the covenant
within the reborn. This was to be the basis for ordering
the life of his congregation.

Otterbein instituted his reform with the conviction that
he was adhering to the true intent of the Catechism, as well
as the "Formula of Unity" to which he had subscribed before
his departure from the Netherlands. His opposition to separatism is indicated by his criticism of the so-called "Congregation of God in the Spirit"--a Pennsylvania movement
originating in 1736 with Zinzendorf, which had as its goal
the union of all "earnest" Christians, regardless of denominational affiliation, under the auspices of the Moravians. 15
The movement arose as the result of an appeal for the union
of the colony's sects which was issued by one Johann Adam
Gruber of Oley, an "Inspirationist" of the school of Johann
Friedrich Roch. 16 It received tangible form when Henry
Antes, a Reformed missionary from the Palatinate, secured
the assistance of Count Zinzendorf in organizing a conference
to which representatives of eight sects came. The Ephrata
brethren were well represented and, as might be expected,
there were sharp contentions which prevented the movement
from attaining its objective of spiritual unity among sectarian
diversity. The "Dunkers," the "New Dunkers" at Ephrata,
and the abortive "Congregation of God in the Spirit" each
tried to meet the crisis of unbelief by perpetuating the old
sectarian solution, only now the Antichrist (the old fallen
world) was not the coercive but the worldliness engendered
by the socially and religiously dispossessed German immigrants.

What, then, was the character of Otterbein's ministry
at Lancaster if he aligned himself neither with the sectarian
ecumenists nor with the externalized, "respectable" religion
which had impoverished his congregation? The answer lies
in his personal discovery that holy affections are not born of
private revelation nor of man's moral attainment; they are
a gift of grace which is always mediated through the Word,
according to the divinely-instituted order of salvation in
Scripture and Catechism. Because of this discovery, he later characterized this period of his ministry as the dawn of
his "conscious spiritual life." 17 There is a tradition that, on
a certain Sabbath morning during the early part of his Lancaster ministry, Otterbein preached with unusual "unction" on

the necessity of thorough repentence and faith in Christ as a
"full and conscious Saviour. "[18] At the close of the service,
a convicted seeker anxiously approached him for counsel, but
Otterbein, though he had preached with such potency, felt so
overwhelmed and humbled by the very power of the Word he
had proclaimed that he could only reply, "My friend, advice
is scarce with me today. "[19] Berger, an early United Brethren historian, sees the following significance in this event:

> The fact that his earnest sermon, full of truths
> which he had theoretically learned and as yet but
> partially experienced, was but the strong outcrying
> of his own unsatisfied soul, and he went away from
> his pulpit to the seclusion of his closet, there to
> struggle in prayer until the problem of a more per-
> fect consciousness of salvation in Christ was fully
> solved. [20]

Whether Otterbein would have described his experience as a
"problem which became fully solved" is doubtful. Yet, he
testified much later to the importance of this event, in answer to one of a series of questions which were asked him
not long before his death by Methodist Bishop Asbury. Asbury, in one of his famous fraternal meetings with Otterbein,
asked "By what means were you brought to the gospel of God
and our Saviour?" Otterbein's reply was, in accordance
with the temporal process of the "order of salvation," that
"By degrees was I brought to the knowledge of the truth,
while I was at Lancaster. "[21]

The privilege to pursue this pilgrimage of faith was
open to all, but only those who have followed it may participate in the "outward" sacrament. Otterbein did not reject
the external aspects of the faith but he was convinced that
externals are superfluous without an inward appropriation by
the heart. Hence, Otterbein's plea to negligent church members to "shun irregularities," as the mystical excesses emanating from Ephrata, and to submit to self-examination before partaking of Holy Communion seems to have been deeply
rooted in his own quest for a fuller experience of grace.

Otterbein's dissatisfaction with the results of his pastoral efforts led him, in 1758, to consider returning to Germany to take a pastorate, perhaps in the vicinity where his
brothers were serving. However, his new apprehension of
Christian truth prevented him from retreating or adopting the
position of those Reformed pastors who increasingly tended to

confuse an emphasis upon the devotional life with the excessive subjectivism that had become manifest among many sectarians. [22]   Such pastors, even though they had been trained
under pietistic influences in Europe, often mitigated the necessity for the experiential appropriation of Christian truth in
view of the pressure from the sectarians.   The leaders of
the coetus, notes Dunn, opposed the Pietism of the German
sects and were cool toward the New Light Presbyterians.
They were not pietistic, but they piously insisted on uncom-
promising adherence to doctrinal standards.   Otterbein was
pietistic, yet the coetal letter of 1788 notes that "though the
purpose of his ministry ... may not in the strictest sense
have always accorded with the opinion of everyone, it was
edification and blessing, and ... he has done a great deal of
good, he has labored earnestly for the salvation of many
souls. "[23]   For Otterbein, the goal of a well-ordered parochial life was attained not by circumventing the affective
meaning of Christian truth but by restoring it to its rightful
place in the center of the life of the worshipping congregation.

Otterbein could not have returned to Germany in 1758
even if he had desired, for the exigencies of the French and
Indian War constrained him.   On the one hand, it was not
safe to make the long sea voyage with conditions of war prevailing, and on the other, he received word that he was
desperately needed at the little frontier village of Tulpehocken,
where recent Indian massacres had worsened the plight of the
people.   By Otterbein's time, the Reformed people of Tulpehocken were badly fragmented because of their contacts with
nearby Ephrata.   There was no middle position in their feel-
ings toward the cloister.   Either they had openly embraced
it and had become communicants to the secular congregation
at the cloister, or perhaps even members of the celibate
brotherhood or sisterhood, or they had raised a defensive
wall against all types of religious affection.   In their zeal to
exclude fanatics, their fellowship harbored a noticeably un-
charitable spirit.   Hence, when Otterbein arrived on the
scene in 1758, he confronted emergencies which were both
physical and spiritual in character.   The latter he considered
to be the greater.

After painting this dark picture of Otterbein's Tulpehocken, there are certain compensating factors to be considered which made his two years here, in some respects,
the Galilean period of his ministry.   A group of refugees
from the Palatinate who had recently arrived at Tulpehocken

had been given devotional books by the court chaplain of St.
James, London, when they passed through the city en route
to America.   Chief among these books was Arndt's True
Christianity, which undoubtedly helped to initiate the people
to the experiential religion which Otterbein would introduce
to them. It was here that the Reverend Johann Christian
Stahlschmidt, a colleague of Tersteegen[24] and author of Die
Pilgerreise, visited with Otterbein. He devotes two chapters
in his narrative to his meeting with Otterbein, noting that

> Otterbein was a truly pious and kind-hearted man,
> and was universally esteemed for his godly life ...
> After conversing a while with him, and feeling a
> confidence in him from his friendly deportment, I
> communicated my inward circumstances to him,
> and also something of my inward state. [25]

Here is a manifestation of the kind of psychological probing
that Domine Otterbein found effective in his role as a leader
of souls, according to the path prescribed by the "order of
salvation. "

     Though Otterbein was less mystically oriented than
Stahlschmidt and Tersteegen, who were both nurtured in the
German Reformed tradition, he made use of the nomenclature
of "inner-worldly asceticism" within the doctrinal framework
of the Catechism.   An early United Brethren hymnal, printed
in 1856, contains Tersteegen's "Lo, God is Here, " as well
as hymns from Neander and Lampe. [26]

     Because Otterbein's spiritual crisis was behind him
when he took up his labors at Tulpehocken, his ministry here
was characterized by the successful use of various pastoral
innovations which bore the mark of the Herborn pietistic influence.   He abandoned the manuscript in the pulpit because
he now preached a practical, "experimental" theology which
he urgently proclaimed in church and in homes.   He also introduced conventicles or private prayer meetings held in the
homes of those who manifested evidence of regeneration.
These meetings were for mutual spiritual examination and edification, and their members were to assist the pastor in reforming the congregation.   They were to be in addition to
regular church attendance.   Though Drury claimed they were
the first to be held in this country, [27] they had also been popular among the Dutch Reformed people (Frelinghuysen) and
the New Light Presbyterians (the Tennents).   In his parish in
Ockersdorf (Germany), neither he nor his congregation had

received that "spiritual quickening"--the sense of true holy
affection which is centered in evangelical repentance and
faith--which would have made such a venture a success, and
he had been repulsed by his congregation.

Because of his Lancaster experience, he introduced
interviews before Communion, which indicates that he would
then recognize no visibility of morals apart from the visibility of faith as a qualification for full communion in the
church. Now, by introducing the prayer meetings at Tulpehocken, he erected on this foundation the theme of intensify-
ing the personal faith of those who were recognized as being
regenerate church members. An early account of these
meetings notes that

> On these occasions his custom was to read a por-
> tion of Scripture, make some practical comments
> on the same, and exhort all present to give place
> to serious reflections. He would then sing a sa-
> cred hymn, and invite all to kneel and to accom-
> pany him in prayer. At first, and for some time,
> but few, if any, would kneel, and he would be per-
> mitted to pray alone ... After prayer he would en-
> deavor to gain access to their hearts by addressing
> them individually with words of kindness and love.[28]

These techniques were not practiced by most of his Reformed
colleagues. Otterbein often proved more effective than his
colleagues in preventing parishioners from lapsing into sec-
tarianism because, like the sectarians, he sought to gain ac-
cess to the hearts of people and to inspire them to holy living by his own testimony of Christian experience; but, unlike
them, he did so by adapting the resources of the institutional
church to this end. However, it was only a small step from
this position to the place where only a converted or visibly
regenerate minister is believed to be able to fulfill the office
of the ministry. This brings us to the account of Otterbein's
role in the emergence of the United Brethren.

b. Otterbein and the United Brethren

As a result of these activities, Otterbein would henceforth exhibit a new openness to what constitutes the marks of
true faith in other men, regardless of their denominational
affiliation. Two important encounters, which were significant
in the rise of the major institutional expression of German-

American evangelicalism, serve to exemplify this openness.

The first encounter was with the Mennonite Martin
Boehm, who was born in Lancaster County in 1725. His
deacon-father introduced him to Mennonite devotional books[29]
which were printed at the Ephrata press in the 1740's. As
a youth, he would wander alone in the forest for long periods
of time in deep spiritual agony. In 1756, he was chosen by
lot for the ministry, as was the Mennonite custom, but this
only increased his distress, for he felt that he could not hope
for grace to teach others the way of salvation if he had not
himself attained it or did not at least possess the hope of attaining it. He prayed for himself without ceasing until finally, while plowing in the field, the words "verlohren, verlohren," haunted him until he sank behind the plow and cried
for mercy. Spayth, a near-contemporary of Boehm, record-
ed the joy with which Boehm now undertook his preaching
responsibilities on the next Sabbath:

> This caused considerable commotion in our church,
> as well as among the people generally. It was all
> new; none of us had heard or seen it before. A
> new creation appeared to rise up before me. Now
> Scripture, before mysterious, and like a dead let-
> ter to me, was plain of interpretation, 'alles geist
> und leben.'[30]

Boehm of course, had not the range of theological understanding which Otterbein had, and though he was certainly affirming, as the Otterbeins had in their theology of the Heidelberg
Catechism, that the whole meaning of Christian faith was tied
to the matter of experiential piety, the scope of this meaning
was for him considerably narrower and more simplified.
Boehm soon left his local congregation to make itinerary
trips to preach to the Germans of the upper Shenandoah Valley of Virginia, where numerous Mennonite families had mi-
grated. Here he met converts of George Whitefield and thus
came into contact with the fruits of the Anglo-American first
Great Awakening. He returned with one of these "English
preachers" to Pennsylvania, where the two of them conducted
a "grosse Versammlung," or great meeting, which was the
eighteenth-century forerunner of the camp meetings and pro-
tracted meetings of the second Great Awakening. These
"great meetings" were two or three days in length (unlike
the longer camp meetings of the next century) and attracted
"inquirers" from all religious faiths. They were short on
liturgy and long on preaching, but they often closed with "love

feasts" (which reflects the Dunker influence) in which the
newly converted participated in order to "seal" their experience.

At the Isaac Long barn in Lancaster County, Boehm
conducted such a "big meeting" on Pentecost, 1767, in which
Lutherans, Mennonites, and Dunkers participated--the German forerunner of the Scotch-Irish camp meetings of the Old
Southwest some fifty years later. Otterbein, who was now
serving the Reformed congregation at York, Pennsylvania,
was also in attendance, though he had never before met
Boehm. Otterbein's visitation while at Lancaster had brought
him within a few miles of Boehm's home. The long controversy between the Mennonites and the Reformed in Europe
surely explains why they were strangers. How different these
two men were! Otterbein, the university-trained minister,
sat at the feet of the frontier lay preacher. Both had been
brought to this confrontation by the sectarian ferment of their
environment, which had been fed by the diverse streams of
continental Pietism. Both had hungered for an experience of
grace, though both rejected the subjectivism of a mystical as-
sent which explicitly embraced human merit, in the manner
of the Zionitic Brotherhood at Ephrata. Otterbein, with his
loyalty to church and Catechism, was not ashamed of the gospel, even when it came in power and might, just as the profound Edwards, when listening to the preaching of Whitefield
in 1740, was moved to tears because his own ministry
seemed by comparison so unprofitable. After Boehm unfold-
ed his testimony which so nearly paralleled Otterbein's own
experience (apart from the formal structure of the Catechism
in which it was expressed), the Pastor leaped from his feet,
embraced Boehm, and exclaimed, "Wir sind Brüder."[31]
United Brethren historians have dated this as the origin of
their movement, and Drury describes it as "A present Pentecost" in which "some in the congregation, unable to repress
their emotions, praised the Lord aloud; but the greater part
were bathed in tears, and all hearts seemed melted into
one."[32] Despite such outward expression, the moment of
Christian truth which shaped this occasion was ennobled by a
strongly biblicist dimension which was lacking in the mystical experientialism which characterized the revivalism of such
sectarians as Beissel and Miller. The sense of holy affection through union with Christ which drew Otterbein and
Boehm together also contrasted sharply with the German sectarians' theosophic speculation applied to deduce a philosophy
of the universe and a precise calculation of the end time.
The scope of their quest was less grandiose than that of the

mystics of Ephrata, but it was eminently more practical and
social.

The brief and terse confession of faith which was later adopted by the United Brethren should not obscure the
fact that the Otterbeins themselves were greatly interested
in adapting evangelical doctrine to the understanding of all
ages and educational levels, in language which was meaning-
ful to them.   Hence, when Otterbein heard the testimony of
Boehm, the ancient antagonism between Anabaptists and mag-
isterial Protestants was completely forgotten and he perceived
a sound expression of evangelical doctrine.   Georg Otterbein's instruction in the Catechism had been concerned with
"explaining and illustrating" the questions and answers for
the promotion of "reflection and self-understanding" on the
basis of their content. [33]   When Philip Wilhelm Otterbein re-
sponded to Boehm, he reflected the affirmation of Question
55 that "believers, all and every one, as members of Christ,
have part in Him and in all His treasures and gifts," and
that "each one must feel himself bound to use His gifts,
readily and cheerfully, for the advantage and welfare of other
members."

A second encounter, in addition to the one with Boehm,
was Otterbein's association with Georg Adam Geeting (1741-
1812), who had come from Nassau to Maryland as a youth.
He had settled on the Antietam Creek near the site where a
Sabbatarian called "Schneeberg" was founded by members of
the Ephrata Community in 1763.   Great love feasts were held
here, after the Dunker style.   The Journal of Christian Newcomer, the pioneer United Brethren bishop, notes that Otterbein began preaching on the nearby Geeting farm while he
served the Reformed church in Frederick, Maryland, and his
great meetings were here for the first time called "sacramental meetings"--undoubtedly their style was influenced by
the love feasts at the nearby cloister.   The following entry
in Newcomer's Journal, for June 3, 1797, is typical of the
meeting in which Geeting was converted in the 1770's:

> Today a sacramental meeting commenced near the
> Antietam.   The Lord was present from the begin-
> ning.   We held a prayer meeting in the evening at
> Br. Samuel Baker's ... We had an excellent time.
> Sunday 4th--This forenoon William Otterbein preached
> from Ephesians 2:1-6.   O, how conclusively did he
> reason.   How he endeavored to persuade his hear-
> ers to work out the salvation of their souls!   How

he tried to convince all of the necessity of vital,
experiential religion and a thorough change of heart!
The congregation was unusually large, and all
seemed to pay profound attention. Poor unworthy
me had to exhort after him; then Otterbein and
Geeting administered the Lord's Supper--we had a
glorious time! A great number of young people
and hoary-headed sinners were convicted, and some
happily committed to God. [34]

Geeting was converted by Otterbein, and through Otterbein's
example and assistance he became sufficiently educated to be
ordained by the Reformed coetus. Otterbein was one of two
Reformed pastors who had been regarded by the coetus of
1755 as "fit persons" to give private catechetical instruction
to ministerial candidates, which was an emergency measure
to provide qualified ministerial leadership without waiting for
university-trained candidates from Europe. [35] The fathers in
Holland had agreed, providing the two men "have a desire
that way and know how to find time, without the pulpit work
and the care of the congregation entrusted to them, suffering
loss thereby ... "[36] However, Geeting, whose piety displayed
an uninhibited quality of religious emotionalism, was expelled
from the Reformed Church in 1804 because, in the words of
the Reformed historian, Dubbs, "he was an enthusiast of the
most pronounced type. "[37] Geeting, notes Dubbs, continued
to conduct the "big meetings" on the Antietam "which are not
forgotten to this day" (1902), and "in this respect he went
much farther than did Mr. Otterbein, who was more quiet
and reflective. "[38]

In the 1770's, Otterbein entered a period of dual relations with the Reformed authorities and with the emerging
movement of German-American evangelicals, who represented
several theological traditions and regarded themselves as "unsectarian. " He not only maintained a close association with
his Reformed colleagues in America, but also with his brothers in the ministry in Germany. In April, 1770, he was
able to make his long contemplated visit to his family in
Germany, including Johann Charles, teacher at Herborn;
Johann Heinrich, pastor at Burbach; Johann Daniel, pastor
at Berleburg; Heinrich Daniel, pastor at Kecken; and Georg
Gottfried, pastor at the major city of Duisburg. [39] Each
eagerly related his own personal progress in the "pilgrimage
of faith, " which was prescribed for them in the Catechism.
After the American brother described his conversion experience at Lancaster, and such events as his meeting with

Boehm, Georg embraced him with affection and exclaimed,

> My dear Wilhelm, we are now, blessed be the
> name of the Lord, not only brothers after the flesh,
> but also after the spirit. I have also experienced
> the same blessing. I can testify that God has pow-
> er on earth to forgive sins and to cleanse from all
> unrighteousness [a paraphrase of Question 56 of the
> Catechism] ... I have a very strong impression
> that God has a great work for you to do in Amer-
> ica. [40]

Though he was never again to see his brothers, he continued
to share their interest in promoting evangalical doctrine according to the "order" of the Catechism. He included an article on catechetical training in his rules for the Church Book
at Baltimore three decades later; there is evidence that in
1803 he was still importing and distributing the volumes of
sermons on the Catechism by Georg Otterbein. In addition,
the charity school of which he served as trustee used the
primer by this same brother, containing doctrinal sections
based on the Catechism and interspersed with biblical citations as well as geographic and scientific information in the
form of an almanac.

Otterbein's dual relationship with the Reformed authorities in America and with the German-American evangelicals
emerged during the course of his final pastorate at Baltimore
(1774-1813). The congregation had been served by a pastor
named Faber, who had been negligent in his pastoral duties
and had not been a member of coetus. [41] When he had neglected a demand by the congregation that he resign, a large
party was attracted to the evangelical preaching of Benedict
Schwope, who had applied for ordination. [42] Schwope was ordained, despite his lack of formal theological training and
against the advice of the Dutch authorities. Both parties re-
ferred the dispute concerning the congregational schism to
coetus for adjudication, and for several years the minutes of
coetus are burdened with the accounts of the difficulties at
Baltimore. [43] Finally, a call was extended to the well-known
Otterbein, in the hope that he would be acceptable to both
parties, and, with the persuasion of coetus, he accepted.
The Faber party refused to cooperate, and Otterbein called
his congregation, which remained loyal to coetus, the "German Evangelical Reformed Church" of Baltimore. [44]

Though the church was a member of coetus, its name

implies a certain distinction. The Church Book of 1785,
drawn up by Otterbein, contains certain distinctive regula-
tions. Rules for holy living were explicitly affirmed (Article
2); attendance at Sunday worship was strictly enforced (Article 3); regular fasting was observed (Article 4); open communion for professing believers was practiced, providing all
communicants would first publicly declare their willingness
to submit to the church discipline (Articles 6 and 7); and
stated prayer meetings were inaugurated as follows:

> The members of this church, impressed with the
> necessity of a constant religious exercise, of suf-
> fering the word of God richly and daily to dwell in
> them,... resolve that each sex shall hold meetings
> apart, once a week, for which the most suitable
> day, hour, and place shall be chosen ... In the ab-
> sence of the preacher, an elder or trustee shall
> lead such meetings.
>
> The rules for these special meetings are these:
> (a) No one shall be received into them who is not
> resolved to flee the wrath to come, and, by faith
> and repentance, to seek his salvation in Christ,
> and who is not resolved willingly to obey the dis-
> ciplinary rules which are now observed by this
> church for good order and advance in holiness ...
> (b) These meetings are to commence and end with
> singing and prayer; and nothing shall be done but
> what will tend to build up and advance holiness ...[45]

In addition, members were to engage in daily private and
family worship. In teaching from the Catechism, Drury notes
that Otterbein "reserved the liberty to modify and construe."[46]
However, as we have seen, this was no innovation with him;
he was only implementing the long-standing Herborn tradition
of catechizing "without bondage to word and form."

The progress of the revival movement in which Otterbein participated with like-minded preachers such as Boehm
and Geeting is indicated in Article 14:

> No preacher can stay among us who will not to the
> best of his ability care for the various societies
> ('Gemeinden') in Pennsylvania, Maryland, and Vir-
> ginia, which churches, under the superintendence
> of William Otterbein, stand in fraternal unity with
> us.[47]

In 1774, Otterbein held a series of conferences, known as
the "Pipe Creek conferences," with other evangelical-minded
Reformed pastors such as Hendel and Schwope, for the purpose of invigorating the Reformed Church through the promotion of Bible and prayer groups, and class meetings.[48] Because there were no extant documents bearing on the progress of this movement after 1775, Dubbs concluded that pe-
culiarities of doctrine and worship appeared which affected
the character of the unity. The participating ministers of
this "United Brotherhood" had apparently begun to assume
that "Christians of various denominations might participate
in a higher unity without renouncing one's ecclesiastical relations."[49] It is known that Otterbein began conversations with
Methodist Francis Asbury in 1774, which would continue until Otterbein's death in 1813, concerning the degree to which
the United Brotherhood might adapt Methodist forms (such as
the class meeting and Methodist discipline).

Though Otterbein's friendship with Asbury was such
that he even took part in Asbury's ordination as a Superintendent in the newly-formed Methodist Episcopal Church in
1784, he steadfastly refused to carry out Asbury's expecta-
tions that he "make proposals to the German Synod this year,
to lay a plan for the reform of Dutch congregations."[50] It
is quite possible that Otterbein had decreased his involvement with nonsectarian movements out of a desire not "to set
forth competitive agencies against the established church"--
a tendency which appeared when the participants in the United
Brotherhood movement included fewer Reformed churchmen
and more who had broken from established churches.[51] Otterbein continued to adhere to the older pietistic concept of a
fellowship of earnest Christians within the established
churches, and he did not look favorably upon permitting such
movements to take on the structure of a new church. The
pattern of nineteenth-century denominationalism, which was
to become the institutional expression of American evangelical Protestantism, remained forever unfamiliar to this es-
sentially eighteenth-century pietistic churchman. Asbury,
who spoke affectionately of Otterbein as being one of the
"best scholars and greatest divines in America,"[52] always
acknowledged that his friend was the greater in spiritual re-
source (he venerably called him "Father Otterbein") and in
preaching talent. However, Asbury undoubtedly had a greater organizing ability and a more extensive (English) field in
which to labor.

After Otterbein disengaged himself from active partici-

pation in the "United Brotherhood" (1776), he was to meet
with them again only irregularly, though he continued regularly to attend the sessions of the Reformed Church, so long
as his health permitted. In 1789, the participants in the
former "United Brotherhood," which now included many non-
Reformed, met at Otterbein's Baltimore parsonage. Otterbein, with his missionary zeal, agreed with the participants'
objective of reaching as many of the frontier populace as possible with the claims of the gospel, but there was little concern with matters of creed and discipline. The first regular
Annual Conference was held in 1800 at Peter Kemp's house
near Frederick, Maryland. The participants, who included
Boehm and Otterbein, emphasized that the character of their
movement was that of an "unsectarian society."[53] Under
this condition, Otterbein, together with Boehm, accepted the
position of superintendent over the societies of the newly con-
stituted Vereinigte Bruederschaft zu Christo.[54] The minutes
also refer to the group as the "unsectarian preachers," and
unofficial names which soon became popular included "The
Freedom People," "The New Reformed," "The New Mennonites," "The General People." Sometimes, they bore the
names of local elders, such as "Neiding's People," "Light's
People," or "Crider's People."[55] Commenting upon this
loosely-organized body of Germans in 1803, Asbury noted
"There are now upwards of twenty German preachers some-
how connected with Mr. Philip Otterbein and Martin Boehm;
but they want authority, and the church wants discipline."[56]

Otterbein was less active in the movement after 1805,
partly because of illness and partly because of a renewed
commitment to his parent church after its reorganization as
the Reformed Church in America and the publication of its
constitution as the Synodal Ordnung. The active leadership
of the movement now passed to Christian Newcomer, who
had fully separated from the Mennonites. In 1809, the Methodist Annual Conference sent a resolution to Otterbein which
expressed a desire for closer relations between Methodists
and United Brethren. The latter approved in Annual Conference a reciprocal reception of members in good standing to
the Lord's Table and granted Methodists permission "to
preach in all our meeting places."[57] In a final meeting with
the Annual Conference of the United Brethren in 1813, Otterbein granted the request of the "Brethren in the west" that
he ordain Newcomer through "the laying on of hands, to the
office of elder and preacher of the gospel."[58] He replied,
"I have always considered myself too unworthy to perform
this solemn injunction of the Apostle, but now I perceive the

necessity of doing so, before I shall be removed."[59]

Thus, though Otterbein remained to his death in the church of his fathers, he sent the new movement forth with his blessing. Two years after his death, the first General Conference adopted a confession of faith and a book of discipline (1815). Remnants of the Otterbeins' "order of salvation" theology persisted in this document--notably in the article on the holy Scriptures, which affirms that the Bible "contains the true way to our salvation."[60] The Word of God in Scripture is still thought of as a logical order which corresponds to the temporal order whereby man comes to faith and which will lead the reader on through the whole order of salvation. The observance of the "outward means of grace" (the sacraments) is recommended, though the mode is not specified. This freedom of form reflects the old tradition of the great meetings in which three modes of baptism were used in the baptism of converts by the "unsectarian preachers" (e. g. , the Mennonite Boehm practiced pouring, Otterbein practiced sprinkling, and an unidentified "Virginia preacher" practiced immersion).

The transition from an evangelical fellowship united by a common concern for the ungodliness of the post-revolutionary era, to a denomination, was quite unintentional and gradual. It caught these German-Americans unaware, and Otterbein, to his death, regarded his office primarily as that of pastor in the Reformed Church. He was not an organizer of a new denomination, despite the fact he was recognized as such by nineteenth-century denominational historiography, and one almost senses that increasingly, after 1800, he was not a man of the hour. His tradition of Reformed pietistic orthodoxy--which appeared to his German brothers to be dying out amid the apostasy of the Enlightenment--fed a stream which became a torrent in nineteenth-century America. In the decades after Otterbein's death (1813), United Brethren and Evangelical itinerant preachers reached hundreds of thousands of German-Americans from Pennsylvania to the Pacific coast, established over fifty colleges and seminaries, and made their way to dozens of foreign lands--including the German homeland which they had left a century or more earlier. Thus it was that the Otterbeins' affirmation of "true Christianity," as the "knowledge of the truth for godliness," took shape in history.

Notes

1. James Tanis, Dutch Calvinistic Pietism in the Middle
   Colonies. (The Hague, 1967). See paragraph on
   book jacket.

2. These symbols were embodied in the "Formula of Unity"
   of the Netherlands, which included the standards of
   the Synod of Dort, of which the Heidelberg Catechism
   was a part.

3. The Pietists' name for conventicles was "churches within
   the church" ("ecclesiolae in ecclesia").

4. J. D. Otterbein, "Letter to the Counselor of the Consistory of Burbach," tr. H. B. Stehman; published in
   The Monthly Itinerant, IV, No. 9, (Harrisburg, 1880),
   65.

5. Herman Harmelink, III, Ecumenism and the Reformed
   Church. (Grand Rapids: Eerdmans, 1968), 10.

6. Charles H. Maxson, The Great Awakening in the Middle
   Colonies. (Chicago: University of Chicago Press,
   1920), 123ff.

7. Ibid., 124.

8. Ibid., 59.

9. Especially J. D. Otterbein, during his pastorate in the
   radical Pietist center of Wittgenstein-Berleburg.

10. Julius F. Sachse, The German Sectarians of Pennsyl-
    vania, 1742-1800. (Philadelphia, 1900), 441-3.

11. J. H. Dubbs, "Otterbein and the Reformed Church"
    (pamphlet reprint found in J. I. Good Collection, n. d.),
    111.

12. W. Stuart Cramer, History of the First Reformed Church
    of Lancaster, Pennsylvania, 1736-1904, I. (Lancaster:
    Wickersham, 1904), 31.

13. Otterbein's Rules of Order, quoted in A. W. Drury, Life
    of Otterbein. (Dayton: United Brethren Publishing
    House, 1898), 66.

14. Ibid.

15. See A. W. Drury, A History of the Church of the United Brethren in Christ. (Dayton: The Otterbein Press, 1924), 63ff.

16. Joseph Henry Dubbs, The Reformed Church in Pennsylvania. (Lancaster: New Era, 1902), 113.

17. Daniel Berger, History of the Church of the United Brethren in Christ. (Dayton: U. B. Publishing House, 1897), 49.

18. Ibid., 48.

19. Ibid.

20. Ibid.

21. Drury, Life, 49.

22. Such as Domine Pomp, who later accused Otterbein of schism and the teaching of heretical doctrines.

23. David Dunn, et al., A History of the Evangelical and Reformed Church. (Philadelphia: Christian Education Press, 1961), 46.

24. Gerhard Tersteegen (1697-1772) was a German Reformed mystic and hymn writer.

25. Johann Christian Stahlschmidt, A Pilgrimage by Sea and Land; or, Manifestations of the Divine Guidance and Providence in the Life of Johann Christian Stahlschmidt, tr. S. Jackson. (London: Hamilton, Adams, and Company, 1837), 242-6.

26. Hymns for the Use of the United Brethren in Christ (English). (Dayton: United Brethren Publishing House, 1856).

27. Drury, Life, 42.

28. Henry Spayth, History of the United Brethren in Christ. (Circleville, Ohio: United Brethren Publishing House, 1851), 23ff.

29. Especially Die Ernsthaffte Christen-Pflicht and Guldene Aepfel in Silbern Schalen.

30. Spayth, 29.

31. Ibid., 41.

32. Drury, History, 89.

33. "Zergliederten und erläuterten," "zum Nachdenken, zur Selbsterkentniss."--G. G. Otterbein, U. H. C., VII.

34. Christian Newcomes, Journal, tr. John Hildt. (Hagerstown, Maryland: G. W. Kapp, 1834), entry for June 3, 1797, 23.

35. The other pastor was H. W. Stoy--Dunn, 40.

36. Letter of the Classis of Amsterdam to the Coetus of the Reformed Churches in Pennsylvania, April 4, 1757; quoted in Arthur C. Core, Philip William Otterbein: Pastor, Ecumenist. (Dayton: The Board of Education of the Evangelical United Brethren Church, 1968), 21.

37. Dubbs, The Reformed Church in Pennsylvania, 243.

38. Ibid.

39. Drury, History, 92.

40. Unity Magazine, III, No. 1, quoted in Drury, Life, 93.

41. Dubbs, "Otterbein and the Reformed Church," 114.

42. Ibid.

43. Ibid., 115.

44. Drury, Life, 155.

45. Otterbein's Church Book of 1785, quoted in Core, 110. Drury notes that "now these meetings (1785) had more of the class meetings than belonged to the social meetings as first introduced by Otterbein at Tulpehocken." (Ibid., 125).

46. Ibid., 126.

47. Ibid., 127.

48. Drury, History, 127; and Core, 32ff.

49. Dubbs, History of the German Reformed Church, 310.

50. Asbury, Journal, March 28, 1775.

51. Paul Herman Ackert, "The Evangelical United Brethren Heritage," United Theological Seminary Bulletin, LIV (second quarter, 1955), 28; quoted in Core, 34.

52. E. Clark, ed., Journals and Letters of Francis Asbury. (Nashville: Abingdon, 1958), III, 478.

53. Minutes of the Annual and General Conferences of the United Brethren in Christ, 1800-1816, tr. and ed. A. W. Drury. (Dayton: United Brethren Publishing House, 1897), Minutes of September 25, 1800, 9ff.; cited in Core, 41.

54. Ibid.

55. Paul Eller, These Evangelical United Brethren. (Dayton: Otterbein Press, 1957), 41.

56. Asbury, Journal, August 2, 1803, II, 400.

57. Minutes of the Annual and General Conferences of the United Brethren in Christ, May 10, 1809; item 5, 24; quoted in Core, 35.

58. Newcomer, Journal, October 2, 1813, 219ff.

59. Ibid.

60. Disciplines of the United Brethren in Christ, Part I, 1814-41, ed. A. W. Drury. (Dayton: United Brethren Publishing House, 1895), 1-3.

Chapter 8

THE LEGACY OF THE OTTERBEINS

It is indeed a truism to proclaim, as bespeaking wisdom, that the church today is "in transition." The only sane
response might well be, "Has it ever been otherwise?" And
yet, the evidences of its current disarrangement, as reflected
in declining membership and financial statistics and in the
rise of a popular, somewhat anti-institutional revival of Christianity among youth, may be of a magnitude without parallel
in this century. At the 1971 United Methodist Conference on
Evangelism at New Orleans, Albert Outler ventured the prophetic suggestion that American Protestantism might well be
on the verge of a third Great Awakening--an Awakening that
will not come as another planned achievement of man but as
the doing of God. [1] In every true revival of prophetic religion
in the past, large-scale dislocation in the structures of the
church has been accompanied by an urgent need to reexamine
the roots of that faith which has given rise to those structures.

It has been our purpose here to bring to life that
germinal spirit which gave birth to the major institutional expression of German-American evangelicalism, which has now
become a constituent part of United Methodism. Unlike later
nineteenth-century revivalism, whose crusades tended to become the planned achievement of professional evangelists,
this spirit was at heart truly evangelical--that is, it came
as the surprising, unannounced visitation of God to men of
faith and humility. It came with such power that its effects
outlived the men who were its instruments. But this spirit
of evangelicalism is not what is unique about the Otterbeins'
message. After all, it was a spirit shared alike by Spener,
Wesley, Edwards, and a host of others. What was distinctive
in their message was that fusion of German and Dutch Pietism, with its practical, "experimental" point of view, with
the rich, evangelical themes of German Reformed theology,
as embodied in the Heidelberg Catechism. This fusion of the
"experiential" or the "experimental" with the sublime and the
transcendent helped distinguish the Otterbeins from that later

189

stream of American revivalism which sundered feeling from thought and will from intellect.

Although the name Otterbein has become recognized in United Methodism since the Evangelical United Brethren-Methodist merger of 1968, available studies have concentrated almost exclusively upon the later career of Philip W. Otterbein, the American brother. We have been cut off from the rich tradition of Reformed Pietistic theology in Germany in which he was nurtured and in which he continued to labor as a Reformed missionary among the Germans in Pennsylvania and Maryland. It was this tradition which shaped his understanding of God, man, and the world, and which guided his involvement in new forms of ministry in the Middle Colonies. To evaluate the legacy of the thought which informed his activities, it has been necessary to consider the written documents from the Herborn theological tradition of his day--the volumes of sermons and exegetical treatises on the Catechism by his German brothers, whose works he distributed in the Colonies.

A reading of these works makes clear that these men were among the leaders in the fight against the encroachments of an anti-Christian rationalism in the Reformed churches of eighteenth-century Germany. They pitted their resources against a tide of secularism, in which the historic ties of family and church were being superseded by an omnipotent state administered by "enlightened despots." The battle which Georg and Johann Otterbein were waging was taken to the American shores by a third brother, Philip W. who envisioned the prospect that here God would enact a "more glorious state of the church." It was predominantly through his labors that German Reformed Pietism became a constituent element in the rise of American Evangelical Protestantism, just as Puritanism was mediated by the New England divines, and Dutch Pietism by Frelinghuysen in New Jersey.

The theme of the Otterbeins, which has remained until now concealed in its eighteenth-century German idiom, reminds us that although we speak much about religion being concerned with the whole of life, these men were among the last for whom this was generally true. It is a theme which was anchored in the affirmation of the Heidelberg Catechism "That I, with body and soul, both in life and in death, am not my own, but belong to my faithful Saviour Jesus Christ ... "[2] and it was integrally related to a Pietistic view of Scripture and history. This is a heritage that survived in the credos of the early Evangelicals and United Brethren. It is a heritage that continues at times to sustain and at times to burden our lives, although the roots of this heritage in the theology of the Otterbeins have long been obscured from our consciousness.

What was the essence of their pietistic theology, which provided such a durable legacy for the mission and institutions of German-American evangelicalism? The intention of Otterbein's catechetical work was to present "true Christianity" as a "knowledge of the truth for godliness."[3] The heart of the matter was an intense experience of conversion that led to a concentrated effort to make the Christian life visible and an expectant conviction that God was preparing them to share in a "more glorious state of the church than ever has been."[4]

Their most distinguishing feature lay in the way the "experiential" or "experimental" was bound to the teaching of the Catechism. Its order, in three sections, "follows the going forth of the Holy Spirit" in the conversion of sinners.[5] Ursinus and the Reformed scholastics had regarded the Catechism as the basis for constructing an intricate system of dogma which would be the Protestant counterpart to the Summa theologica of St. Thomas Aquinas. The Otterbeins perceived that this evangelical symbol of the German Reformation was best suited not as a textbook for doctrines but as a practical guide for the Christian life. It was profoundly human in orientation, emphasizing the first person singular, and its point of view is set forth in the first question: "What is your only comfort in life and in death?" It presented a tripartite construction based on the recognition of one's sin and guilt, the recognition of one's redemption and freedom, and the recognition of one's gratitude and obedience. This was the order which the Otterbeins perceived as following the "going forth" of the Spirit in the work of conversion. For them, it meant that the Christian life was not to be judged exclusively on the grounds of right doctrine but more as a course of spiritual exercises or steps whose completion, under God's grace, is necessary for the new birth to reach fruition.

Every individual is a pilgrim at some stage in this order of salvation. This helps to explain the Otterbeins' tireless efforts in their catechetical writings to adapt this order to the particular level of each individual, whether he be young

or old, simple or erudite. The import of the historic meetings of Philip W. Otterbein with the unlettered German farm-
ers of colonial Pennsylvania can only be understood by recog-
nizing this overarching concern which impelled him. Every
pilgrim had to know what it meant to be broken and healed
by God's judging, redeeming love. He had to know how deep,
subtle, and pervasive is sin, and this had to be existential
and not merely cognitive knowledge for it to be effectual.
He also had to experience the wondrous depths of grace, and
all his self-searching and rigorous discipline were henceforth
to be rooted there. This order contained in the Catechism
is not, as Karl Barth has suggested, the "one indivisible act
of faith which lies beyond our control."[6] To Georg Otterbein, it refers to the experience of the steps of the moral
life, for "the order which our Catechism has chosen is in accordance with the movement of thought of our souls."[7] The
Otterbeins saw through the weakness of orthodox catechization: instruction, they felt, should appeal not only to the understanding but also to the deeper levels of the human psyche,
which involve the reordering of the will and the entire life.

     The theme was expressed in one all-embracing con-
cept, the idea of covenant. For the Otterbeins, the covenant
was not one idea among others. It was the basic motif which
pervaded the whole of their lives and determined their total
understanding and feeling for existence. As with the Puritans,[8] it controlled their outlook on marriage, church, and
society. It conveyed the sense of the intimate, personal relationship of God to man and man to man that had been lost
in the abstract, deductive methodology employed by the scholastic interpreters of the Catechism. The covenant motif
was the basic model with which the Otterbeins helped to displace the older hierarchical pattern of family, church, and
social order, though it was itself destined to be displaced by
the mechanical pattern in the course of the scientific revolu-
tions of the nineteenth century. When Johann Otterbein im-
plored the condemned convict with whom he was counseling
to close with Christ, it was done from the conviction rooted
in Scripture and Catechism that God was a promise keeper,
and that what distinguished man was his ability to commit
himself. He sensed that the doctrines of the Catechism had
for so long proved ineffectual in producing reformation of
life in Germany because their promises had remained concealed as external laws imposed by a hierarchical state
church system. If the whole of life is to be reordered by
these promises, the order of salvation must be internalized
by the oath of fealty so that duties to God and man might be

freely accepted. The influence of this covenant motif meant
that the decision of faith was a work of grace and not a human, rational possibility, as in the case of many eighteenth-
century Arminians. It has become an important aspect of
the Otterbeins' legacy to American Protestantism, though all
too often covenantal promise has given way to contractual
convenience and the notion that religious organizations are
to be joined to achieve personal or social respectability.

If this pilgrimage of faith which the Otterbeins
preached is to have any content and purpose for those of us
who would stand in their spiritual lineage, we must inquire
about the identity of the pilgrim and also about his intended
destiny. Here we find them reflecting upon the nature of
history with a seriousness that is not paralleled in the subsequent annals of American denominationalism.

When the pilgrim passes from his misery to the
promise of redemption, he is empowered to live in hope of
the fulfillment of that promise, which will not come merely
as his private, invisible reward in heaven but as the approaching "more glorious state of the church" on earth. In
short, the final stage in the pilgrimage of faith is as fully
rooted in history as are the others. The pilgrim finds his
identity as a member of the new fellowship of regenerate
Christians which is supplanting the old fallen order of human
society. The eschatological thinking which was manifested in
their interest in the millenial doctrine--a subject that had
been banned by all Roman and Protestant church traditions
in their day--had also undergirded the dynamism within their
portrayal of the "way of salvation." The Incarnation, notes
Philip W. Otterbein, represents Christ's personal attack upon
the "kingdom of Satan" over mankind, whose rule is the
"judgment of divine abandonment" of man because of sin. [9]
His work had only launched the initial attack by reconciling
God to man; He now reconciles us individually to God by
creating in us lives of holiness. This means that the transformation of man in Christ must withstand empirical description if it is to be at all valid.

In making "practice" the supreme test of faith, Otterbein was reflecting the conviction of eighteenth-century man
that the folly of polemical strife in past centuries was to be
attributed to the fact that men had only a theoretical understanding of the Christian credos. Their lives had been rendered helpless by dialectical subtlety, which had robbed
truths of faith of their true content and changed them into

unfruitful theologizing.

The Otterbeins expressed the idea of the spiritual rebirth in terms of the distinction between the visible and the
invisible. The death of the old man in repentance, which is
the inward work of the Spirit, finds its outward expression
in the penitential struggle of the penitent, and the moment of
rebirth finds its outward expression in the peace and joy of
the believer. In a like manner, the fellowship of the regenerate tends toward the invisible church by emphasizing the
kingdom which is growing within the pilgrims, which transcends the historical institutions of the passing age and is universal and spiritual. It is the invisible church amid the actual church. Yet, to the extent that the regenerate become
recognized by outward marks of holy living, the emphasis on
the invisible becomes the new definition of the visible, historical church of the dawning age of the kingdom. As members of the new age, true believers are visible to one another, but not to the world. [10] They are identified as those
who are fit to partake of the Lord's Supper as the sign and
seal of their rebirth, and their conventicles become the new
definition of the visible church in the United Brethren movement.

Their view of history pressing toward a glorious consummation is also a part of the legacy which has passed
deeply into our American ethos in an altered fashion, for the
old sense of divine calling and mission was to become thoroughly fused with a dynamic nationalism. The profoundly
moral tended to become the moralistic, and the more glorious state of the church and of the nation tended to become
the planned achievement of men rather than the doing of God.
For the Otterbeins, the progress of history was always submitted to the divine purpose, and the vast increase in human
knowledge during the Enlightenment was to be only a prologue
to "the promised growth in the knowledge of the ... godly
Word ... in the last times. "[11] Without the latter, human
knowledge would serve only to augment arrogant human pride.
They describe this condition as the time preceding the last
age, which they call the age of the Antichrist, the man of
sin, when true Christians are persecuted. It is the time
when they are to make their calling and election sure.

The question now is: What stance ought we to assume
toward this heritage? In what direction do we desire this
tradition to be turned? Much emphasis has recently been
given to the "catholicity" of Philip W. Otterbein, in view of

his association with non-Reformed in the United Brethren
movement and with the leaders of early American Methodism,
while retaining his loyalty to the Reformed Church. [12] Although this emphasis represents a healthy reaction against the
tendency of nineteenth-century denominational historians to
emphasize Otterbein's deviation from the Reformed tradition
and to portray him as the organizer of a new denomination,
care should be taken to distinguish between different types of
catholicity in Christian tradition. When Otterbein spoke of
the higher unity in which believers could share, he did not
have in mind the Roman Catholic ideal of a universal, divine-
human community, by analogy with the God-man. [13] He affirmed with the Catechism that all believers "as members of
Christ have part in Him" (Question 55), but for Otterbein,
catholicity finds its point of reference in the ethos of his
age. The propensity to form voluntary associations arose at
the time when the old obligatory institutions, including the
church, were losing authority as the expression of community.
In Otterbein's conventicles within the Reformed Church or in
the new United Brethren movement, members of different
families, classes, congregations, or even denominations
could become brethren, as opposed to the anonymous masses
of the unregenerate. It was a place to wait, and to induce
others to join, until the better future when their triumphant
Lord would bring human history to an end. It was the institutional norm for those who were on a pilgrimage of faith,
according to the "order of salvation" which the Catechism
provided.

        This is the conceptual mode in which the catholicity
of Philip W. Otterbein is to be evaluated. It was the vision
of a latter-day Pietist who sought to provide for those who
displayed a "knowledge of the truth for godliness. " It was
a quest which, if duly heeded, might provide direction and
insight in the current stirring of evangelical interest within
and without the existing structures of the church.

<h3 style="text-align:center">Notes</h3>

1.   See Newman Cryer, "Where Are We in Evangelism? "
        Together, XV, (April, 1971), 13-21; "Delegates Share
        Ideas on Evangelism, " The Interpreter, XV (March,
        1971), 46 (an unsigned magazine article); Russell
        Chandler, "Shattering Stereotypes, " Christianity To-
        day, XV, (January 29, 1971). Outler's Denman lec-
        tures at the New Orleans conference have now been

published under the title Evangelism in the Wesleyan Spirit. (Nashville: Tidings, 1971).

2. Question 1, The Heidelberg Catechism.

3. Georg Gottfried Otterbein, Predigten über den Heidelbergischen Katechismus, I. (Duisburg, 1800), VII.

4. Philip Wilhelm Otterbein, "Letter Concerning the Millenium," printed in Core, Philip William Otterbein: Pastor, Ecumenist, 102ff.

5. Georg Gottfried Otterbein, Predigten..., I, 8.

6. Karl Barth, The Heidelberg Catechism for Today. (Richmond, Virginia, 1964), 28ff.

7. Georg Gottfried Otterbein, Predigten..., I, 77.

8. See Gordon Harland, "American Protestantism: Its Genius and its Problem," The Drew Gateway, XXXIV, (Winter, 1964), 74.

9. Philip Wilhelm Otterbein, "The Salvation-Bringing Incarnation and Glorious Victory of Jesus Christ over the Devil and Death," translated by Erhart Lang and printed in Core, Philip William Otterbein: Pastor, Ecumenist, 81.

10. Whereas, in the Reformers (notably Luther), true believers are not visible even to each other; rather, one believes, as a believer, in their presence where the marks of the true church are present. See Martin Luther, Lectures on Galatians (1535).

11. The Otterbeins derived this theme from Friedrich Lampe, whose Geheimnis des Gnadenbundes they read at Herborn. See Jurgen Moltmann, Zeitschrift für Kirchengeschichte, 71, (1960), 128.

12. See Core on the "active Ecumenism" of Otterbein, 28-37.

13. See Thomas Aquinas, Summa theologica, 2a-2ae, 1-10; translated in Thomas Gilby, (ed.), St. Thomas Aquinas: Theological Texts. (London: Oxford, 1955), 345ff.

BIBLIOGRAPHY

1. Texts and Translations

Arndt, Johann. True Christianity. Philadelphia: Smith, English and Company, 1869.

Calvin, John. Calvin's New Testament Commentaries. 12 vols. Edited by D. W. and T. F. Torrance. Grand Rapids, Michigan: Eerdmans, 1959-

————. Commentaries on the Old Testament. 30 vols. Edinburgh: Calvin Translation Society, 1845-1855.

————. Institutes of the Christian Religion. Edited by J. T. McNeill, translated by F. L. Battles. Volumes XX and XXI of the Library of Christian Classics. Philadelphia: Westminster, 1960.

Cocceius, Johann. Summa Doctrinae de Foedere et Testamento Dei. Edited by Alexander Schweizer. Die Glaubenslehre der Evangelisch-Reformierten Kirche Dargestellt und aus den Quellen Belegt. Zürich: Orell, Füssli und Comp., 1844.

Lampe, Friedrich Adolph. Geheimnis des Gnadenbundes. 6 vols. Bremen: Verlegts Nathanael Saurmann, 1748.

————. Milch der Wahrheit nach Anleitung des Heidelberger Katechismus zu Nutzen der lernbegierigen Jugend aufgesetzt ... Herzfeld and Frankfurt, 1746.

Luther, Martin. D. Martin Luthers Werke: Dictata Super Psalterium. Weimar: Böhlau, 1885, 1886.

Newcomer, Christian. Journal. Translated by John Hildt. Hagerstown, Maryland: F. G. W. Kapp, 1834.

Otterbein, Georg Gottfried. Der Geist des wahren Christenthums nach Paulus: eine Reihe praktischer Erklärungen des Zwölften Kapitels des Briefes an die Römer;

ein Erbauungsbuch. Erste Halfte. Frankfurt and
Leipzig: F. A. Jülicher, 1792.

_____. Das Leben Henoch's oder die Art und Weise mit
Gott zu wandeln, von dem Englischen Gottesgelehrten
Joseph. Verdeutsch ... herausgegebin von Georg
Gottfried Otterbein. Duisburg: Helwing, 1778.

_____. Lesebuch für deutsche Schulkinder; herausgegeben
von Georg Gottfried Otterbein; mit Veränderungen und
Zusätzen, zum Gebrauch Nor-Amerikanischer Schulen.
Philadelphia: Carl Cist, 1795.

_____. Predigten über den Heidelbergischen Katechismus.
2 vols. Duisburg: Helwing, 1800; (and) Lemgo:
Meyer, 1803.

_____. Unterweisung in der Christlichen Religion nach
dem Heidelbergischen Catechismus ... Zweyte Auflage.
Frankfurt: Jülicher, n. d. (1778?).

Otterbein, Johann Daniel. Dissertatio Sacra II, ad pium S.
Coenae usum invitatoria, Ministerio Gratiae, Minis-
trorumque sub N. T. vera indole, ad locum illustrem
II. Cor. VI. 3-11. Th. Stad. Schoenbaco-Nassovius,
Resp., 1773.

_____. Jesus und die Kraft seines Bluts Ganz besonders
Verherrlichet an Johann Jost Weygand einem armen
Sünder, der einen Mord begangen; und den 21ten Octo-
ber, 1785. auf der Richtstätte vor Berlenburg, mit
dem Schwerd vom Leben zum Tod gebracht worden.
Lancaster: Neuen Buchdruckerey, 1790.

Otterbein, Philip Wilhelm. Die Heilbrigende Menschwerdung
und Der Herliche Sieg Jesu Christi Deu Teufel Und
Tod. Edited by Arthur C. Core and translated by
Ehrhart Lang. Philip William Otterbein: Pastor,
Ecumenist. Dayton: Otterbein Press, 1968.

_____. Letters of 1753-1812 and miscellaneous items.
Edited by Arthur C. Core. Philip William Otterbein:
Pastor, Ecumenist. Dayton: Otterbein Press, 1968.

Rambach, Johann Jakob. Christus in Mose, oder Einhundert
Betractungen über die vornehmsten Weissagungen u.
Vorbilder auf Christum in den funf Büchern Moses.

Cleveland: Buchdruckerei des Evangelische Gemein-
schaft, 1886.

Stahlschmidt, Johann Christian. A Pilgrimage by Sea and
Land; or Manifestations of the Divine Guidance and
Providence in the life of Johann Christian Stahlschmidt.
Translated by Samuel Jackson. London: Hamilton,
Adams, and Company, 1837.

Tersteegen, Gerhard. Letters and Writings. Translated by
Samuel Jackson. London: Hamilton, Adams, and
Company, 1837.

Ursinus, Zacharias. Commentary on the Heidelberg Catechism. Translated by G. W. Williard. Columbus,
Ohio: Scott and Bascom, 1852.

Vitringa, Campegius. Aphorismi, quibus Fundamenta Theol.
Comprehenduntur. Edited by Alexander Schweizer.
Die Glaubenslehre der Evangelisch-Reformierten Kirche
Dargestellt und aus den Quellen Belegt. Zürich:
Orell, Füssli, und andere, 1844.

Voetius, Gisbert. Selectae Disputationes Theologicae. Edited
and translated by John W. Beardslee, III. New York:
Oxford University Press, 1965.

2. Critical Works

Albright, Raymond. A History of the Evangelical Church.
Harrisburg: Evangelical Press, 1956.

Althaus, Paul. Die Principien der deutschen reformierten
Dogmatik im Zeitalter der aristotelischen Scholastik.
Darmstadt: Wissenschaftliche Buchgesellschaft, 1967.

Barth, Karl. Church Dogmatics. Edited and translated by
G. W. Bromiley. 4 vols. Edinburgh: T. & T.
Clark, 1956-.

_____. The Heidelberg Catechism for Today. Translated
by Shirley C. Guthrie, Jr. Richmond, Virginia: John
Knox Press, 1964.

_____. Die Protestantische Theologie im 19 Jahrhundert.
Zürich: Evangelischer Verlag A. G. Zollikon, 1947.

_____. Protestant Theology from Rousseau to Ritschl.
Edited and translated by Brian Cozens. New York:
Harper and Row, 1959.

Beardslee, John W., III. Theological Developments at Geneva
under Francis and Jean-Alphonse Turretin (1648-1737).
Ph. D. Dissertation, Yale University, 1956.

Bemesderfer, James O. Pietism and its Influence upon the
Evangelical United Brethren Church. Harrisburg:
Printed at the Evangelical Press, 1966.

Berger, Daniel. History of the Church of the United Brethren in Christ. Dayton: United Brethren Publishing
House, 1906.

Bizer, Ernst. "Die reformierte Orthodoxie und der Carte-
sianismus," Zeitschrift für Theologie und Kirche, 55,
306-371.

Bohatec, Joseph. Die cartesianische Scholastik in der Philosophie und reformierten Dogmatik des 17. Jahrhunderts. I Teil. Leipzig: A. Deichert'sche Verlags-
buchhandlung.

Brothers Lamech and Agrippa. Chronicon Ephratense.
Translated by J. Max Harck. Lancaster, Pennsylvania: S. H. Zahm Company, 1889.

Brown, Dale. The Problem of Subjectivism in Pietism: A
Redefinition with Special Reference to Philip Jakob
Spener and August Hermann Francke. Ph. D. Disser-
tation, Northwestern University, 1962.

Brumbaugh, Martin Grove. A History of the German Baptist
Brethren in Europe and America. Mount Morris,
Illinois: Brethren Publishing House, 1899.

Cherry, Conrad. The Theology of Jonathan Edwards: A Reappraisal. Garden City, New York: Doubleday and
Company, 1966.

Core, Arthur C. Philip William Otterbein: Pastor Ecumenist.
Dayton: The Board of Education of the Evangelical
United Brethren Church, 1968.

Cragg, G. R. The Church and the Age of Reason, 1648-1789.

Harmondsworth, England: Penguin Books, 1966.

Cramer, W. Stuart. History of the First Reformed Church.
Lancaster, Pennsylvania: Wickersham, 1904.

Cremer, H. "Samuel Collenbusch," The New Schaff-Herzog
Religious Encyclopedia, 3, 160ff.

Cuno, J. W. "Johann Daniel Otterbein, weiland Inspector in
Berleburg," Reformirtes Wochenblatt. 26-31 (26
Juni. -31 Juli, 1874), 161-246.

Dillenberger, John. Protestant Thought and Natural Science.
New York: Doubleday, 1960.

_____ and Welch, Claude. Protestant Christianity. New
York: Scribners, 1954.

Discipline of the Evangelical United Brethren Church. Harrisburg and Dayton: The Board of Publication, 1959.

The Doctrines and Discipline of the Evangelical Association.
Cleveland: The Board of Publication, 1905.

Drury, A. W. A History of the Church of the United Brethren in Christ. Dayton: The Otterbein Press, 1924.

_____. Life of Otterbein. Dayton: United Brethren Pub-
lishing House, 1898.

Dubbs, Joseph Henry. "Otterbein and the Reformed Church."
(Pamphlet reprint found in Good Collection, n. d.)

_____. The Reformed Church in Pennsylvania. Lancaster,
Pennsylvania: The New Era Publishing Company, 1902.

Dunn, David, et al. A History of the Evangelical and Reformed Church. Philadelphia: Christian Education
Press, 1961.

Eller, Paul. These Evangelical United Brethren. Dayton:
Otterbein Press, 1957.

Empie, Paul C. and McCord, James, editors. Marburg Revisited. Minneapolis: Augsburg, 1966.

Ensign, Chauncey David. Radical German Pietism, c. 1675-

1750. Ph. D. Dissertation, Boston University, 1955.

Evjen, John O. "Luther's Ideas Concerning Polity," Lutheran Church Review, XIV (1926), 207-235; XV (1927), 339-367.

Gausted, Edwin Scott. The Great Awakening in New England. New York: Harper and Brothers, 1957.

Goebel, Max. Geschichte des christliche Lebens in der rheinisch-westphalischen evangelischen Kirche. 3 vols. Coblenz, 1852-1862.

Good, James. The Heidelberg Catechism in its Newest Light. Philadelphia: Publication and Sunday School Board of the Reformed Church in the United States, 1914.

_____. History of the Reformed Church in the United States, 1752-1792. Reading: Daniel Miller, 1899.

_____. History of the Reformed Church of Germany, 1620-1890. Reading: Daniel Miller, 1894.

Graffmann, Heinrich. "Erklärung des Heidelberger Katechismus in Predigt und Unterricht des 16. bis 18. Jahrhunderts," in Handbuch zum Heidelberger Katechismus. Herausgegeben von Lothar Coenen. Duisburg-Ruhrort: Joh. Brendow u. Sohn, 1963.

_____. "Der Unterricht nach dem Heidelberger Katechismus im Zeitalter der Orthodoxie und des Pietismus mit besonderem Blick auf Rheinland und Westfalen," in Monatshefte für evangelische Kirchengeschichte des Rheinlands. IX (1960).

Gustagson, James M. Christ and the Moral Life. New York: Harper and Row, 1968.

Hardon, John A., S. J. The Protestant Churches of America. Westminster, Maryland: Newman Press, 1966.

Hazard, Paul. European Thought in the Eighteenth Century. New Haven: Yale University Press, 1954.

Heppe, Heinrich. Die Dogmatik der evangelisch-reformierten Kirche. Darmstadt: Neukirchener Verlag, 1958.

_____. Geschichte des Pietismus und der Mystik in der reformierten Kirche. Leiden: Brill, 1879.

_____. Reformed Dogmatics Set Out and Illustrated from the Sources. London: George Allen and Unwin, 1950.

"Herborn Pamphlets." (a bound collection of miscellaneous pamphlets on Herborn found in the Good collection).

Hildebrandt, Franz. Melanchthon: Alien or Ally? Cambridge: The University Press, 1946.

Hinke, William J. Ministers of the German Reformed Congregations in Pennsylvania and Other Colonies in the Eighteenth Century. Lancaster, Pennsylvania: Ridisill and Company, 1951.

Hirsch, Emanuel. Geschichte der neuen evangelischen Theologie, Band III. "Die Neuen philosophischen und theologischen Anfänge in Deutschland." Gütersloh: C. Bertelmanns Verlag, 1952.

Hollweg, Walter. Neue Untersuchungen zur Geschichte und Lehre des Heidelberger Katechismus. Erste Folge. Lemgo: Neukirchener Verlag, 1961.

_____. Neue Untersuchung zur Geschichte und Lehre des Heidelberger Katechismus. Zweite Folge. Lemgo: Neukirchener Verlag, 1968.

Hurst, John F. History of Rationalism. New York: Phillips and Hunt, 1865.

Kidd, B. J., editor. Documents Illustrative of the Continental Reformation. Oxford: Clarendon Press, 1911.

Koontz, Paul Rodes and Roush, Walter Edwin. The Bishops of the Church of the United Brethren in Christ. Dayton: Otterbein Press, 1950.

Lawrence, John. History of the United Brethren Church. Dayton: United Brethren Printing Establishment, 1868.

Lechner, C. S. Genealogie Otterbein. Leiden: Brill, 1927.

McCoy, Charles S. The Covenant Theology of Johannes Cocceius. Ph.D. Dissertation, Yale University, 1957.

McNeill, John T. The History and Character of Calvinism.
New York: Oxford University Press, 1954.

Manschreck, Clyde L. Melanchthon: The Quiet Reformer.
New York: Oxford University Press, 1958.

Manuel, Frank. Shapes of Philosophical History. New York:
Scribners, 1961.

Martin, James P. The Last Judgment in Protestant Theology
from Orthodoxy to Ritschl. Grand Rapids, Michigan:
William B. Eerdmans, 1963.

Maurer, H. "History of the Herborn High School," (found in
Good Collection--pamphlet, n. d.).

Maxson, Charles Hartshorn. The Great Awakening in the
Middle Colonies. Chicago: The University of Chicago
Press, 1920.

Möller, Grete. "Föderalismus und Geschichtsbetrachtung im
XVII und XVIII Jahrhundert," in Zeitschrift für
Kirchengeschichte, L (1931), 292-440.

Moltmann, Jürgen. "Jacob Brocard als Vorläufer der Reich-
Gottes-Theologie und der symbolisch-prophetischen
Schriftauslegung," in Zeitschrift für Kirchengeschichte,
71 (1960), 110-129.

_____. "Zur Bedeutung des Petrus Ramus für Philosophie
und Theologie im Calvinismus," in Zeitschrift für
Kirchengeschichte, 68 (1957), 295-318.

Müller, E. F. Karl. Die Bekenntnisschriften der Reformierten Kirche. Leipzig: A. Deichert'sche Verlagsbuch-
landlung, 1903.

_____. "Lampe," in The New Schaff-Herzog Religious En-
cyclopedia, VI (1910), 405.

Mutch, V. E. "Otterbein and his Lesebuch," in Religious
Telescope, CXII: No. 27 (July 3, 1946).

Nicholson, Harold. The Age of Reason. New York: Scribners, 1961.

Oak, D. "Centennial Notes on Otterbein," in Religious Telescope, XL (Dec. 23, 30, May 27, June 3, 10, 17, July 1, 8, 22, 29, and August 5, 1874).

Ong, Walter J. Ramus, Method, and the Decay of Dialogue. Cambridge, Massachusetts: Harvard University Press, 1958.

Ott, Heinrich. Theology and Preaching. Translated by Harold Knight. Philadelphia: Westminster, 1961.

Pelikan, Jaroslav. From Luther to Kierkegaard. St. Louis: Concordia, 1950.

Pinson, Koppel S. Pietism as a Factor in the Rise of German Nationalism. New York: Columbia University Press, 1934.

Richardson, Alan. A Theological Word Book of the Bible. New York: Macmillan, 1962.

Ritschl, Albrecht. Geschichte des Pietismus. I. Bonn: Adolph Marcus, 1880.

Sachse, Julius Friedrich. German Pietists of Pennsylvania. Philadelphia: P. C. Stockhausen and Company, 1895.

_____. The German Sectarians of Pennsylvania, 1708-1742. Philadelphia: P. C. Stockhausen and Company, 1899.

Schaff, Philip. The Creeds of Christendom. III. Grand Rapids, Michigan: Baker Book House, 1966.

Scharlemann, Robert. Aquinas and Gerhard. New Haven: Yale University Press, 1964.

Schrenk, Gottlob. Gottesreich und Bund im alteren Protestantismus. Gütersloh: C. Bertelsmann, 1923.

Schwab, Ralph Kendall. The History of the Doctrine of Christian Perfection in the Evangelical Association. Menasha, Wisconsin: Banta Publishing Company, 1922.

Snijders, Gerrit. Friedrich Adolph Lampe. Harderwijk: Drukkerij Flevo v. h. Gebr. Mooij, 1954.

Spayth, Henry. History of the United Brethren in Christ.

Circleville, Ohio: United Brethren Publishing House, 1851.

Steck, K. G., et al. Um evangelische Einheit. Herborn: Oranien Verlag, 1967.

Steitz, Heinrich. Geschichte der evangelischen Kirche in Hessen und Nassau. 3 vols. Marburg: Verlag Trautvetter u. Fischer Nachf., 1961-1963.

Steubing, Johann. Geschichte der Hohen Schule Herborn. Hadamar, 1823.

_____. Kirchen und Reformations-Geschichte der Oranien-Nassauischen Lande. Hadamar, 1804.

Stoeffler, F. Ernest. The Rise of Evangelical Pietism. Leiden: Brill, 1965.

Tanis, James. Dutch Calvinistic Pietism in the Middle Colonies. The Hague: Martinus Nijhoff, 1967.

_____. "The Heidelberg Catechism in the Hands of the Calvinistic Pietists," unpublished article.

Tappert, Theodore. Introduction to Pia Desideria (Spener). Philadelphia: Fortress Press, 1964.

Thompson, Bard, et al. Essays on the Heidelberg Catechism. Philadelphia and Boston: United Church Press, 1963.

_____, translator. "The Palatinate Liturgy," in Theology and Life, 6/1 (Spring, 1963), 49-67.

Tonkin, John. The Protestant Reformation and the Institutional Church. Ph.D. Dissertation, Drew University, 1968.

Torrance, T. F. Kingdom and Church. Edinburgh: Oliver and Boyd, 1956.

Trinterud, Leonard John. "The Origins of Puritanism," Church History, XX (1951), 37-57.

Troeltsch, Ernst. The Social Teaching of the Christian Churches. (Translated by Olive Wyon.) New York: Harper, 1960.

_____. Vernunft und Offenbarung bei Gerhard und
Melanchthon. Göttingen, 1891.

Van Buren, Paul. Christ in our Place. Grand Rapids,
Michigan: Eerdmans, 1957.

Weber, Emil. Reformation, Orthodoxie, und Rationalismus.
I. 2 Darmstadt: Wissenschaftliche Buchgeselischaft,
1966.

Wendel, Francois. Calvin. (Translated by Philip Mairet.)
New York: Harper and Row, 1964.

White, R. J. Europe in the Eighteenth Century. New York:
St. Martin's Press, 1965.

Wiebe, Orlando H. Johann Arndt: Precursor of Pietism.
Ph. D. Dissertation, State University of Iowa, 1965.

Williams, George H. The Radical Reformation. Philadelphia:
Westminster, 1962.

Wundt, Max. Die Deutsche Schulmetaphysik des 17. Jahrhunderts. Tübingen: J. C. B. Mohr, 1939.

INDEX

Alsted, Jakob 15
Anabaptism 134f., 157
Apostles' Creed 118
Aquinas, St. Thomas 24, 191
Aristotle 20, 23f., 44f., 53f., 56, 118
Arndt, Johann 45, 103, 174
Asbury, Francis 172, 182
Augsburg Confession 3ff.

Baltimore 166, 180-184
baptism 138
Barth, Karl ix, 135, 192
Berger, Daniel 172
Berleburg Bible 97, 169
Beza, Theodore 24, 27, 69, 112
"big meetings" 140, 176f.
Boehm, John Philip 167
Boehm, Martin 176, 183f.
Boehme, Jacob 97
Bohatec, J. 53
Bremen 65ff., 75
Bruchhausen, Heilmann 2

Calvin, John ix, 3f., 7, 11f., 16, 24ff., 69f., 70, 73, 75f., 109ff., 117, 119, 128, 131f., 136f., 141, 151-153, 159
Cartesianism 48, 53, 57
Christ, Jesus (doctrine of) 109, 111f., 116, 119f., 126, 129, 143, 157-160, 177
Church, The 75, 128-143
Church of the United Breth-

ren in Christ x, xi, 94, 126, 128, 135, 140, 175-184, 194
Clauberg, Johann 54f.
Cocceius, Johannes 30, 46, 48ff., 56, 59f., 68, 76, 98, 103, 118, 128, 142
Collenbusch, Samuel 95
Communio sanctorum 136
covenant of grace 48, 53, 67f., 110, 116, 118
creation 118
"Crypto-Calvinism" 4, 6, 23
Cuno, F. 2

de fijnen 60
Denck, Hans 117
Descartes, Rene 53
Dieterici, Wilhelm 77
Dillenburg x, 2f., 5, 7, 10, 15
discipline 139
Donatism 11
d'Outrein 72
Drury, A. W. 174, 181

Edwards, Jonathan 142
Enlightenment 95-104, 157, 166
Enoch 159
Ephrata, Pa. 170f., 173, 177f.
Evangelical Association, The 128
Evangelical United Brethren Church, The 190

faith 71f., 117, and practice 152-160
Fall, The 114f.
Formula of Concord, The 6, 9
Formula of Unity, The 171
Franck, Sebastian 52
Franeker 65, 69
Franklin, Benjamin 169
Frederick III, the "Pious" 4, 8
Frelinghuysen, Theodore x, 166, 174

Gabriel, Petrus 5
Galileo 44
Geeting, George Adam 178f.
Gelassenheit 117
Geneva 109
Goebel, Max 64
Graffmann, Heinrich 17, 50

Hasenkamp, J. G. 95
Heidelberg 4, 8, 15, 23, 25, 27
Heidelberg Catechism ix, x, xi, 3-28, 44, 46-61, 67, 69-77, 94-104, 109-120, 126-140, 151-160, 166-171, 174, 176-184, 189, 190ff.
Heilsordnung 51, 70, 76, 110, 129, 142, 160
Helvetic Consensus Formula 109
Heppe, Heinrich 8
Herborn ix, 2, 13ff., 23, 26, 28, 30, 48, 54-60, 76f., 94, 98-109, 128
Hollweg, Walter 4, 8, 22
Holy Spirit 131, 136, 166, 174
Horch, Heinrich 77

image of God 118, 155

Joachim of Floris 51
Johann VI 2f., 3, 5ff., 13ff., 54, 58f.
Joris, David 52

Kant, Immanuel 96
Kingdom of Christ, The 65f., 128-143, 157
Koelman, J. 60

Labadie, Jean de 61
Lampe, Friedrich A. 61, 64-77, 98f., 110, 126, 128, 174
Lancaster, Pa. 169-173, 179
Leibniz, Gottfried W. von 53
Lentulus, Cyriscus 55
Lodensteyn, Jodocus von 45, 60f.
Lord's Supper, The 138, 170f.
Louis XIV 60
love 155, 157
Ludwig, The Elector 6
Luther, Martin 3, 12, 21, 72, 135, 152

McCoy, Charles S. 49
Marck, Johannes à 127
Martinius, M. 15, 48, 54
Melanchthon, Philip 2ff., 15, 18f., 21, 44f., 190
Mennonites 177
Methodism xi, 137, 182, 189f.
Millenium, The 75, 126f., 141ff.
Miller, Perry 23
Moltmann, Jergen 23, 51
Moravians 97, 169, 171

Nassau x, 2f., 7ff., 13, 59, 77, 95, 98
Nassau Church Order 8f., 11ff.
Nassau Confession 9, 14
natural theology 54, 100ff.,

natural theology (cont.) 119
Newcomer, Christian 178
Newton, Isaac 53

Olevianus, Caspar 4, 7f.,
16, 22f., 48, 56, 59,
76, 94f.
Ong, Walter 24
Otterbein, Georg Gottfried
ix, 95f., 98f., 99-104,
110-120, 126, 136, 142,
151, 155, 157, 159, 160,
179f., 190
Otterbein, Johann Daniel
(Senior) x, 95
Otterbein, Johann Daniel
(Junior) ix, xi, 97, 153-
155, 158-160, 167, 179,
190
Otterbein, Philip Wilhelm x,
xi, 94, 112f., 126-132,
135, 140-143, 157, 166-
184, 190, 192f., 195
Outler, Albert 189

Palatinate, The 4f., 15, 60,
167
Palatinate Church Order 7f.,
57, 75
Peace of Westphalia 58
Pelikan, Jaroslav ix
perfection 73, 156
Pipe Creek Conferences, The
182
Piscator, Johannes 12, 15f.,
23, 26, 56
"practical syllogism" 151,
153
"precision" 46f.
predestination 49, 70, 112f.
Presbyterians 168, 173f.
Providence 118f.

radical Pietism 97
Rambach, J. J. 128f.

Ramus, Peter 23-27, 48,
56f.
rationalism 45, 53f., 60, 114
Romans, The Epistle to the
158-160
Ruysbroeck, Jan van 98

sacraments 137
sanctification 73, Chapter VI
Schlatter, Michael 168
Schleiermacher, Friedrich ix
Scholasticism Chapter I, B.,
45, 114
Schrenk, Gottlob 51, 75
Schwope, Benedict 180
Scripture, use of 44, 49ff.,
56, 61, 67f., 99, 101, 103f.,
128f., 130
separation (from the world)
61, 64, 135, 156
sin 69, 95f., 115, 153
Spener, Philip Jakob 45, 58f.,
72
Stähelin, Christoph 98
Stahlschmidt, J. C. 174
Steitz, Heinrich 2
Steubing, H. 98
Synod of Dort, The 45, 61

Taffin, Jean de 60
Teelink 60, 76
Tersteegen, G. 174
Thirty Years' War 58, 60
Trinity 118
Troeltsch, Ernst 19
Tulpehocken, Pa. 173-175
Turretin, Francis 109

Udemans, Gottfried 60, 76
Untereyck, Theodore 45, 61,
68, 77
Ursinus, Zacharias 4, 11,
17-24, 27, 44, 51, 100
Utrecht 66

211

Van Til, Solomon   50, 56
Villiers, Pierre L. de   5
Vitringa, Campegius   62f.,
  65, 67, 75, 77, 128, 142
Voetius, Gisbert   30, 45f.,
  47-50, 54, 60, 127, 155

Westphal, Joachim   4
Whitefield, George   169
Willem the Silent   54
Wittich, C.   54ff.
Wolf, Christian   53, 95f.
Word, The   131, 137

Zepper, Wilhelm   22, 56, 76
Zinzendorf, Count Nicholas L.
  171
Zwingli, Ulrich   3f.